DISCOVERING

JOHN G. MAISEY

Department of Vertebrate Paleontology
American Museum of Natural History

Illustrations by
DAVID MILLER
IVY RUTZKY

Photography by
CRAIG CHESEK
DENIS FINNIN

FOSSIL FISHES

a PETER N. NEVRAUMONT *book*

A Henry Holt Reference Book
HENRY HOLT AND COMPANY
New York

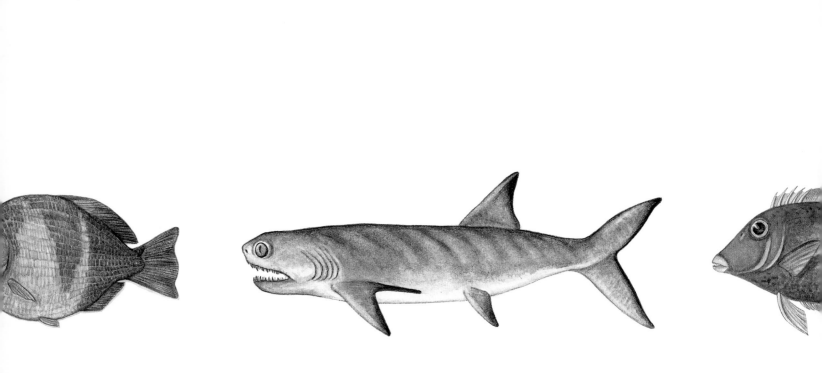

contents

~~~~~~~~

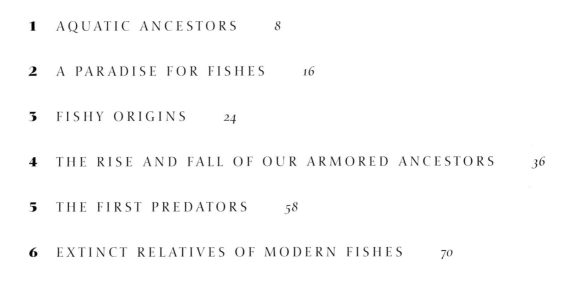

To Bobb Schaeffer,
colleague, mentor, and friend.

A Henry Holt Reference Book
Henry Holt and Company, Inc.
Publishers since 1866
115 West 18th Street
New York, New York 10011

Henry Holt ® is a registered trademark of Henry Holt and Company, Inc.

Published in Canada by Fitzhenry & Whiteside Ltd.,
195 Allstate Parkway, Markham, Ontario L3R 4T8

Library of Congress Cataloging–in–Publication Data is available upon request.

Henry Holt books are available for special promotions and premium.
For details contact: Director, Special Markets.
First Edition — 1996

Book design: José Conde, Studio Pepin, Tokyo

Printed in Italy by EBS – Editoriale Bortolazzi-Stei (Verona)

10 9 8 7 6 5 4 3 2 1

Created and Produced by
Nevraumont Publishing Company
New York, New York

Ann J. Perrini, *President*

ANCESTORS

⇒⫴⫷ What's in a Name?

*f*ISHES have a unique evolutionary history that stretches back in time more than 450 million years. They are incredibly ancient, older than the dinosaurs, and include the ancestors of all the limbed vertebrates living on land, even humans. Human evolution is rooted in fishes; and scientists have discovered traces of 360-million-year-old fossils of transitional aquatic creatures that had both gills and limbs. Not only are humans and fishes related, some fishes are more closely related to humans than they are to other fishes! We commonly think of ourselves as completely separate from our aquatic ancestors when instead we should be marveling at the similarities.

Let's see where we fit in. Humans are classified as **tetrapods** (*four-footed*; more generally, having two pairs of limbs). This same designation applies to all the air-breathing land vertebrates with which we are familiar: all other mammals, birds, reptiles, and amphibians. The tetrapods in turn are a highly specialized offshoot of a very ancient class of animals, the Sarcopterygii. The only other living members of this group are the coelacanths and the lungfishes. It seems that we have very important, and very fishy, ancestors!

We no longer look like fishes, of course, and that is because most modern fishes evolved from different ancestors than did tetrapods. Our tetrapod ancestors left the water and found a new environment on land.

PLATE 1
Calamopleurus, an Early Cretaceous relative of the modern bowfin about 1m long, lunges from concealment at a passing group of filter-feeding *Vinctifer*, members of the extinct teleost group known as aspidorhynchids. These fishes lived in a shallow inland sea covering parts of northeastern Brazil about 110 million years ago.
(see Plates 67 and 77)

In making this transition, they lost or modified many of their aquatic adaptations. Fishes stayed in the water, and evolved new adaptations to this environment. [Plate 1] Both fishes and tetrapods, however, share common *distant* ancestors. These were highly mobile, *aquatic* creatures with a sophisticated brain, complex sensory systems, and a muscular tail. These features, which first appeared more than 450 million years ago, characterize a group known as the **craniates** (*having a cranium*, the part of the skull that encloses the brain). (Another name frequently used for the group is **vertebrates**, but, as we shall see, the terms vertebrate and craniate are not strictly interchangeable.) Tetrapods have superimposed their adaptations to *terrestrial* life upon their aquatic (craniate) features; fishes have built more adaptations to *aquatic* life on top of theirs. [Figure 1]

As we go back in time, we can trace our tetrapod lineage to a common ancestry with fishes. When we try to trace the lineage forward from the earliest craniates, however, we find that tetrapods have been segmented, by classificatory fiat, from the fishes. This poses a problem, for we see that fishes do not form a natural group, because tetrapods have been excluded, but instead represent a heterogeneous assemblage. The term "fish" is therefore generally used to refer to a life form that has many different representatives. The basic form is a craniate that has retained some primitive features (evolved in the common ancestor of all craniates), such as gills and a tail fin, but may also have other features representing a long series of evolutionary adaptations. Often the sense in which the word is used is merely conventional; from a practical viewpoint, fishes are what we study in fish classes! Here is a paradox, for although most of us have no difficulty recognizing a fish, collectively fishes have no unique features by which they can be classified.

Our first discovery, then, is that fishes do not represent an entire natural lineage of creatures that evolved from a common ancestor, for the group is incomplete without tetrapods. Why, then, write a book about an incomplete group? Precisely because there *is* so much misunderstanding about the early evolution of craniates, it is more convenient to discuss various issues under a blanket title of "fishes." And let's face it—few people would have read a book entitled *Discovering Primitive Fossil Non-Tetrapodan Craniates*!

Fishy Diversity

From their ancient ancestors, the craniates, fishes evolved not once, in a single lineage, but multiple times, filling countless biological niches. The various classes of living and extinct fishes (for example sharks, lungfishes, coelacanths, ray-finned fishes, acanthodians and placoderms) are as different from each other as mammals are from birds. Fishes are spectacularly diverse, with around 25,000 living species described so far and untold thousands more awaiting discovery. Fishes make up slightly more than half of the approximately 48,500 described living species of vertebrates. The remaining known vertebrate species, about 23,500, are represented by the tetrapods.

Given their long evolutionary history, it is not surprising that so many species of fishes exist today; one new fish species evolving every 18,000 years, or about 55.5 species evolving per 1 million years, would account for the numbers. Such an orderly, regular pace of evolution is unrealistic, of course, for no living species has existed for 450 million years.

The sum total of fishy diversity through time is far greater than now, and the evolutionary history of fishes is a vast and complex subject. It is impossible to give an accurate estimate of how many species of fishes have existed through time, because the diversity of many groups has waxed and waned, and because there are significant gaps in the fossil record, but the total is likely to have been in the millions. As more fossil fishes are uncovered, we will know better what the ancient world looked like and come to discover more of our own ancestors.

FIGURE 1
◦⊚◦

Diagram to show the diversity of craniates. Groups inside solid boxes are monophyletic (descended from a single ancestor, the line leading to box). Groups inside dashed boxes are unreal, because they include members of more than one evolutionary line. For example, gnathostomes (craniates with jaws, an advanced feature) form a monophyletic group, but "agnathans" (craniates lacking jaws, a primitive condition) are unreal because they include two separate evolutionary lineages: hagfishes and lampreys. Similarly, tetrapods (gnathostomes with limbs) are monophyletic, but the group "fishes" (all craniates lacking limbs) is unreal. (Lineages number 1–4 are extinct groups of fishes discussed elsewhere in this book.)

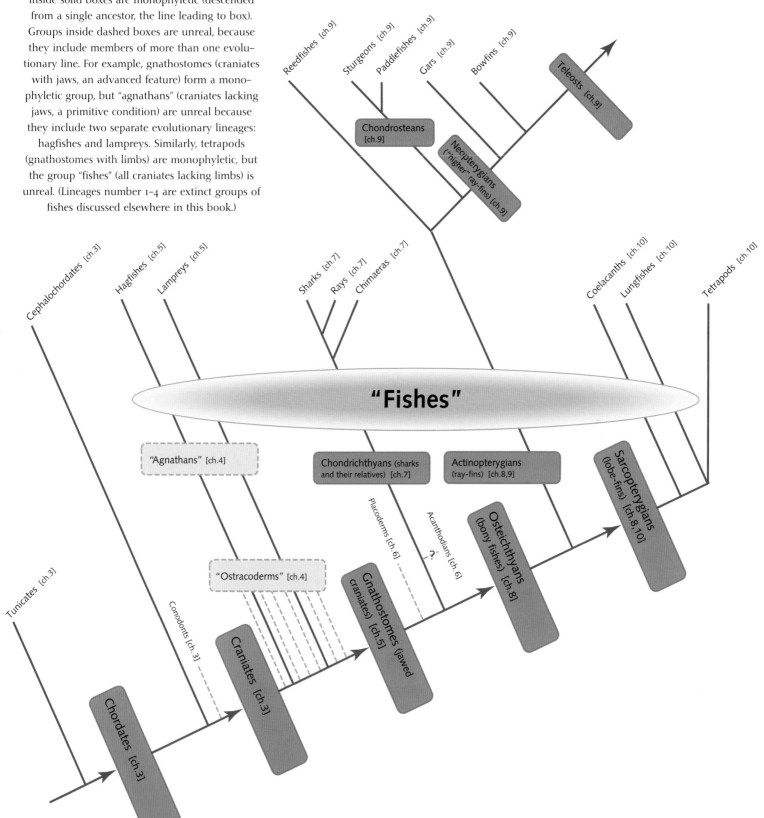

Are Fishes Primitive?

Some fishes (sharks, for example) are classified as primitive, while others (such as spiny-finned teleosts or lungfishes) are classified as advanced. But scientists use words like "**primitive**" and "**advanced**," (or "lower" and "higher") in an evolutionary sense only to provide a perspective on the hierarchy they have created. For example ray-finned fishes are intuitively regarded by scientists as advanced fishes (relative to sharks or extinct placoderms), yet within ray-fins the reedfishes, paddlefishes and sturgeons are all regarded as primitive. In the sense that tetrapods came later on the craniate evolutionary tree, and evolved many new adaptations to a terrestrial environment, they have been considered more advanced than fishes. While it is true that fishes (as they are construed here) certainly include the earliest and most primitive of all craniate animals, they nevertheless also include groups (teleosts, for example) that possess their own suites of unique advanced features and which evolved much later in geologic time. Fishes did not stop evolving after tetrapods left the water some 350 million years ago. Teleosts first appeared about 200 million years ago, and the oldest fossil perchlike fish is now celebrating only its 60 millionth birthday, along with the earliest ducks, frigate birds, and some mammalian groups such as horses and primates. In other words, the anatomical features that define perchlike fishes, frigate birds and horses appeared at roughly the same moment of geologic time.

One way to measure how **evolved** a group is, in the biological sense, is to look at the number of species in that group relative to the length of time the group has been around. Each new species represents a change in one or more characters from the previous state; if changes did not occur, there would be no new species! Hypothetically, the original species had only original characters, which we call primitive. The appearance of new anatomical features (which we call advanced) in the descendants of the ancestral species provides a measure of evolutionary change, and allows us to distinguish new species. The greater the degree of anatomical diversity within a given group, the more species we may recognize. A species-rich (i.e. anatomically diverse) group having only a short duration (in terms of geologic time) presumably underwent rapid speciation and had a high rate of anatomical change. Speciation rates among coelacanths (one living species and about one hundred fossil species over 350 million years) and acanthomorph teleosts (about 18,000 living species plus innumerable fossil species over 100 million years) are clearly very different. In essence, a creature that has undergone a large number of evolutions, producing new species, in a defined time is considered to be more evolved than a creature that has undergone few or no changes in a comparable or longer time. Thus, the number of species can be taken as a general indicator of a group's evolvedness—in a biological sense.

Let's look at some examples to compare the diversity and the geological age of the spiny-rayed (acanthomorph) fishes (the largest and most advanced group of living ray-finned fishes) with the diversity and geological age of birds, which most people would place high on the vertebrate evolutionary tree. In other words, we will be comparing speciation rates—the number of new species that have evolved over a defined time interval. The oldest fossil bones from acanthomorph fishes are a mere 100 or so million years old, and fossilized ear stones (**otoliths**) like those of acanthomorphs are known about 160 million years old. *Archaeopteryx*, the oldest undisputed fossil bird, is about 150 million years old, so birds and acanthomorphs have virtually the same geological range. Acanthomorphs have close to 18,000 described living species, whereas there are around 10,000 described species of birds. These numbers show, in a very crude way, that the phenomenal diversity of modern acanthomorphs has arisen in about the same span of geologic time as that of birds. And based on the criterion of number of species, acanthomorphs are more evolved than birds. We can see a similar story in virtually every group of modern fishes, even among those supposedly primeval creatures, the **sharks** (see Chapter 7).

⩉⫸ A Long Way Down!

The human species is the only one on Earth to have looked back over its shoulder, to see where it came from. No other species has ever had this ability, for history and prehistory—like religion, politics, and economics—are uniquely human concepts. For a few millennia our history is clear, because people wrote things down and kept souvenirs of the past. What they wrote down and what they buried and discarded all form the tangible basis of human history. But what can we know of the time before writing, burial, and garbage?

Fortunately, some fragments of our prehistoric ancestry still exist as fossils, preserved by naturally occurring processes on Earth. These fossils, painstakingly extracted from the rocks, then reassembled and reconstructed in the laboratory, provide tantalizing glimpses into the prehistory of humans, and beyond, into the unrecorded history of our biological ancestors. Religious fundamentalists may deny that evolution exists, but in the natural world it is religion that does not exist.

Frequently our view into our prehistoric past is obscured by the mists of antiquity and the ravages of erosion. The origins of *humanity*—the totality of the cultural and social relations that distinguish humankind from other animals—can be followed into the past a few thousand chilly years, to glacial and postglacial caves and rift valleys where small groups of individuals lived who divided their labors, cared for their sick and elderly, cooked, painted, dreamed, and planned for their future: the funeral of a loved one tomorrow, the bison returning with the sun's warmth in the spring, the tribal gatherings at harvest time.

The origins of the *human species* are more distant. They have been traced back in time a few million years, to the dry sands and muds of lakeshores in eastern Africa. There, unique and curious creatures, our forebears, walked upright, used crudely worked tools, and planned, in a simple way, for the future. They looked forward to shaping the new stone with its razor-sharp cutting edge, to the movement of a pride of lions, to the ensuing hunt. Farther back in time, the existence of primates, to which humans and our simian cousins belong, is known from the fragile bones of 60-million-year-old lemurs and tarsier-like animals from Europe and North America, Morocco, and Asia. Beyond that the fossil record reveals no more traces of those peculiar traits by which we define humanity or the human species, and we see only the relics of a once living world.

Our mammalian origins are even more remote in the past, and we have only fleeting glimpses of the earliest mammals, tiny fossilized bones of shrew-sized creatures that must have cowered in the shadows of early dinosaurs more than 200 million years ago. Beyond that point, the fossil record reveals many bizarre extinct animals, large and small, that to us seem increasingly reptilian and share progressively fewer anatomical features with modern mammals. Rarely, we find the fossil bones of even earlier four-legged animals, primitive semi-aquatic tetrapod amphibians, in strata that were laid down in lakes, swamps, and estuaries more than 360 million years ago.

Even these animals do not represent the base of our evolutionary ladder, for it stands in the water and extends deep beneath the surface. Many of the most fundamental physical features of humans, even the legs that support us, first appeared in nascent form in an aquatic environment. Our basic vertebrate design—jaws, brain, nerves, internal organs, even the bones that provide anchorage for our muscles—first evolved in animals that lived in water. In reality, this book is not only about fishes; it is also about humans, and about our earliest aquatic ancestors.

Our bodies reveal many clues to our ancestry. Hair and mammary glands are shared by our mammalian cousins. The amniotic membrane that ruptures when "the waters break" at the start of birth is shared by all amniotes, whether they give birth to live young, as cats, mice, and kangaroos do, or lay eggs, as do reptiles, birds, and the platypus. Our arms and legs—and the bones within them—are shared by frogs and salamanders, and our backbone with its many vertebrae is shared by sharks and **bony fishes**. Our brain and sensory capsules are shared by lampreys and hagfishes, and our spinal nerve cord and its supporting notochord are shared by the lancelet, a tiny fishlike sea creature that lacks a head and true fins.

We share Earth with countless millions of other living organisms, all of which have managed to evolve and survive to the present day in spite of their supposedly inferior anatomy. They are not inferior, of course, nor are they superior: they simply *are*. While the human species is distinctive, every living species has its ancestors and its own evolutionary lineage comparable to our own. Each and every one of those lineages is continuing to evolve and will continue to do so unless some untoward event snuffs it out.

Medieval representations of the universe show tiny humans in the foreground, larger angels, archangels, and saints in the middle distance, and a gigantic deity in the background. The perspective had symbolic meaning: to the medieval mind, this image served to keep mankind in its place. We would not now portray the universe this way. Oddly enough, though, most books on vertebrates tend to a similar distortion of the natural world by devoting far more space to mammals and other tetrapods than to fishes. The writers simply added a fishy footnote to the image, enlarged the humans, and dispensed with the angels and deity.

Just as the Renaissance discovery of perspective changed the way reality was represented, so our modern understanding of the fossil record has reduced humankind to a single thread in the tapestry of the living world. The history of *Homo sapiens* is interconnected with the history of every other species, living and extinct, that has rented space on Earth. Uniquely, however, humankind has discovered its own origins. Like all species, we evolved from forgotten ancestors, we exist briefly, and we will be gone. This is perhaps the strongest message sent by the fossil record, and we would do well to listen. ❧

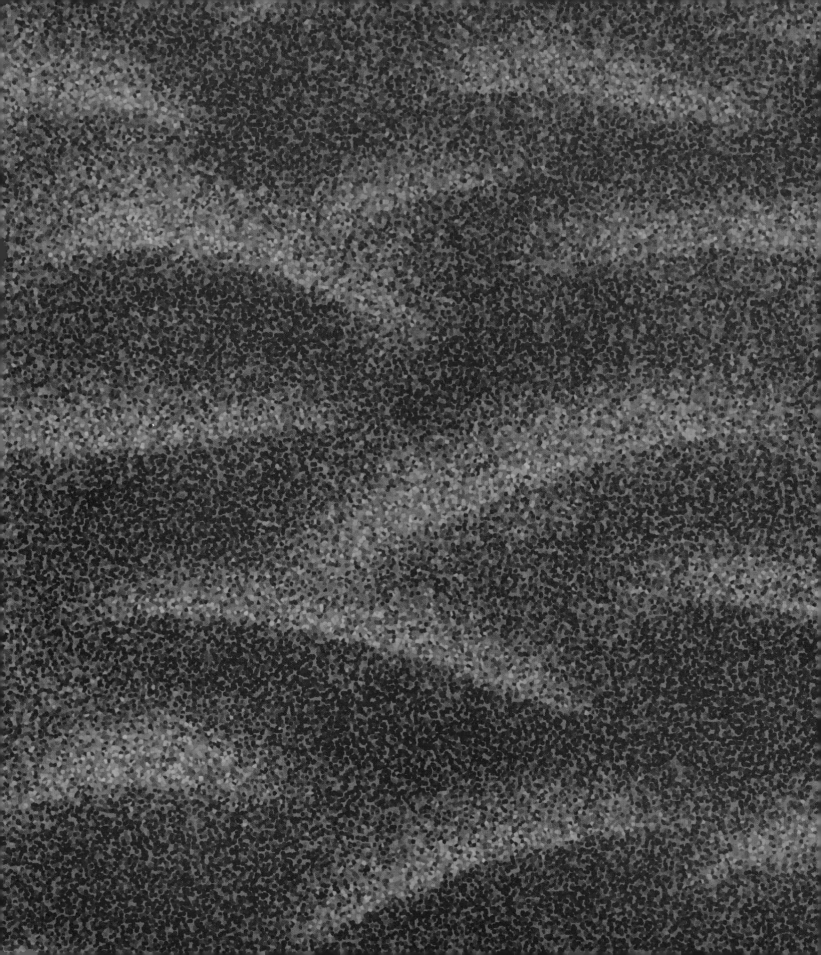

FOR FISHES

"**Water, water, every where...**"
Samuel Taylor Coleridge, "The Rime of the Ancient Mariner," 1834

T*HE GLOBE* we live on is a very different place from the neighboring planets. Its surface is lumpy and uneven, with vast basins filled with seawater and great mountain chains towering high into the atmosphere. These basic physical features—lots of water, with intermittent patches of dry, high land—are inextricably interwoven with the development of life on Earth as we know it today.

Earth is unique among the planets of our solar system, for only on Earth are the surface conditions just right for liquid water to exist in vast quantities. Without liquid water there would be no fishes, and without fishes there would be no land vertebrates, including humans, for humans evolved from fishes. Without water, it is unlikely that life would have developed here at all. And not only is there liquid water on this planet, there is a *lot* of it. Earth is a very wet place, a paradise for fishes! Some 71% of Earth's surface is covered by oceans, and if we could bulldoze flat the continents, we would all be sitting under 2.6 kilometers of salt water. The only reason we are not sitting in water is that the lighter granitic rocks forming the continental land masses form a thick pile, floating on the upper mantle in gravitational equilibrium with the thinner but denser basaltic crust beneath the oceans.

About half the continental crust lies between 1 and 2 kilometers above sea level, whereas most of the oceanic crust lies 2 to 6 kilometers

PLATE 2

A dead *Phareodus*, related to modern southern-hemisphere osteoglossids (bony tongues), lies on the shore of an Eocene lake in western North America (40–65 million years ago), accompanied by small herrings (*Knightia*) and a perch-like fish (*Priscacara*). All these fishes are teleosts, the largest group of living fishes. Although osteoglossids first appeared in the Early Cretaceous, many modern teleost families appeared in the Eocene, along with many modern mammals and birds; the earliest fossil ducks and frigate-birds are found in the same strata as *Phareodus*.

beneath the waves. When we consider the overall size of Earth, this difference in altitude between continental and oceanic crust may seem trivial, but with all that water sloshing about on Earth's surface, the difference of even a few kilometers becomes crucial. Although the continents form high spots above sea level, the volume of seawater on Earth exceeds the space available in the ocean basins, so that the oceans slop over the edges of the continents, in places referred to as the continental shelves. If the sea level were lowered globally by about 1.7 kilometers, the continental shelves would be almost entirely exposed. Conversely, if the sea level were raised by a few hundred meters, many of the great cities of the world would be standing in water.

≈||||⦿ "...Nor any drop to drink"

It may come as a surprise to learn that only a little more than half of the fish species on Earth live in salt water. The rest, between 40% and 45%, either are restricted to fresh water or spend an appreciable part of their lives in it. In other words, about one quarter of all ver-tebrate species (mostly fishes) live in the seas and oceans, and three quarters of vertebrate species–the freshwater fishes and most tetrapods–live on the conti-nents. Because the continents make up lit-tle more than a quarter of the Earth's surface, the continental vertebrates have proportionately much less habitat to live in than the sea-going vertebrates.

Melanie Stiassny, an **ichthyologist** at the American Museum of Natural History, in New York, has shown that for freshwater fishes, the available habitat is tiny indeed. Of all the water in the world, fresh water accounts for a mere 2.5%, and almost all of this is locked up in the polar ice caps or stored underground in aquifers and soil moisture. Very little fresh water is actually available for fishes to live in: *a quarter of the world's vertebrates, and almost half of its fishes, live in only 0.01% of the world's water*. In a striking image, Stiassny has likened the lakes and rivers of the world

to fragile islands of fresh water surround-ed and isolated by land. These tiny islands of water also must supply human needs: for drinking water, irrigation, hydroelectric power, and industrial coolant. Small won-der that humans' demand for fresh water is having catastrophic effects on the world's fishes!

Although we have emphasized the importance of an aquatic environment in the evolutionary history of Earth's ani-mals, it is clear that the continents also were important to vertebrate evolution, not only for terrestrial animals but for many fishes as well. Slightly over half of the world's fishes are dispersed through-out 97.5% of its surface waters; the rest live on small "islands" of water scattered across the continents. [Plate 2]

≈||||⦿ Where Did All the Water (and Salt) Come From?

Liquid water could not have existed at the surface of early Earth when the sur-face temperatures were much higher than they are today. Quite probably, much of the water was present in the embryonic planet, but was locked up in water mole-cules, first as part of a gaseous cloud, then within the mantle of the solidifying plan-et. As Earth's surface cooled, the oceans and atmosphere were both probably formed by gradual leakage of water, nitro-gen, carbon dioxide, hydrogen, sulfur dioxide, and carbon monoxide from Earth's mantle, in a process known as degassing. This gradual first accumulation of the oceans and atmosphere may even have been integral to the formation of Earth's crust.

As the first surface waters began to accumulate, they would quickly have become saturated with soluble salts. The salt content of these smaller early seas may have been much higher than it is today, and dropped only as more and more water was gradually added through continued degassing. If, as some scientists believe, early Earth lacked any continents and was entirely covered by oceanic crust, like that forming the modern seafloor, it may have been completely covered by a shallow sea, lacking any fresh water except that provided by ephemeral rains and floating ice caps.

Although the outer crust eventually became solid, it probably remained fairly mobile, much as it is today, and a process of recycling the oceanic waters then began. Seawater became trapped within the sediments and crystalline rocks of the ocean floor and was removed by seafloor spreading and subduction (the sinking of crustal rocks) of parts of the ocean floor beneath the continents, where the water and other volatiles accumulated in the mantle layer of Earth. Much later these volatiles were returned to the surface via volcanic eruptions through the crust. In this manner they have been recycled over millions of years.

Sea levels have changed repeatedly during the past 600 million years. The oceans have sometimes inundated vast areas of the continents. At other times they have barely wetted the continental margins. If water was lost by subduction at rates faster than it was replaced by degassing (in volcanic eruptions, for example), there may have been a gradual fall in global sea levels over time. If, on the other hand, water was replaced faster than it was consumed, global sea levels may have risen. This is a process view of a much more complex situation, but outlines one way in which the changes in global sea levels over time may have occurred.

Modern seawater contains between 33 and 38 parts per thousand of dissolved salt, 91% of which is sodium chloride, plus traces of sulfate, magnesium, calcium, potassium, and bicarbonate ions. About 3.5 trillion kilograms of dissolved salts are carried by rivers to the oceans each year. Ocean salinity is remarkably uniform and constant, however, which suggests that salts are removed as fast as they are added. The most likely cause of salt loss is through inclusion and burial in oceanic sediments, as well as from crystallization as seawater evaporates (especially in arid regions such as the Persian Gulf). But there is always enough salt left to maintain saturation levels, and the oceans actually couldn't get much saltier than they are.

The oceans don't get progressively fresher because water is lost through evaporation and incorporation into sediments about as fast as it is added by rivers and rain. The reason that most fresh waters are not salty is that even the vast amount of dissolved salt contained in them is a mere drop in the bucket. But where fresh waters cannot drain to the ocean, salt lakes and dead, salty seas may form as water evaporates and salts accumulate. Fresh waters generally do not exist in the oceans, except at the mouths of large rivers such as the Mississippi or Amazon, where a lens of brackish or even fresh water can sit on top of denser seawater. Without continents, there can be no permanent bodies of fresh water.

How Old Is the Sea?

The oldest known bits of terrestrial matter are 4.2-billion-year-old fragments of zircon crystals found in sediments from Western Australia. [Figure 2] Less than half a billion years after gaseous Earth began to solidify, therefore, it may have possessed some granitic crust, but we have no idea whether seas covered parts of Earth's surface at that time. The oldest rocks at the surface of Earth, from Isua in Greenland, show that about 3.8 billion years ago, lavas formed at Earth's surface and were then eroded by air and liquid water, although we do not know if the water was fresh or salt.

By 2 billion years ago there were ocean basins full of salt water, and continents that separated them. Evidence for this has been found in the Canadian Shield, north of Great Slave Lake, in the Northwest Territories of Canada. Here, some of the oldest known bits of mountain are all that remains of two originally separate granitic continental masses that collided more than 2 billion years ago. The sea floor that once separated them is

FIGURE 2
◎〇

Table of Geologic Time, with some important events in the evolution of fishes. Following the Pre-Cambrian, geologic time is divided into three progressively younger eras, the Paleozoic ("Ancient Life"), Mesozoic ("Middle Life"), and Cenozoic (" Modern Life"). Each era is divided into periods (frequently referred to in the text), and periods are further subdivided into stages. These stages are rarely mentioned in the text, and are not shown here. Note that in the U.S.A., the Carboniferous is usually broken down into two periods, the Mississippian (early Carboniferous) and Pennsylvanian (Late Carboniferous).

gone, long ago subducted beneath the mountains on either side. Squeezed into the ever-diminishing space between the converging continents were sediments including sands, limestones, and muds that had formed on a submerged oceanic continental shelf (similar to the Bahama Banks). Although they are distorted by heat and pressure, and ravaged by time, these sediments are testaments to the existence of ancient oceans.

The seas could actually be older than the granitic continents that now separate the ocean basins. Ancient oceans once covered parts of Earth that are now in the middle of continents.

Ocean Basins and Plate Tectonics

One of the great mysteries of modern geology is the immense difference in age between continental and oceanic crust. The interiors of the continents include the most ancient rocks found on Earth, some more than 4 billion years old. In stark contrast, the oldest bits of ocean floor have been dated to around 200 million years, a mere 1/20th the age of the oldest continental rocks, and most of the oceanic crust is considerably younger than this. How could the ocean floors date only from the time of the dinosaurs when portions of the continents are vastly older?

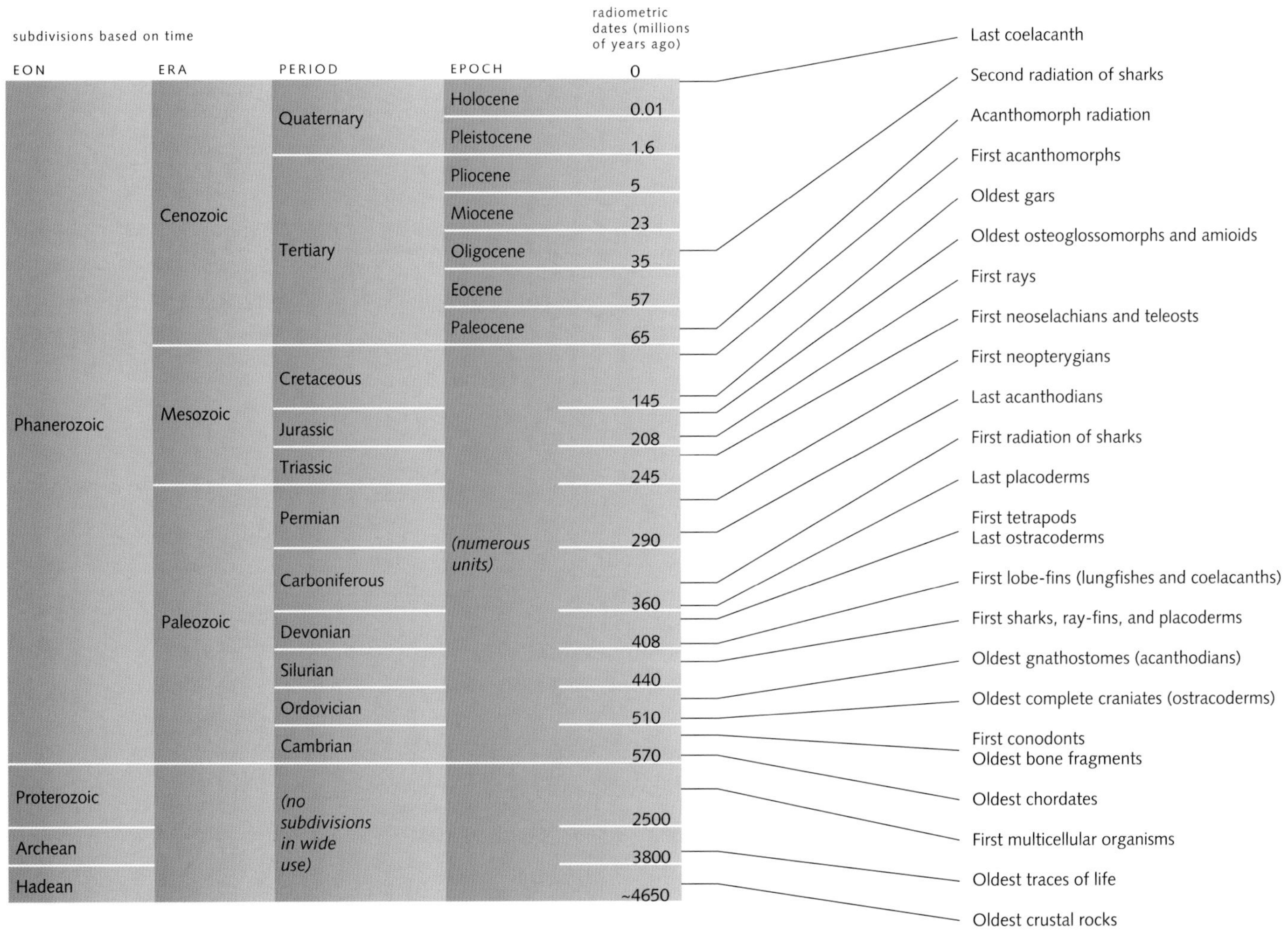

subdivisions based on time				radiometric dates (millions of years ago)	
EON	ERA	PERIOD	EPOCH	0	Last coelacanth
Phanerozoic	Cenozoic	Quaternary	Holocene	0.01	Second radiation of sharks
			Pleistocene	1.6	Acanthomorph radiation
		Tertiary	Pliocene	5	First acanthomorphs
			Miocene	23	Oldest gars
			Oligocene	35	Oldest osteoglossomorphs and amioids
			Eocene	57	First rays
			Paleocene	65	First neoselachians and teleosts
	Mesozoic	Cretaceous	(numerous units)	145	First neopterygians
		Jurassic		208	Last acanthodians / First radiation of sharks
		Triassic		245	Last placoderms
	Paleozoic	Permian		290	First tetrapods / Last ostracoderms
		Carboniferous		360	First lobe-fins (lungfishes and coelacanths)
		Devonian		408	First sharks, ray-fins, and placoderms
		Silurian		440	Oldest gnathostomes (acanthodians)
		Ordovician		510	Oldest complete craniates (ostracoderms)
		Cambrian		570	First conodonts / Oldest bone fragments
Proterozoic		(no subdivisions in wide use)		2500	Oldest chordates
Archean				3800	First multicellular organisms / Oldest traces of life
Hadean				~4650	Oldest crustal rocks

The answer lies in the ongoing geo-tectonic processes that rip up and melt down parts of Earth's crust while replacing it elsewhere. Earth has a cool, rigid, brittle outer layer, the lithosphere, on average less than 100 kilometers thick. The lithosphere consists of crustal rocks and a solid mantle layer that extends beneath the crust. The lithosphere is cracked and broken into 11 large plates and several smaller ones, all constantly in motion and jostling like pieces in a loosely spaced puzzle. Continents represent a light residue of ancient granitic rocks that have gradually accreted on the surface of the lithosphere. They are fragments of crustal scum that have at different times been torn apart and welded together by the motions of the fluid lithosphere beneath them. The surface of our planet actually moves, and we can measure this movement using sensitive equipment in satellites. Although the rates are slower than a snail's pace, centimeters per year translates into hundreds of kilometers per million years. As far as we can tell, the crust has continually flexed and changed, perhaps even before life existed on Earth. Plate motions are driven by still incompletely understood processes that apparently involve movement of the asthenosphere, hot, weak, plastic rock that extends beneath the lithosphere to an estimated depth of 350 kilometers below the surface. Although we do not understand the mechanisms fully, we have coined the term **plate tectonics** for the process.

ꙮ The Magician's Trick
Plate tectonics is responsible for both the creation and the destruction of the dense, heavy oceanic crust, ultimately driving it beneath the lighter continental crust, where it is melted and reabsorbed back into the asthenosphere. Just as a magician whisks the tablecloth out from under the best china while leaving the dishes in place, so plate tectonics is constantly pulling the floor out from under the ocean. Unlike the magician, who cannot slip the tablecloth back under the china, plate tectonics provides a replacement floor to the oceans. Ocean floor is created by basaltic lavas that erupt from fissures along mountainous mid-ocean ridges. Like a gigantic conveyer belt with hiccoughs, the seafloor is jerkily but inexorably widened by successive injections of basalt along the mid-ocean ridge, until it gets shoved beneath another part of the crust, frequently but not invariably a continent, at subduction zones along its margin.

It has taken almost 200 million years for plate tectonics to turn over the entire oceanic floor of the globe. Oceanic crust is continually being created somewhere and continually being lost somewhere else.

ꙮ Fossil Statue of Limitations
The age limit imposed on the ocean's crust by plate tectonics applies equally to the marine sediments that have accumulated on top of the crust, for these muds and oozes are carried along by the same conveyer belt of tectonic activity. Nowhere within the ocean basins can we reasonably expect to find oceanic sediments or oceanic fossils older than 200 million years. Anything older than this either has been lost to subduction and melting or else has been crunched up against some continental margin. Much of Earth's marine history has been obliterated by subduction of the oceanic plates. The magician took the fossils while we were watching him replace the ocean floor!

The only places where marine sediments and fossils have a remote chance of survival beyond the 200-million-year statute of limitations is on continental margins, where shallow seas once extended across the lowest shelf areas. These areas frequently are tectonically stable and quiet for protracted periods, even after they are uplifted and exposed above sea level. It is precisely in such situations that we find the bulk of our marine fossil record and the oldest marine fossils.

Even if we could explore the deep seabed for fossils younger than 200 million years, we probably wouldn't have much luck. First, fossils are buried in layers of sediment, where they are protected from erosion and scavenging, but sedimentation rates in the deep sea are slow, and not much sediment has accumulated so far from shore, so there is little opportunity for burial. Second, the kinds of fossils we are most familiar with are hard shells and bones made from calcium carbonate and calcium phosphate. In ocean deep water there is very little environmental carbonate and phosphate available for forming shells and bones, and many deep-water organisms have poorly mineralized skeletons. Third, carbonate and phosphate minerals in shells and bones deposited on the deep seafloor would dissolve quite rapidly under the intense pressure of the immense body of water pressing down on them; whale ear bones and large shark teeth have been dredged from these environments, but they are invariably pitted and corroded, already partly dissolved.

The principles of physics and geology, the real magicians in this story, conspire to deny us access to much of the history of sea life before 200 million years ago. If we want to learn more about the earlier saga of the ancient oceans, and what lived in them, we must concentrate our efforts on land raised from the sea. The sample is biased, but it is all there is. Paradoxically, it is easier for us air-breathing terrestrial organisms to learn about the early history of the oceans than it would be for any water-bound species.

≈‖‖⊳ Plate Tectonics and Evolution

Living organisms all have their place in the world. Each one occupies an ecological niche and fits at some level into a local hierarchy of who eats whom (called its trophic level). These niches and hierarchies, ephemeral as the species that fill them, exist only because of the prevailing physical environment. The driving forces of plate tectonics have radically altered the distribution of land and sea many times over the past half-billion years. The inexorable reconfiguration of continents and seas undoubtedly had long-term climatic consequences, affecting oceanic circulation patterns, global temperatures and rainfall, and perhaps even the amount of water in the oceans. As the environment changes, the ecological setting is also transformed, denying established populations the conditions in which they once flourished, creating new habitats and opportunities for colonization by different organisms, and setting the stage for new species to evolve. The changing pattern of continents and oceans has influenced the distribution of fishes and played a role in the success or disappearance of many groups.

≈‖‖⊳ If Things Had Been Different, We Wouldn't Be Here

Satellite probes reveal clearly that the surfaces of Mercury and the Moon are covered by impact craters of great antiquity. The Moon is dead, its magma generation having stopped as much as 4 billion years ago. Only the external influence of major meteorite impacts has generated sufficient energy to allow ephemeral melting of its surface rocks. A similar story is told by Mercury. The surfaces of these bodies form single, continuous crustal plates, not broken up into smaller plates as on Earth. The lava plains filling their craters are not torn or crumpled by tectonic movements. The cloudy surface of Venus has proved difficult to image, but we now know that it is fairly smooth, apart from large circular structures. The total relief from the lowest valley to the highest peak is only 13 kilometers—about half that on Earth. There is thus no evidence today of plate tectonic activity on Venus either, but if there ever was any such activity in the past it must have been on a minor scale relative to Earth's, and it must have stopped billions of years ago. Mars is volcanically active (Olympus Mons is the largest volcano of the inner planets), but there is no evidence of plate movements there either.

In fact, space probes have uncovered no evidence of processes akin to Earthly plate tectonics anywhere in our solar system except on Jupiter's moon Ganymede, where that body's ancient, icy surface is broken into dark, continent-sized fragments separated by light-colored, grooved ice terrains with few impact craters. Apparently the mechanisms of plate tectonics work just as well with a crust made of ice. As far as the inner planets are concerned, however, Earth is unique.

Without the continuous process of crustal creation and destruction, it is possible that life never would have appeared, and the surface of Earth would more closely resemble that of Mars or Venus. Even had life appeared, the range of life-sustaining habitats undoubtedly would have been constrained, and it is questionable whether a life-supporting atmosphere could have been sustained indefinitely. A comparison of Earth and the other inner planets of our solar system gives us an acute awareness of its uniqueness; we are lucky to be here!

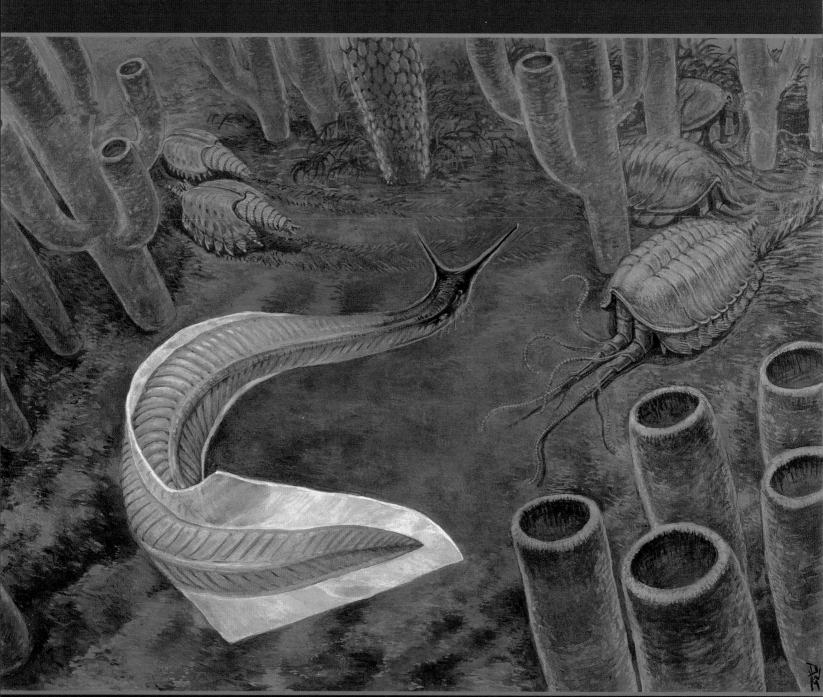

ORIGINS

≡⫸ First Traces of Life

PLATE 3
◌◌

Pikaea, an early chordate similar to the modern amphioxus, lived in Middle Cambrian seas about 540 million years ago, alongside many bizarre invertebrates. Delicate fossils of these sea creatures were discovered in the 19th century from the now-famous Burgess Shale of British Columbia. A slightly older chordate, *Yunnanozoon*, was described in 1995 from the Lower Cambrian of China.

*N*O LIFE could have survived the infernal temperatures of the molten phase Earth passed through 4.5 to 4 billion years ago. Any organic molecules would have been pyrolized – altered by heat – to carbon dioxide, carbon monoxide, nitrogen, hydrogen, ammonia, and water. Most biochemical processes involving DNA or RNA – that is, essentially all processes concerned with life as we know it – occur within a small temperature band, from around freezing to a maximum of 35° C, and it is reasonable to suppose that the earliest life forms were constrained by a similar temperature range for their metabolic processes.

Among the oldest traces of life on Earth are fossilized filaments of blue-green algae about 3.5 billion years old, from South Africa and Western Australia. Life forms with complex DNA molecules containing their own blueprints of life thus existed very soon after Earth's crust was formed. Associated with the fossils from South Africa are sure signs of water, in the form of fossilized ripple marks on the surface of sandstone strata, and pillow lavas erupted into the sea.

Three billion years ago Earth's shallow seas were inhabited by communities of simple-celled or prokaryotic (lacking a nucleus) microorganisms, some of which were capable of primitive photosynthesis, using sunlight to synthesize glucose and sulfur from carbon dioxide and sulfur dioxide. Other microbes were consumers of these photosynthetic products. Yet others, such as cyanobacteria, were more advanced photosynthesizers, capable of producing sugars and oxygen from carbon dioxide and water. Much of the oxygen was absorbed immediately by various chemical reactions to make water, carbon dioxide, and sulfides. The oxygen that was not absorbed would ultimately transform the atmosphere, the hydrosphere, and life on Earth, although another billion years would be needed to accomplish the transformation.

≋ The Oxygen Crisis

Oxygen levels reached a critical level in Earth's atmosphere about 1.75 billion years ago. At about the same time, we find fossils of the first complex cell or eukaryotic life forms, in which most of the genetic material is confined to the nucleus. For about 550 million years eukaryotes were represented mainly by small plankton, called acritarchs, that lived in the upper photic (*light-receiving*) zone of the sea. They evolved slowly, perhaps because they were unable to reproduce sexually and thereby mix their DNA with that of other individuals. About 1.1 billion years ago, planktonic eukaryotes evolved more rapidly, possibly coinciding with the "invention" of sexual reproduction. By about 950 to 850 million years ago these organisms reached a zenith of abundance and diversity, but they disappeared from the fossil record about 600 million years ago. The demise of these planktonic creatures has been linked to a decline in hydrothermal activity, which may have led to a global atmospheric decrease in carbon dioxide and an increase in free oxygen. Strange new life forms, composed of many cells instead of single ones, inherited and began to utilize this oxygen-rich environment toward the end of the Precambrian. These metazoan, **aerobic** (*oxygen-using*) creatures were the forerunners of the animals and plants that dominate the modern world, although many of them looked like nothing we know today. Many fossils from the end of the Precambrian are difficult or impossible to classify within existing groups. It has often puzzled zoologists why complex metazoan life forms did not evolve until comparatively late in Earth's history, but the answer may lie in the build-up of oxygen and the decline in carbon dioxide levels around 600 million years ago. These atmospheric changes may have set the stage for the successful emergence of larger organisms, permitting them to evolve many different kinds of complex tissues, including specialized respiratory structures. Aerobic respiration and metabolism are more efficient than anaerobic respiration and metabolism and created the possibility for a greater complexity of organization. Once organisms could free up parts of their bodies for other functions, such as food gathering, locomotion, and sensory perception, the possibilities for evolutionary diversification were greatly expanded.

≋ Modern Life Appears

Around 540 million years ago, in the Cambrian period, the world became populated by more creatures, including the ancestors of sponges, corals, worms, arthropods, mollusks, echinoderms, and chordates. The oceanic world in which fishes originated almost 500 million years ago probably was much like that of today, although the configuration of land and sea, the flow of ocean currents, and the force and direction of global winds would have been different.

Most Cambrian animals belonged to major groups (phyla) that still exist today, although the individual families to which the animals belonged are now extinct or have only one or two obscure descendants. Fossil representatives of some of those extinct Cambrian animals include a delicate 530-million-year-old creature named *Pikaia*, found in the Middle Cambrian Burgess Shale of British Columbia, and a slightly older Lower Cambrian creature named *Yunnanozoon*, which was recently discovered in China. Both of these soft-bodied animals resemble a modern relative of fishes known as a lancelet. [Plate 3]

Chordates: Creatures With a Nerve

One of the most basic anatomical features of humans is a hollow nerve cord that runs along the back. This nerve cord is found in all animals with a backbone, but its origins lie farther down the evolutionary ladder. All creatures with this nerve, whether or not they have a backbone, are called **chordates**. [Figure 3 and 4]

One of the most primitive chordates is the lancelet or **amphioxus** (*Branchiostoma*; its scientific name is rarely used) , which lives around sandy seabeds of the North Sea, the Mediterranean, the Indian Ocean, and coastal South America. The anatomy of amphioxus, apparently matched by that of extinct lancelets *Pikaia* and *Yunnanozoon* from the Cambrian, is very similar to the hypothetical ancestral condition of vertebrates. Amphioxus has a notochord (an elastic, incompressible structure passing from end to end of the body), a dorsal nerve cord, and serially arranged muscle blocks folded into chevrons (like the body muscle of fishes). The notochord prevents shortening of the body as these muscles contract, making them efficient in bending the body, so providing thrust with the simple tail.

There are gills and gill supports, a fishlike arterial and venous system, and a tail supported by fin rays. Usually under 5 centimeters long, amphioxus has the appearance of a small fish without paired fins or a head (its name means "both ends sharp"). Unable to swim well, amphioxus prefers to burrow in sandy sediments. The notochord extends almost to the tip of the "snout" (in fishes the notochord ends at the level of the hindbrain, so that most of a fish's head lies in front of the notochord). The tail of amphioxus is supported above and below by short rods that resemble the fin rays of fishes. The nerve cord has a swollen anterior extremity (the cerebral vesicle, usually regarded as the equivalent of the forebrain of vertebrates). There are no vertebrae or braincase, and no trace of other brain structures, cranial nerves, or sensory structures such as eyes, ears, or nostrils (although there is a light-sensitive eyespot and a small olfactory pit). There is no heart, but in its place the main blood vessels pulsate, driving oxygenated blood (which in lancelets is colorless) through a dorsal aorta to various organs in the body. Blood is returned to the gills through veins that connect with a ventral trunk beneath the intestine.

FIGURE 3

Some advanced features of a generalized chordate (highly simplified), including the nerve cord underlain by the notochord, and chevron-shaped body muscle segments extending along the entire body.

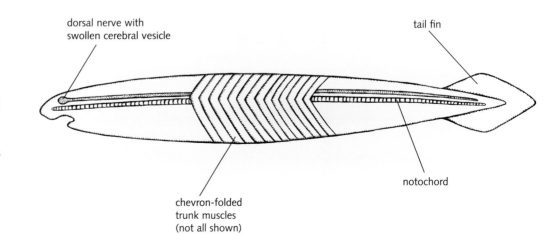

dorsal nerve with swollen cerebral vesicle

tail fin

chevron-folded trunk muscles (not all shown)

notochord

Chordates

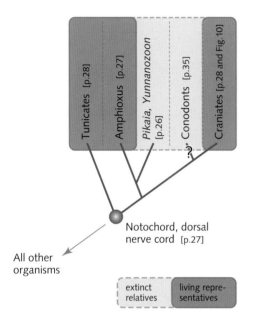

Tunicates [p.28]

Amphioxus [p.27]

Pikaia, Yunnanozoon [p.26]

Conodonts [p.35]

Craniates [p.28 and Fig.10]

?

Notochord, dorsal nerve cord [p.27]

All other organisms

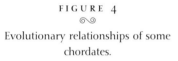

extinct relatives

living representatives

FIGURE 4
∽

Evolutionary relationships of some chordates.

Just about every feature that can be compared is similar in the Cambrian lancelets and modern amphioxus, although *Pikaea* has a pair of antenna–like protrusions on top of its "head," and it is not known if the notochord extended as far forward as in amphioxus. If we were to equate evolutionary success with geological longevity, lancelets would surely be a winner; on the other hand, their anatomy has not advanced much in 530 million years.

Tunicates, or "sea squirts," are also classified as chordates. Although adult tunicates are completely unfishlike, their larvae possess a muscular finlike tail and other chordate features. Lancelets and vertebrates share many features not found in tunicates, such as white and gray matter in the neural tube, a cerebral vesicle or diencephalon, a digestive caecum or liver, specialized cells known as the lateral plate mesoderm, gill supports, the arrangement of blood vessels, and a biosynthetic pathway for thyroid hormone production. On the other hand, tunicate larvae share one important feature with vertebrates that is not present in amphioxus: they have a distinct head region in front of the notochord.

Early in the 20th century it was suggested that amphioxus and higher chordates are creatures that retained many larval features into the adult stage (an evolutionary trend called paedomorphosis). It was argued that ancestral chordates may have had a tunicate–like adult stage that was lost when the onset of sexual maturity shifted to earlier in the life cycle. Although this notion could hold true for amphioxus, it doesn't fit the facts as far as higher chordates such as craniates are concerned. These have many additional features, involving additional steps in their development, with the result that adult craniates have far greater complexity than amphioxus or tunicates. The addition of new developmental steps prior to the onset of sexual maturity (called peramorphosis) is customarily regarded as the exact opposite of paedomorphosis. Are

craniates paedomorphic chordates with highly peramorphic embryos? This paradox does not make much sense, and perhaps there is a simpler explanation; primitive adult chordates may have resembled amphioxus, and adult tunicates and craniates could represent two completely independent peramorphic trends, one toward a sessile mode of life on the seafloor, the other toward active swimming. Fossils such as *Pikaia* and *Yunnanozoon* may eventually provide some clues to this mystery.

Getting a Head: Craniates

Humans and fishes share many anatomical features. Our front end contains a brain with several chambers, surrounded and protected by a skeletal cranium. We have paired sensory capsules (eyes, ears, and olfactory receptors); a dermal skeleton formed within the skin (although not much of it is left); an internal bony skeleton (the endoskeleton), including a vertebral column that encloses the notochord; and many soft-tissue features such as thyroid and pituitary glands, a liver with special vessels to carry blood from the intestine, a gallbladder, a pancreas, and a spleen. All these features reflect early adaptations to a primitive aquatic environment, and all have been greatly modified in humans' 350 million years of terrestrial evolution.

Animals with these features are craniates. Anatomically speaking, a craniate is a chordate with a highly specialized head region. The nerve cord includes a brain and cranial nerves, and there are sensory capsules for smell, vision, and balance–not hearing–all wrapped in a protective skeletal braincase. Although the nerve cord is underlain and supported by the notochord as in amphioxus, in the most primitive craniates there is no indication of discrete vertebrae surrounding the nerve cord. [Figure 5] From this difference it is clear that craniates and vertebrates really represent two different groups, although in some textbooks they are treated as if they were synonymous.

A backbone with vertebrae is not present among primitive jawless craniates such as lampreys and hagfishes, and is not preserved in the most primitive fossil fishes either. It is therefore entirely possible that this structure evolved only after the craniate head region.

The profound anatomical differences between craniates and other chordates such as tunicates and lancelets represent an enormous evolutionary advance. In the past, it was customary to assume this meant a lengthy gap in the fossil record, for it seemed inconceivable that so many features could have evolved rapidly, and the Cambrian lancelets are separated from the first Ordovician bony craniates by almost 90 million years. Today, with a better understanding of genetics and developmental processes, craniate evolution can be viewed in terms of changes to the **genome** (the totality of the DNA sequences an individual inherits from its parents) and the expression of these changes in the embryo. We now know that, in craniates, some regulatory genes (usually very stable) responsible for the earlier stages of development became significantly modified in the course of evolution, and unique patterns of gene **expression** developed in the embryo. Most developmental and anatomical differences between craniates and other chordates stem from this tinkering with regulatory genes. From a geneticist's viewpoint the changes are small, and could have been accomplished in just a few generations instead of millions of years.

Getting a New Head, and Filling It

Craniate structure is the big sum of small but profound genetic differences. The first clues that craniate evolution may not have been so gradual as usually supposed came in the 1980s, when two American anatomists, Carl Gans and Glenn Northcutt, suggested that the craniate head was an evolutionarily new feature, in the sense that it did not exist in any prior organism. Of course, many invertebrates have a head at the front end of their body, but in none of them does the head have the structural complexity seen in craniates. Even though the amphioxus clearly has a front end, there is no equivalent of the

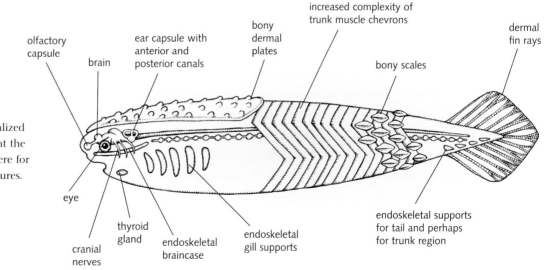

FIGURE 5

Some advanced features of a generalized craniate (highly simplified). Note that the nerve cord and notochord (shown here for clarity) are primitive (chordate) features.

olfactory capsule

brain

ear capsule with anterior and posterior canals

bony dermal plates

increased complexity of trunk muscle chevrons

bony scales

dermal fin rays

eye

cranial nerves

thyroid gland

endoskeletal braincase

endoskeletal gill supports

endoskeletal supports for tail and perhaps for trunk region

craniate head, because the notochord extends forward and occupies the space where the head would be.

The idea that the head was an evolutionarily new structure was widely accepted, since it seemed to provide a developmental rationale for the appearance of the earliest craniates that was broadly in accord with the geologically late appearance of craniate fossils (craniates are one of the few major group of living animals not represented in the Early and Middle Cambrian).

There are actually two parts to the "new head" model, although the distinction is subtle. First, there is the acquisition of the space where the head should be, the process of cephalization. In craniates, this space lies almost entirely in front of the tip of the notochord. Second, the head space has to be filled with new stuff, namely a brain, the cranial nerves and blood vessels, the sensory capsules, and the muscles, cartilage, and bone of the skull—the process of cranialization. The contents of the craniate head represent a remarkable evolutionary advance, greater perhaps than any since the appearance of complex multicellular creatures, and arguably of greater significance than anything that has occurred in subsequent craniate history.

It would be a mistake to think that the first craniates were empty-headed, first acquiring a space and then filling it with all kinds of new structures. The "new head" scenario proposes that the processes of cephalization and cranialization took place simultaneously. But here is a remarkable thing: All of this new stuff in the craniate head is produced by special embryonic tissues that do not exist in any other creatures. And, as scientists delve further into craniate development, it turns out that practically every other unique craniate feature is also derived from these special tissues, which simply do not exist in other organisms. Craniate embryos are as different from "invertebrate" embryos as adult craniates are from adult "invertebrates." So, we can define craniates in

more than one way. To an anatomist, craniates are chordates with a head full of new structures. To an embryologist, however, craniates are characterized by various kinds of unique embryonic tissues, the most important of which are the **neural crest**, **epidermal placodes**, and **hypomere**.

The most crucial of these tissues, in terms of the variety and number of structures it forms, is the neural crest. The neural crest consists of special cells that are located initially at the upper margins of the nerve cord in very early embryos of all craniates, including humans. Actually, the neural crest isn't so much a tissue as a special zone where some cells of the embryonic nerve cord are genetically signaled to migrate to other parts of the embryo and form various structures. Without the genetic signal, these cells remain part of the nerve cord. With the signal, they begin to migrate to far-flung parts of the embryo, where they divide and interact with other cells to form many kinds of connective tissues, pigment cells, nerves, parts of the eyes, and parts of the pharynx, digestive tract, and circulatory system. Most important of all, they are the progenitors of bone cells. Bone is unique to craniates because only they have the embryonic tissue necessary to make it.

Not only do lancelets and tunicates lack the heady stuff of craniates, they also lack the special precursor tissues necessary to form it. Lancelets have a nerve cord but lack the genetic pathway to generate neural crest cells. The acquisition of these novel tissues led to the evolution of a great many new structures, not the least of which was an elaborate bony skeleton. By far the most profound consequence was the formation of a head with a brain, sensory capsules, the complex wiring and plumbing of the cranial nerves and blood vessels, and a protective braincase.

Cranialization represents a great leap in anatomical complexity and allowed highly sophisticated sensory systems to evolve. Those new sensory systems endowed craniates with new levels of awareness of their surrounding environment. Early craniates had a completely new view of the world. Other parts of their bodies changed as well. They developed a cartilaginous skeleton and bony armor to protect all of the new sensory hardware, and they improved their propulsive systems in order to move it all around. The development of specialized mouthparts in the head also opened up new possibilities for feeding, including scavenging and predation, although an effective biting mechanism like that provided by movable jaws was still a thing of the future.

New Head, New Tissues, New Genes

We are all aware that genes inside our cells control our development, but probably few people understand the intricacies of the process. For most of us, genetics was something we learned in high school or college, and our classroom exercises involved looking at who had blue or brown eyes, or the ratios of black and white mice in a litter, and so forth. Such traits are inherited and are regulated by particular genes. But this is only the beginning, for there are many other genes whose function (or *expression*) is less obvious, such as switching other genes on and off and regulating when and where they are expressed. Thus we have structural genes and control genes.

One of the most exciting advances in developmental biology at the close of the 20th century has been the discovery that most (perhaps all) complex multicellular animals share special families of very conservative control genes that regulate development of their fundamental body pattern. Among these is the **Hox gene** family, without which we would not be able to exist as organized multicellular creatures. [Figure 6] Hox genes are remarkably similar in hydras, nematode worms, arthropods, and chordates. The great diversity of features regulated by Hox genes suggests that their evolution has gone hand in hand with the evolution

of new structures and morphologies. They regulate the activities of many other genes and are responsible for some of the earliest and most fundamental events in embryonic development in humans.

At first glance, it might seem paradoxical that these highly conservative genes are responsible for regulating the development of anatomically diverse structures in such obviously different creatures as hydras, flies, and fishes. It turns out, however, that Hox genes are involved in basic aspects of development, such as distinguishing anterior from posterior, where segments will form in the embryo, where limbs or fins will form, and which way is up. Moreover, Hox genes are expressed in a particular chronological order along the main body axis, and each **gene** has a sharply defined domain where its influence is felt. Timing and location are therefore critical for Hox gene expression in the embryo.

In the fruit fly *Drosophila* there is a cluster of just eight Hox genes, arranged in a distinct sequence (by convention, geneticists number the genes sequentially, from 1–8). Other arthropods have remarkably similar Hox genes, and their different body plans (for example, in crustaceans, chelicerates, myriapods, and insects) may have evolved by divergent modifications to the way this set of Hox genes is expressed during development; the same is probably true of other invertebrates.

In amphioxus, a primitive chordate, there is again a single cluster of Hox genes, differing only slightly from that of *Drosophila* in having ten genes (geneticists regard the extra genes as copies of two of the original eight). In jawed craniates (although only a few have been investigated, such as a ray-finned fish, frog, mouse, and chick), a remarkable difference has been discovered, for they all have *four* clusters of Hox genes instead of one (for convenience, geneticists have designated these clusters as Hox A, B, C, and D). Their Hox genes also are more numerous, with up to 11 per cluster (geneticists regard the extra genes as copies of original ones, and also regard the extra clusters as copies of the original one).

Each Hox cluster in jawed craniates differs slightly from the others in lacking certain genes, but all four clusters are clearly similar. If we could lay all four clusters side by side, we would notice that each gene of one cluster has a corresponding one (called a paralogous gene) on at least some (sometimes all) the other clusters (for example, A1, B1, C1, etc.). Because all four clusters have extra genes, they are thought to have been added prior to whatever mutations led to the formation of extra copies of the gene clusters. Thus the hypothetical ancestor of all craniates may have had a single cluster with more Hox genes than the ten found in the lancelet. To a geneticist, craniates could be defined as organisms with multiple copies of the chordate Hox cluster.

Why is all this important? Because *many of the unique anatomical features of craniates, and their unique tissues such as the neural crest, are under the direct regulatory influence of these Hox genes*. The Hox genes are implicated in the development of the craniate head (including the organization of the hindbrain), the arrangement of segments along the body axis, and the development of paired fins and limbs.

A gene is said to be *expressed* by whatever structure it controls; thus a gene that regulates limb development (such as Hox C-5) would be expressed, or "spoken for," by the appearance of the limb bud in the embryo. The expression of a particular gene in one cluster may not be the same as that of a paralogous gene in another cluster, although both may be expressed in the same part of the embryo.

A couple of specific examples will underscore the importance of these changes in Hox gene complexity for craniate development and evolution. Firstly, two genes on a single cluster (Hox A-1, Hox A-3, or the first and third gene on cluster "A") are expressed in the formation of neural crest. Paralogous genes on other clusters have different functions (for example Hox B-3 is expressed in forma-tion of body segments, presumably the primitive gene expression). The "A" cluster thus regulates a fundamental craniate embryonic tissue, and without Hox A-1 and Hox A-3 the tissue fails to develop. Secondly, the development of paired appendages (fins, limbs) is regulated by Hox C-5 (i.e. the fifth gene on cluster "C"), so without this third cluster craniates would not develop paired fins or limbs. No single cluster of Hox genes is responsible for regulating all aspects of craniate development; the responsibility is shared among all the clusters, with little duplication of gene expression.

We have thus discovered that craniates are unique not only in their anatomy, but also in their embryonic tissues and their Hox gene arrangement. The unique anatomical and developmental attributes of craniates are rooted in changes to their Hox genes and involve gene duplications, multiple copies of gene clusters, and new products of gene expression. If the single primitive Hox gene cluster had not been lengthened and copied in the common ancestor of craniates, no fishes or dinosaurs or humans would have evolved.

Hox Genes and Macroevolution

Most scientific discussion about the mechanisms of evolution has focused upon microevolutionary changes in features that are easily studied, such as the shape of certain structures that are presumed to be under the regulation of structural genes. So far, less attention has been paid to the impact of mutations affecting regulatory genes, partly because their expressions (frequently transient and ephemeral) are more difficult to investigate within the developing embryo, and partly because they are so intrinsically stable. The traditional neodarwinian view of evolutionary change is gradualistic, involving micromutations and the complex interaction of genes, with natural selection operating on these genetic mutations. Larger-scale (macroevolutionary) events, such as the evolution of craniates, have generally been viewed as the product of many

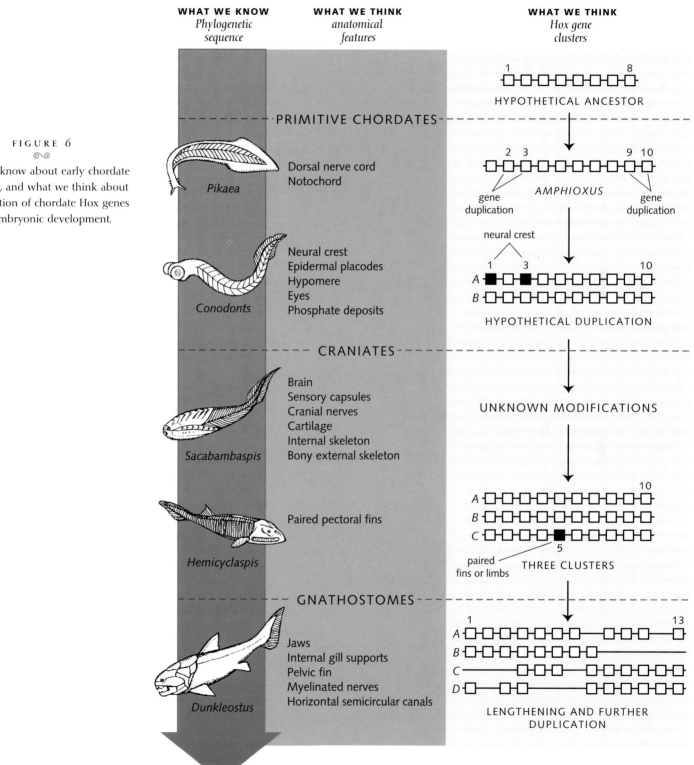

FIGURE 6
⁊୭
What we know about early chordate evolution, and what we think about the evolution of chordate Hox genes and embryonic development.

WHAT WE KNOW
Phylogenetic sequence

WHAT WE THINK
anatomical features

WHAT WE THINK
Hox gene clusters

1   8
HYPOTHETICAL ANCESTOR

PRIMITIVE CHORDATES

Pikaea

Dorsal nerve cord
Notochord

2 3   9 10
AMPHIOXUS
gene duplication   gene duplication

Conodonts

Neural crest
Epidermal placodes
Hypomere
Eyes
Phosphate deposits

neural crest
1   3   10
A
B
HYPOTHETICAL DUPLICATION

CRANIATES

Sacabambaspis

Brain
Sensory capsules
Cranial nerves
Cartilage
Internal skeleton
Bony external skeleton

UNKNOWN MODIFICATIONS

Hemicyclaspis

Paired pectoral fins

10
A
B
C
5
paired fins or limbs   THREE CLUSTERS

GNATHOSTOMES

Dunkleostus

Jaws
Internal gill supports
Pelvic fin
Myelinated nerves
Horizontal semicircular canals

1   13
A
B
C
D
LENGTHENING AND FURTHER DUPLICATION

accumulated smaller (microevolutionary) events.

The revelation that craniate development is regulated by special copies of otherwise very conservative control genes casts new light on how major evolutionary changes may occur. Instead of viewing the rise of craniates as a gradual series of microevolutionary events leading, mutation by imperceptible mutation, from chordate to craniate, maybe we should view it as an evolutionary *fait accompli*, involving just a few mutations to vital regulatory control genes. Such tampering with the regulatory genome is evidently rare, otherwise we should not find such close similarities in the Hox genes of various animals across the board. But when it does occur, as in the craniates, the end result is a profoundly different level of bodily organisation and pattern of embryonic development. It is almost as if there were two kinds of mutations; those affecting structural genes (common, and leading to small-scale or microevolutionary changes), and those affecting control genes (rare, and leading to major shifts in developmental strategies and structural complexity).

While the earliest stages of embryonic development in a human are regulated by essentially the same control genes as in a fish or a frog, we obviously end our development looking completely different. Hox genes in the living zebrafish are practically identical to those of a chick or mouse, yet its Hox C-5 gene is not expressed in limbs or digits, suggesting that Hox gene expression can be altered (an area currently under investigation by geneticists). Such possibilities are insufficient to account for all the anatomical differences between a human, a fish or a frog, however, and expressions of structural genes are probably more important at this level.

Although we are still missing a lot of the genetic data, we can attempt to map a few events in the evolution of craniate regulatory genes and the embryonic development they control. Tunicate larvae,

with their notochord and nerve cord, represent the primitive condition. Amphioxus, with a cerebral vesicle, folded body muscles and a couple of extra genes in its Hox cluster, is more advanced. In hagfishes and lampreys, craniate features (including those fundamental tissues such as the neural crest) are accompanied by duplication and apparent elongation of the original Hox cluster. Jawed vertebrates have a slew of new anatomical features, mostly derived from unique craniate tissues, and seem also to have the most complex Hox clusters. There *is* a hierarchy of anatomy, development, and genes among craniates, but the evolution of **ontogeny** at this basic level does not seem gradual. The evolution of craniates may be characterized as a major reorganization of regulatory genes, leading to profound shifts in development and appearance of many new structures without any ancestral counterpart. The appearance of craniates was arguably the farthest-reaching evolutionary jump in the animal kingdom since the great Cambrian explosion, when the fundamental body plans of several major invertebrate groups were established. [Figure 6]

Are There Craniate "Missing Links"?

Many features of modern craniate head organization, such as the presence of a brain, cranial nerves, sensory capsules, and gills, are present in the earliest fossil fishes. These fossils suggest that such special embryonic tissues as the neural crest had evolved more than 450 million years ago, and that the duplicate genes that regulate these tissues were already present. In the search for a "missing link" between fishes and such primitive chordates as *Pikaia* and *Yunnanozoon*, there is increasing evidence that some extinct creatures possessed some craniate attributes while lacking others. Among the most enigmatic of this group of fossils are animals called **conodonts**. [Plate 4]

At first, conodonts were known only from tiny phosphatic fossils resembling teeth that occur abundantly in strata ranging in age from the mid–Cambrian to the Late Triassic, an impressively long span of about 300 million years. It was not until the 1980s that a few complete conodont fossils were discovered, in 340-million-year-old Carboniferous strata near Edinburgh, Scotland. To the untrained eye, the complete conodont animal is disappointing. It consists of a pair of rounded lobes at one end and a slender, tapering tail at the other. The conodont animal apparently was little more than a set of teeth with a tail, lacking features to provide guidance or direction. Based on their fossil occurrences, conodonts were exclusively sea creatures, and they spread widely throughout the world's oceans.

Some scientists have concluded that conodonts possessed important chordate features, such as segmental muscular segments and a notochord, and it has even been suggested that they should be classified as craniates, based on interpretations of some hard tissues as cellular bone, enamel, and calcified cartilage. In fact, three conodont features seem to tie these ancient animals in to craniate evolution.

First, within the conodont tail are short rods that resemble the fin rays of fishes and lancelets. It is widely thought (perhaps incorrectly) that fin rays in fishes are derived from the neural crest, which is unique to craniates. On the other hand, the non–craniate lancelets also have fin rays but lack a neural crest, so conodonts could also have had fin rays derived from non–neural crest tissue. Second, it has been suggested that conodont animals had eyes that were supported by cartilaginous rings. Neural crest tissue is involved in the formation of craniate eyes, and eye lenses form from another unique craniate tissue, epidermal placodes. If

conodonts had eyes like those of fishes, they probably also had a neural crest and epidermal placodes. Conodonts, however, lack any trace of an internal skeleton other than the paired rings that supposedly supported their eyes. Third, conodont teeth were arranged internally, apparently within a pharynx. If the tooth array was movable, as some scientists have suggested, muscular action may have been required, and in craniates the **pharyngeal** muscles are formed by the hypomere, the third kind of unique craniate tissue.

Did conodonts possess a neural crest, epidermal placodes, and a hypomere? If we accept the existence of any of these features as evidence, conodonts may be an extinct group of chordates, perhaps related to the ancestors of craniates. If that is correct, some duplications of Hox genes and clusters may already have occurred in the common ancestors of conodonts and craniates, since segmentation and neural crest formation apparently are controlled by paralogous genes on different clusters (Hox A–3, Hox B–3). Conodonts may represent a group of simple craniates that diverged from the mainstream prior to the advent of more complex structures, such as an elaborate brain, an internal skeleton, and bony external plates and scales. But conodonts lacked olfactory organs and a labyrinthine organ of balance, and had no bones or scales in the skin. The main event was going on elsewhere, among creatures that peered at their watery environment through eyes encased by bones.

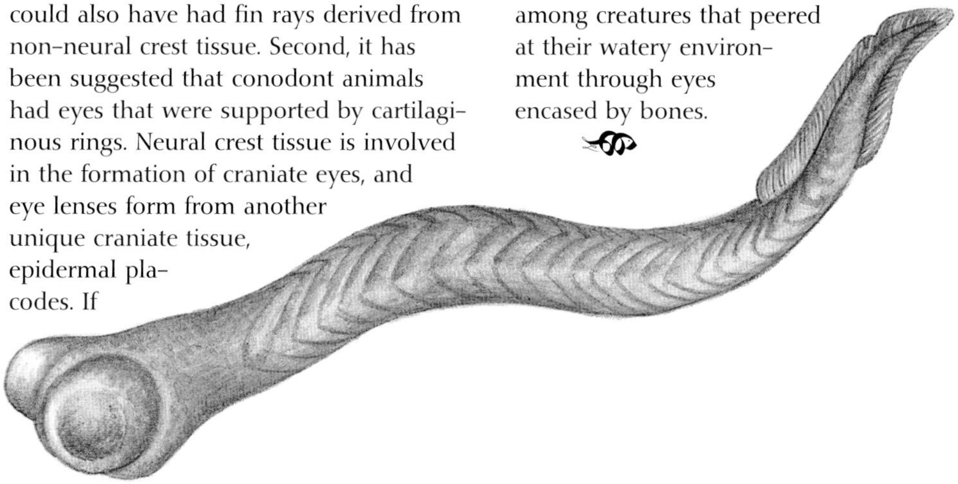

PLATE 4

Restoration of a conodont animal from the Early Carboniferous of Scotland (about 350 million years old). Conodont animals are supposed by some scientists to be a craniate "missing link", lying between amphioxus and fishes. Estimated length approximately 40mm long (microscopic teeth from other localities suggest that many conodonts were much smaller).

⋙ Fishes Take Over the World: The Ostracoderms

PLATE 5

Sacabambaspis lived in shallow seas covering parts of Bolivia about 450 million years ago, during the Late Ordovician. Its head was heavily armored with bony plates that formed a solid unit, but its body was covered in narrow scales arranged in chevrons that provided flexibility. It is the earliest ostracoderm craniate for which we have complete fossils, and was approximately 25cm long.

⋙ The Oldest Bones

*T*HE FIRST CLUES that the primeval world once teemed with bizarre and unfamiliar fishes came early in the young science of paleontology. In the 1830s the Swiss anatomist Louis Agassiz was sent some fossils of bony armored fishes from ancient sandstone strata of Scotland. The fossils were unlike any living creature, and Agassiz had a hard time trying to decipher their anatomy. His first reaction was to compare them with modern armored fishes such as catfishes and sturgeons, a view that he published in 1835. In subsequent work, published in 1844, Agassiz came to realize that the fossils, which lacked movable jaws, were in fact very different from these fishes.

In 1889 the American paleontologist Edward Cope placed these fossils (from the Devonian period) and some even older Silurian ones from Estonia into a new group, which he named **ostracoderms**, meaning "shell-skinned." We, too, can use Cope's old name, ostracoderm. It is convenient and less long-winded than "ancient armored jawless fishes," although ostracoderms collectively do not form a natural group with a common ancestor. Remember that ostracoderms are different from **placoderms** (*armor-skinned*), which are "ancient armored *jawed* fishes."

The oldest claimed bits of ostracoderm bone are from the Upper Cambrian, dating from around 510 million years ago. In 1978 John Repetski, of the United States Geological Survey in Washington, published a detailed description of supposedly bony fragments, referred to *Anatolepis*, from the Deadwood Formation of Wyoming. Writing in 1989, Swedish anatomist and paleontologist Tor Ørvig was undecided whether these fossils were bone, even after looking at thin sections of samples under the microscope. In late 1990, Australian paleontologists reported finding similar small fragments of ostracoderm bone in Cambrian strata, but this material has not yet been described.

Charles Walcott, discoverer of the famous Burgess Shale fossils from the Upper Cambrian of British Columbia, was prospecting in the 1890s for ancient fossils in Colorado, near Canyon City. He discovered unmistakable evidence of ostracoderm bones and scales, about 450 million years old, in Upper Ordovician strata known as the Harding Sandstone. This was a remarkable discovery, not only because those bones were at the time the oldest bones known, but also because two different kinds of bony plates were recognizable, leading Walcott to describe in 1892 two new Ordovician ostracoderms,

which he named *Eryptychius* and *Astraspis*.

Eryptychius was poorly preserved and its anatomy is still not well known. The other fossil, *Astraspis*, was represented by the external impression of a bony shield that covered the head and consisted of many closely interlocking polygonal bony plates. Almost 80 years after Walcott's first amazing discovery, a second, more complete specimen of *Astraspis* was discovered in 1968, providing an opportunity to gather additional information about this ancient fish. Subsequent microscopic histological studies of thin sections from both of the original fossils of the Harding Sandstone have confirmed their bony composition and that Walcott was correct in recognizing two entirely different ostracoderms.

With ostracoderms inferentially diverse in the Ordovician of North America, vertebrate paleontologists wondered if they could have existed in other parts of the world as well. After many years, two major discoveries were made, in places far distant from Colorado, confirming that ostracoderms were widespread more than 400 million years ago. In 1977 fragments of an ostracoderm called *Arandaspis* were

PLATE 6

Sacabambaspis janvieri, an ostracoderm from the Late Ordovician of Bolivia (cast), about 450 million years old. Length 24cm.

described from Middle Ordovician strata of the Amadeus Basin in central Australia (slightly older than the Harding Sandstone), and in 1986 complete fossils of another ostracoderm, *Sacabambaspis* [Plates 5 and 6] were discovered in the Upper Ordovician of Bolivia. The earliest jawless fishes were indeed spread across the globe!

These fossil discoveries are informative for several reasons. They indicate that ostracoderms definitely existed at least 450 million years ago, and from their shape and structure we may infer that they swam and functioned in ways that are perfectly familiar today. The bones (all of which were formed superficially, within the skin) imply the presence of soft internal organs (for example, nostrils, eyes, a pressure-sensitive lateral line system, a brain, and gills) that are not otherwise preserved as actual fossil material. Most informatively, these fossils show no trace of internal bony tissue. We are so used to our own skeletons and to those of fossil prehistoric animals such as dinosaurs that we tend to overlook the fact that many of these internal bones are entirely absent in the oldest ostracoderms!

≋⦙⦙⦙⧽ Our Two Skeletons

Although we usually think of ourselves as having one skeleton, in fact we have two [Figure 7] They are formed differently, they have different evolutionary histories, and as far as we can tell they evolved separately. With the passing of time, distinctions between the two have become blurred, and our two original skeletons are now merged into one. In our extinct fishy ancestors, such as the first ostracoderms, only one of these skeletons is present, and in our living fishy cousins, the two skeletons are still distinguishable, providing clues to the history of craniate evolution.

FIGURE 7
⊙⊙

Craniates have a dermal skeleton (formed in the skin) and an endoskeleton (formed in and around cartilage), as in this Devonian fish, *Moythomasia* (about 375 million years old). [see page 141 and Plate 14]

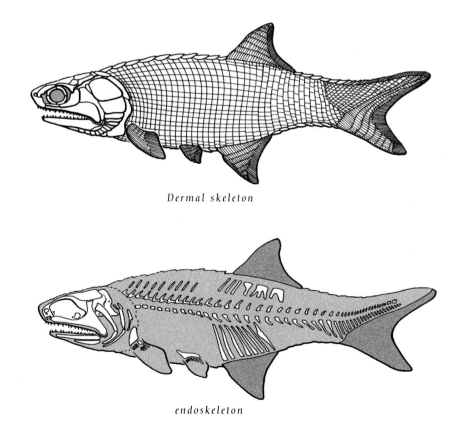

Dermal skeleton

endoskeleton

One of these skeletons is formed superficially, just beneath the skin, and is called the **dermal skeleton**. It is always bony, but the hard "bony" tissue is variable in composition and includes specialized structures that we do not usually consider bone, such as teeth with their hard enamel layer. The dermal skeleton typically does not form deep within the body (there are rare exceptions), and is never cartilaginous. The earliest bones in the fossil record, which are from ostracoderms, are exclusively from the dermal skeleton, so we know that this evolved at least 450 million years ago. In the human skull, much of the facial region is made of dermal bones, including the cheek bones, the tooth–bearing bones, and those of the forehead.

Our second skeleton forms deeper within the body, around the spinal cord and brain and within the fins and limbs, and is called the **endoskeleton**. It is not preserved in early ostracoderms. Unlike the dermal skeleton, the endoskeleton is not always bony, but is sometimes cartilaginous, for example in modern hagfishes, lampreys, sharks, sturgeons, paddlefishes, and even some amphibians. Endoskeletal bone is formed either around cartilage (perichondral bone) or within it (endochondral bone), for example in our vertebrae, limb bones, and pelvis. A cartilaginous endoskeleton without bone may have evolved very early in craniate history, but we find evidence for it only in fossils with endoskeletal bone, which evolved comparatively late in craniate history.

⇒⏅⏅⏅⏅▹ What's So Special About Bone?

Bone is not a dead mineral deposit but a unique kind of living tissue. It can form only in certain parts of the body, and it requires one kind of special cell to produce an organic framework and other kinds to secrete calcium phosphate, the primary mineral component of bone, around this framework. It is not an easy matter to define bone, because a tremendous variety in bony tissues is recognized in living craniates, chiefly in the extent and arrangement of cell spaces and canals for blood vessels within the bone, the arrangement of the organic framework (made up of bundles of a fibrous protein called collagen), and the density of bony phosphate. Craniate bone has no invertebrate precursor and is different from the hard skeletal tissues of invertebrates.

As far as we know, the cells responsible for constructing craniate skeletons are derived from those mysterious craniate tissues we call the neural crest and epidermal placodes. Both the dermal skeleton and the endoskeleton are new features in craniates, and the development of both is regulated by copies of genes that never existed even in more primitive chordates or other invertebrate animals.

Bone is constantly changing within our bodies and, as many people learn to their cost, it can break and be repaired, it can be deformed and diseased, and it can be cruelly robbed of its calcium content, especially in later life. Clearly our bones serve us in different ways than in the first fishes, but in some regards our respective skeletons are still the same. There has been a great deal of speculation about the function of bone in the first ostracoderms. It is worth while considering some of the possibilities.

⇒⏅⏅⏅⏅▹ Bumps and Scratches?

Protection from the rough–and–tumble of a high–energy nearshore environment would seem like a good reason to have a hard outer layer. Bone just beneath the skin protects from abrasion, and it can be repaired when broken, chipped, or cracked. Calcium phosphate is marginally harder and therefore more resistant to physical damage than the calcium carbonate from which invertebrate shells are mostly made.

There is evidence of abrasion on some ostracoderm bones, where their bumpy ornament has become worn and scratched, but evidence of predation in the form of healed wounds is rare. Although predators such as eurypterids (large, extinct "sea scorpions," distantly related to modern horseshoe crabs) certainly existed during the Ordovician, it has not yet been shown that they lived in the same environments as the earliest ostracoderms. Although ostracoderm bone might have been modified toward a protective function through natural selection, it doesn't seem likely that it originated to protect these early fishes from abrasion or attack. Thus, protection is more likely to be a secondary rather than original function of ostracoderm bone.

Swimming?

External rigidity and protection against abrasion are offset by the need for flexibility of the muscular body. Small dermal plates and scales offer a compromise. Designers of medieval suits of armor understood this problem well, and devised many ingenious ways to protect the more flexible parts of armor-wearing knights.

In modern fishes an internal bony skeleton provides support and attachment for muscles and ligaments and is crucial to movement and other bodily functions, especially in supporting the body muscles used in generating forward thrust by the tail fin. Although it has been suggested that bone evolved in connection with locomotion and muscular support in the earliest fishes, a few moments' thought will show that this is really unlikely.

First, the fossil evidence shows that the oldest ostracoderms had no internal bony tissue, and bone was confined to the dermal skeleton of the body and head. Second, there is no bone in the vertebral column of modern lampreys and hagfishes, coelacanths and lungfishes, sturgeons and paddlefishes, and various deep-sea fishes, yet they all swim very well despite this supposed handicap. Bony vertebrae occur only in advanced members of several groups, for example among "modern" sharks and advanced bony fishes. Clearly, the presence of bone per se has no correlation with a fish's ability to swim or perform other functions.

Ostracoderm streamlining and surface ornament (it isn't merely decorative) are hydrodynamic responses to the watery environment. A bony covering of scales could also have provided a stiffer tail surface for improved thrust, but this bony covering surely evolved after the appearance of the muscular body with all its chevron segments, and would not have provided support for the internal muscles of the tail. Bone therefore seems to have only a secondary purpose in locomotion, which would not represent its original function.

Preventing Leaks?

Bone has several important physiological functions today, and some of these functions undoubtedly were important to the earliest bony fishes. Many years ago, back in the days when craniates were thought to have evolved in fresh water, it was suggested that dermal bone served to prevent seepage of fresh water by osmosis into the body fluids of ostracoderms, much as a layer of tar painted on the outside of an old boat keeps water from leaking in. The preponderance of fossil evidence today points to a seawater origin for these fishes. Organisms living in salt water have the opposite problem, that of retaining water against a reversed osmotic gradient, as terrestrial animals do. Most likely the earliest ostracoderms were in osmotic equilibrium with surrounding seawater, with glomerular kidneys, another unique craniate feature, to remove waste products more efficiently from the body.

Calcium Metabolism and Storage?

Many paleontologists have suggested that bone was first used by ostracoderms as a place to store calcium. When it is first laid down as new bone, much of the calcium phosphate in living bones is in an amorphous (non-crystalline) state. In this condition it is more readily mobilized by the body. As blood levels of calcium fall, hormones signal bone cells to liberate more by removing calcium from the bone.

The ability to regulate calcium hormonally is present even in the most primitive living craniates and may have been an important first step in the evolution of bone tissue. Crystalline calcium phosphate (hydroxyapatite) of mature bone is less readily mobilized and does not provide the body with such rapid access to calcium. What we invariably see in fossils is this mature bone, but we should not forget that it was probably associated with amorphous new bone that either did not fossilize or became crystalline during fossilization.

What would be the value of calcium storage to an ostracoderm? Calcium in dilute seawater (in estuaries at the mouths of large rivers, for example, where the level of dissolved salts is appreciably lower than in normal seawater) can greatly enhance the ability of marine organisms to regulate the intake of water. Some marine fishes are capable of entering fresh waters that have a high calcium content but experience distress where calcium levels are lower. By carrying a supply of calcium along in their dermal skeleton, some ostracoderms may have been able to enter fresh waters that had low calcium levels.

Bone is also an obvious source of phosphate, which is essential to the energy cycle involving adenosine phosphate, a substance that plays a pivotal role in cell metabolism. Phosphate ions could be mobilized (especially in new bone) as the demand arose, and a portable phosphate store may have provided the first bony ostracoderms with the ability to make extended forays into environments with low phosphate levels. Free phosphate availability is lowest in fresh waters, and ostracoderms venturing into brackish or fresh waters might have drawn on their bones for additional phosphate. Bone is also the principal storage site of carbonate in the body.

We have looked at the physiological advantages of an on-board store of calcium, phosphate and carbonate in freshwater fishes. Those same resources would also be beneficial to a sea-going ostracoderm. If bone arose first in sea-going ostracoderms, any physiological advantages it provided in fresh waters would be secondary.

⋙ Little Bones or Big Bones?

Some scientists have suggested that the most primitive bones must have been small individual dermal plates that formed, rather like teeth or shark **denticles**, within little dermal papillae in the skin. This micromeric (*small part*) hypothesis presupposes that the skeleton consisted primitively of lots of little denticles, some of which fused together to form larger plates of bone in more advanced fishes. Other scientists have suggested that the primitive skeleton consisted of large plates that secondarily were subdivided into smaller elements.

The macromeric (*large part*) hypothesis assumes either that the earliest craniate body was primitively encased by rigid bone, which is absurd, or that only the inflexible head was cloaked in bone, which is not what the fossils tell us. The micromeric hypothesis cannot be refuted – there are primitive fossils called thelodonts (see page 55) from the Silurian with just such a skeleton – but the oldest fossil bones are not micromeric. Large plates and smaller scales appear at about the same time, and the oldest Ordovician ostracoderms had both. The earliest vertebrate dermal skeleton could therefore have been platelike in the head region, where rigidity was advantageous, and at the same time have consisted of smaller plates or scales over other parts of the body where flexibility of movement was at a premium.

⋙ What Were the First Bony Fishes Like?

Ordovician ostracoderms had a blunt, rounded head shield made up of both large and small plates. The eyes of *Astraspis* were larger and set farther apart than in the other forms, with ample room for olfactory organs between the eyes and the mouth. The body behind the head armor was gently tapered and covered by many

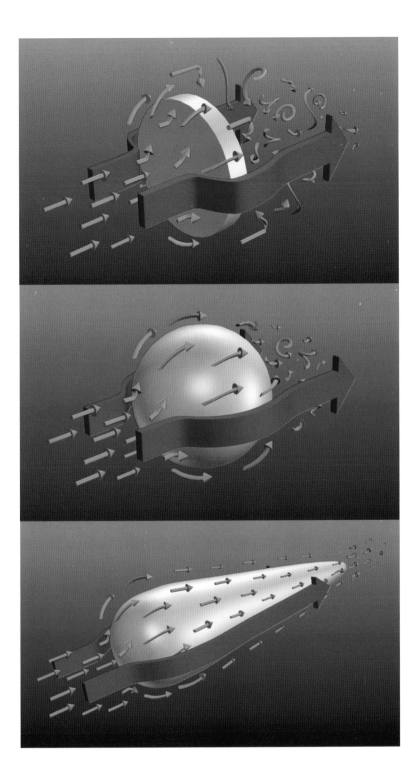

FIGURE 8
∽

Flow of water around different shapes:
disk (top), sphere (middle), and teardrop (bottom).

rows of scales arranged in a series of chevrons so that their overall shape was that of a teardrop. There was a well–developed pressure–sensitive system (the lateral line) embedded in the surface of their bony armor. The detection of pressure changes in the water caused by currents or the movement of prey, for example, may have been particularly sensitive. Modern fishes have a comparable lateral line system, and in sharks the sensitivity of this device in detecting the weak movements of distant prey is well documented.

⇛ Ostracoderm Physics

The teardrop shape of *Astraspis*, as well as that of *Arandaspis* and *Sacabambaspis*, is deceptively simple, for it is actually one of the most hydrodynamically efficient shapes we can imagine. The same physical constraints apply equally to guppies, whales, sailboats, nuclear submarines, and ostracoderms. [Figure 8]

Any object moving through a fluid, such as a fish through water, will experience resistance that tends to impede its motion. This resistance is known as **drag**, and it is the chief factor in ship hull design. Water can flow past an object in two ways, either smoothly (laminar flow) or in a disorganized fashion (turbulent flow). It is in a fish's (or a ship's) best interest to minimize the amount of turbulent flow and to maximize laminar flow over its surface.

Drag comes in two principal forms. Pressure drag is related to the density of the fluid. Imagine a flat disk or plate at a right angle to a current of water. Water reaching the disk is displaced around and behind it and generates tremendous turbulence. It will take a great expenditure of energy to move the disk forward against the current. If we rotate the disk so that it is side–on to the current (which the flow of water will try to do anyway), we will have a much easier time moving it forward, because the only pressure drag now is created by the thickness of the disk (a thinner disk is easier to move forward than a thick one for this reason). But even though forward motion is easier, there is still another kind of drag having its effect.

This second force is friction drag, and it is caused by the viscosity, or stickiness, of the fluid (for example, water has a lower viscosity than honey, and objects will move through water and honey at different rates). Between a fish and water there is a transitional boundary layer. Water immediately adjacent to the fish is essentially stuck to the fish by viscosity, while overlying water molecules of the boundary layer progressively farther from the fish are able to move more easily past each other. If the boundary layer is disrupted, turbulent flow will develop and the fish will have all the swimming agility of a brick. A fish shaped like a disk (for example, a sunfish or discus) swims edgewise to the water in order to minimize pressure drag, but its large surface area generates much higher friction drag than a narrow, pointed shape. The highest pressure drag is produced by a flat disk facing upcurrent instead of edgewise. A sphere moving through water generates only half the drag produced by a disk. If the back side of the sphere is drawn out to a point downstream, pressure drag falls even more.

The optimal shape, producing only 5% the drag of a disk, is a teardrop, with its maximum diameter between one third and one half of its length, and with a fineness ratio (length divided by diameter) between 4 and 5 (that is, the fish is 4 to 5 times longer than wide). From published illustrations of Ordovician fishes, the fineness ratio of *Astraspis* was probably around 3.75, that of *Sacabambaspis* was about 4.57, and that of *Arandaspis*, for which the estimate is least reliable, was about 4.8. All three ostracoderms are close to the optimal teardrop shape for the lowest pressure drag, with *Sacabambaspis* right on the button!

Ostracoderm physics also suggests these first fishes had different swimming speeds. The scales and bones of *Astraspis* are strongly overlapped and ornamented. Overlapping scales suggest a need for streamlining in order to reduce pressure drag, which in turn may reflect higher relative velocities between the fish and the surrounding water. Bumpy scale ornamentation tends to improve laminar flow of water over the skin. Both features suggest either that *Astraspis* was a faster swimmer than other Ordovician ostracoderms, or that it lived in a higher energy regime with stronger tides or currents.

Physics also determines how ostracoderms maneuvered in their watery environment. [Figure 9] The tail of *Sacabambaspis* is perfectly symmetrical, an arrangement that would have thrust the body forward. The upturned tail of a shark not only produces forward movement, it also tends to raise the tail, causing the head to pitch downward. This effect is compensated for in sharks and many other fishes by large paired front fins (**pectoral fins**) just behind the head. A downturned tail has just the opposite effect, driving the tail down and the head up. No known Ordovician ostracoderm had paired fins, a lack that would have limited their ability to compensate for up-and-down pitching movements. Similarly, the absence of median fins on the back (**dorsal fin**) and belly (**anal fin**) would have made it difficult to control roll around the body axis and side-to-side movement. Some ostracoderms and all jawed fishes have paired front (pectoral) fins and at least one dorsal fin (jawed fishes additionally possess paired **pelvic fins** behind the pectorals, and a median anal fin under the belly), providing these fishes with improved stability (control of **roll**, **pitch**, and **yaw**), turning, and braking.

Although the structure of the ear region is unknown in Ordovician ostracoderms, fossils from the Devonian reveal traces of a labyrinthine organ similar to that of lampreys, with two vertical semicircular canals arranged at right-angles to each other. In life, movement of fluid (endolymph) inside these passages provided perception of turning motion and vertical orientation. This sense was less developed than in jawed craniates, in which there is an additional horizontal canal. It may have been more important for primitive bottom-dwelling craniates to distinguish up from down than left from right; maybe down meant food and safety, whereas up meant strong currents, waves, and death.

≋⫸ Where Did the First Ostracoderms Live?

The Harding Sandstone is thought to have been deposited close to shore in a shallow sea that stretched across parts of North America during the Ordovician. Ostracoderm bone fragments within it are angular and have suffered little erosion, which suggests they did not drift very far after death. Some *Sacabambaspis* fossils from Bolivia are almost complete and were almost certainly buried in the bottom sediments of the environment where they lived. These fossils, like those from Australia, are associated with fossils and other evidence of sea life, including distinctive "*Cruziana*" trackways thought to have been made by trilobites, an extinct group of jointed-limbed marine arthropods. The presence of tracks indicates that the bottom environments were habitable by

detritus feeders such as trilobites and ostracoderms. All these Ordovician ostracoderms are therefore from nearshore, high-energy *marine* environments. As yet we have no evidence of Ordovician freshwater fishes.

The modern geographic positions of these fossils are not an accurate indication of where the first ostracoderms swam and died, because the sites have moved profoundly since the Ordovician period. The first ostracoderms apparently lived in warm, shallow seas not far from the equator, in sandy nearshore intertidal or subtidal environments. Deeper shelf sea sediments of Ordovician age are full of shelly invertebrate fossils but lack ostracoderm bones, suggesting that the first ostracoderms were incapable of swimming across vast reaches of open ocean. From time to time, shallower waters or island arcs may have existed between continents. Over tens of millions of years, these geologically ephemeral links may have permitted some dispersal from one marginal marine environment to the next, but the first ostracoderms probably did not venture into deep waters.

Ordovician ostracoderms from Aus-

FIGURE 9
෨෨
Swimming and stability in a primitive craniate such as *Sacabambaspis*. The tail provides forward thrust but produces side-to-side (yaw) movements that may have impaired directional stability.

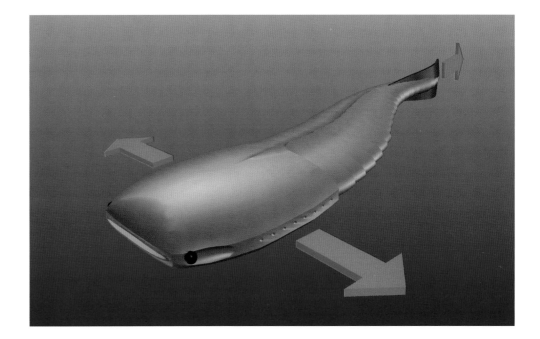

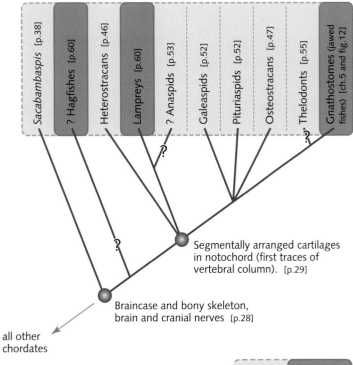

Craniates

Sacabambaspis [p.38]
? Hagfishes [p.60]
Heterostracans [p.46]
Lampreys [p.60]
? Anaspids [p.53]
Galeaspids [p.52]
Pituriaspids [p.52]
Osteostracans [p.47]
Thelodonts [p.55]
Gnathostomes (jawed fishes) [ch.5 and fig.12]

Segmentally arranged cartilages in notochord (first traces of vertebral column). [p.29]

Braincase and bony skeleton, brain and cranial nerves [p.28]

all other chordates

extinct relatives | living representatives

FIGURE 10

Evolutionary relationships of some living and extinct craniates, including various ostracoderms discussed in the text. Living craniates include lampreys, hagfishes and gnathostomes or jawed craniates.

tralia and Bolivia both lived in the ancient southern supercontinent of **Gondwana**, and this could have been the cradle of craniate evolution. But within less than 40 million years, this pattern of distribution was profoundly altered. By the Silurian, about 440 to 430 million years ago, ostracoderms had spread to many other parts of the globe. By about 410 million years ago, in the Early Devonian, they had diversified into many new habitats (including fresh waters), and several distinct groups of bony ostracoderms groups were by then well established.

The anatomy of these new ostracoderms is of interest to paleontologists because of its variety. These supposedly simple fishes exhibited considerable diversity of form, much more than is seen among living hagfishes and lampreys. Some closely resembled Ordovician ostracoderms, while others had progressed in several new evolutionary directions. This period of craniate diversification produced many bizarre body plans, most of which are no longer around. In other words, the modern palette of craniate diversity has lost much of its early richness. [Figure 10] Let's look at some of that lost color.

Heterostracans: Conservative Ostracoderms

Heterostracans (*different shell*) are Silurian and Devonian ostracoderms that closely resemble the Ordovician ones, differing from them mainly in having all the gills venting to the outside through a single opening on each side of the body. Most heterostracans were no more than several centimeters long, but some reached far greater size, with a head shield width of about 1 meter. Some had symmetrical tails, but in others the body extended into the lower lobe. Like earlier ostracoderms, heterostracans had no paired fins and no dorsal fin, although some had a bony spine projecting from the head shield. Without paired and median fins, the hydrodynamic stability of heterostracans was limited. A sharp turn of the head in a strong current would probably cause loss of stability and a dramatic increase in drag, causing a sudden stall. It is unlikely that water could be pumped over the gills inside the rigid head armor, so ram respiration (flow of water over the gills produced only by forward motion of the fish) was probably the preferred method. Unless the fish could return quickly to a position appropriate for ram ventilation following a stall, it would probably die from asphyxiation.

A "reversed" tail and flattened body may have been advantageous in keeping heterostracans close to the ocean floor, where water currents were slower and where the fish would be relatively undisturbed. One of the most extreme examples of flattening is seen in *Drepanaspis*, [Plates 7 and 8] a sea-living heterostracan from the Devonian of Germany, which was about 25 centimeters across and about 2.5 centimeters from top to bottom.

Despite their conservative anatomy, heterostracans fared well, at least for a time. One measure of heterostracan success is their high diversity and rapid evolution, and they were also among the first craniates to colonize fresh waters. In fact, so well documented is their invasion of freshwater environments, that different species have been used to divide up some sequences of Devonian strata into distinct horizons (successive layers of strata, each with a distinctive suite of heterostracan fossils.)

Osteostracans

Among the first fossils studied by Louis Agassiz from the Old Red Sandstone were curious fishes with a horseshoe-shaped head and a long armored body, which Agassiz named *Cephalaspis*. Today, *Cephalaspis* is classified along with many other ostracoderm fossils as an osteostracan (*bony shell*). These peculiar ostracoderms were widespread, and several distinct groups evolved.

Osteostracans were restricted to a northern area (the "Euramerica Province" or "Old Red Sandstone Continent"), including North America, Greenland, and northern Europe. Their earliest occurrences in the late Silurian include both very primitive and very advanced species, indicating that diversification of the group must have transpired even earlier. The most advanced forms were restricted to lagoons in what is now the Baltic region in the Late Silurian. They spread to adjacent parts of Europe, where some were successful in the Early Devonian, but the most specialized—represented, for example, by *Tremataspis*—became extinct at the end of the Silurian. *Hemicyclaspis* [Plates 9 and 10] was a member of a large middle-of-the-road osteostracan group that thrived in fresh waters through most of the Devonian period.

Osteostracans had a more elaborate skeleton than heterostracans, with bone partly enclosing the brain, major nerves, sensory capsules, and even the course of some major blood vessels. By studying these internal features of the head, we can identify many anatomical similarities with modern jawed vertebrates. It is difficult to assess the evolutionary significance of these observations, however. Were the internal organs more advanced in osteostracans than in heterostracans, or were they simply more extensively encased in bone?

Osteostracan bone contains microscopic spaces for bone cells, showing that these cells actually continued to live within the bone after it was deposited. Human bones are likewise full of cells, and the presence of cellular bone is therefore a strong link between us and osteostracans. In the 1980s some scraps of bone from the Ordovician Harding Sandstone were found to contain bone cells. Whether this bone came from an early osteostracan, or from a common ancestor of osteostracans and jawed vertebrates, or even from some incredibly ancient fish with jaws is not known at this time.

Many osteostracans have a pair of front fins, an important feature shared with jawed fishes, attached to the rear of the head at its widest point. [Figure 11] A pair of pectoral fins offers many advan-

PLATE 7

Drepanaspis, a heterostracan ostracoderm
from the Early Devonian of Germany
(about 400 million years old) was a
flattened ostracoderm about 35cm long
that probably lived on the sea floor,
feeding on particles of organic matter it
sifted from the mud using its jawless
mouth. The absence of paired or dorsal fins
in such ostracoderms probably restricted
their ability to maneuver in the water.

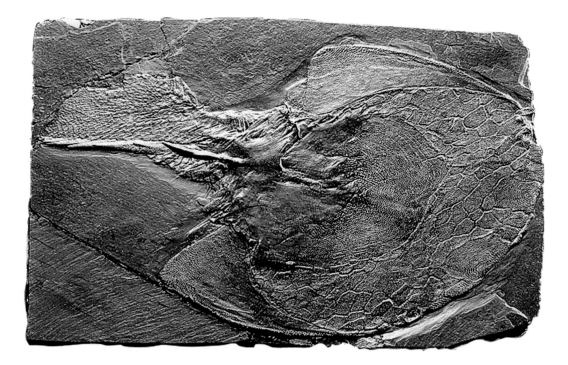

PLATE 9

Hemicyclaspis, from the Early Devonian of
Scotland (about 400 million years old), is a
typical osteostracan, a group that lived in
nothern hemisphere fresh waters through–
out most of the Devonian. It had paired
pectoral fins and a dorsal fin, like more
advanced craniates with jaws, and grew
about 20cm long.

THE RISE AND FALL OF OUR ARMORED ANCESTORS

PLATE 10

Several *Hemicyclaspis murchisoni*, a cepha-
laspid from the Early Devonian of
Herefordshire, England (cast), about 400
million years old. Length 19cm.

tages to a swimming fish, especially in generating lift and stabilizing roll. Paired pelvic fins are absent; these occur only in jawed vertebrates. Osteostracans also have a small dorsal "fin," formed by enlarged scales on the back, and a sharklike tail fin; they were evidently much better equipped for swimming than the heterostracans.

Osteostracans' mouth and gill openings are located beneath the head, as in modern rays, which suggests that they lived close to the bottom and fed either by filtering organic debris from muds or perhaps by sucking in soft algae or very small invertebrate animals. Some osteostracans may even have been able to pump water over their gills by means of muscular contractions of the skin beneath the head.

The top of the head was equally bizarre, with a pair of close-set eyes and a curious median opening, apparently for a single nostril. The head shield had three areas (one in the middle and one to each side) that lacked a surface of "finished" bone but were well innervated, and probably were for chemosensory or electrosensory perception.

The last osteostracans lived in the Middle Devonian; an example is *Alaspis*, from Quebec. [see Plate 120] They differed little from their Early Devonian relatives except that the head skeleton was broken up into numerous small polygonal bones instead of forming a solid head shield. The significance of this is not clear; it may be a reversal to a pattern seen in earlier Silurian osteostracans.

≋⤳ **Wonders of the Orient and Down Under: Galeaspids and Pituriaspids** 19th and early 20th century paleontology focused strongly on European and North American discoveries, and provided a distinctly biased view of evolution. Exciting new discoveries, such as Ordovician fishes in Australia and South America, and a plethora of new finds in Asia are demonstrating that for years we have been missing large and important parts of the puzzle of ancient life. One such example of a missing piece is provided by galeaspids (*hekmet shield*), a diverse group of bizarre fishes with a passing resemblance to osteostracans. They are unique to parts of

FIGURE 11
ᕈᕤ
Swimming and stability in an osteostracan such as *Hemicyclaspis*. Forward thrust is provided by the tail, while vertical pitch and rotation (roll) are limited by fins and the shape of the head.

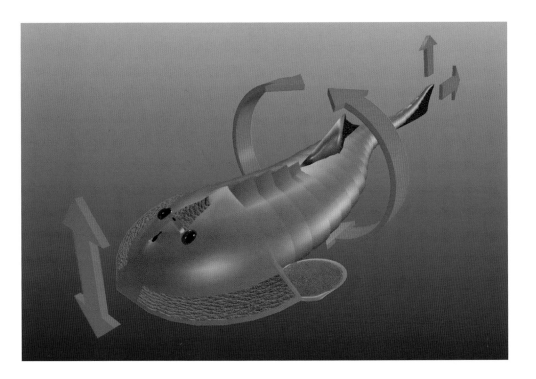

THE RISE AND FALL OF OUR ARMORED ANCESTORS

modern-day China and northern Vietnam, where they arose in the Silurian and died out in the Devonian, having gone nowhere. Perhaps they were the Asian equivalent of the osteostracans from Euramerica, and may have occupied comparable ecological niches. A peculiarity of galeaspids is a large hole in the middle of the head, which apparently communicated with paired nasal cavities and the pharynx. Galeaspids have no pectoral fins and

PLATE 11
≪∽

Pterolepis nitidus, an anaspid from the Late Silurian of Rigerike, Norway (about 410 million years old). Length 8cm.

their bone tissue apparently lacks cell spaces, two important differences from osteostracans and jawed vertebrates.

Another missing piece of the puzzle is represented by *Pituriaspis*, with a stretched-out head shield surmounted by a long spine on the end of its snout. Two different pituriaspids (*hallucinatory shield*) are now known, both from the Middle Devonian of Australia. These fishes apparently have pectoral fins behind the head shield, and small paired areas resembling the "sensory fields" of *Cephalaspis* and other osteostracans. At present it is not certain whether pituriaspids shared a common ancestry with osteostracans and

galeaspids, nor whether these fishes represent separate groups that are sequentially closer to the jawed craniates.

Anaspids

Among all the ancient jawless fishes, perhaps the most controversial are the anaspids (*no shield*). According to some scientists, they are related to modern lampreys, but it has also been suggested that they were related to jawed bony fishes, although the evidence either way is slender. Anaspid fossil preservation usually is poor. Until very recently, anaspids were thought to be restricted to the Silurian [Plate 11], but new discoveries from the Late Devonian of Canada have changed that view. Their total time range from the Early Silurian to the Late Devonian is almost 60 million years, but with no fossils from the middle of this range, we are looking at a big gap in their history. The oldest fossil lampreys (and hagfishes) are about 300 million years old, while the last known anaspids are about 75 million years older.

Anaspids were among the most streamlined ostracoderms, suggesting that they were active swimmers, and some had paired fins behind the head. They had an upside-down tail like that of many heterostracans, and the body may have been covered by thin scales. Behind each eye there was a row of gill openings that gradually got closer to the belly. A similar arrangement occurs in lampreys and Ordovician ostracoderms such as *Sacabambaspis* and *Arandaspis*. In some anaspid fossils, there are traces of a structure resembling the annular cartilage (a ring of cartilage around the mouth) of lampreys. On the other hand, the presence of paired front fins is an important similarity with

PLATE 12

Phlebolepis, a thelodont from the Late
Silurian (about 410 million years old).
Unlike other ostracoderms, these small
marine fishes (usually under 10cm long)
lacked bony plates and were covered
instead by small scales.

osteostracans and jawed fishes, and there are additional similarities with jawed fishes, such as a series of dermal bones around the eyes, and a large dermal plate beneath the mouth. Thus the evolutionary relationships of anaspids are poorly resolved, with contradictory evidence both for a relationship with lampreys and with jawed fishes.

⇒⊪⊪▷ Thelodonts

Thelodonts (*feeble tooth*) were sea-dwelling fishes that achieved a worldwide distribution and had a lengthy history from at least the Late Ordovician to the Late Devonian, a total span of some 70 million years. [Plates 12 and 13] Probably they were capable swimmers, with flexible body muscles under their sharklike shagreen of tiny scales. Some thelodonts had paired finlike pectoral expansions on each side of the body; a dorsal and sometimes an anal fin were also present. Complete thelodont fossils are rare, but their isolated microscopic scales are abundant and have been used by geologists to correlate strata of similar age in different places. The

oldest thelodont scales are from the Ordovician of Siberia and the USA, and it is suspected that the group originated in waters around the northern continents. Thelodonts survived until the Early Devonian in the Northern Hemisphere, but fared better around the southern continent of Gondwana, where they survived until the end of the Devonian. Thelodont scales covered the body and also lined the mouth and pharyngeal region. Different kinds of thelodont scales are recognized, but it is often uncertain whether they originally came from different species or from various parts of the skin.

Apart from these scales, we know little about thelodont anatomy, because there was no internal ossification. Although thelodonts are treated in most classifications as **agnathans** (*jawless*; examples are lampreys and hagfishes), it is really not clear whether they had jaws or not. New thelodonts, described in the 1990s from the Northwest Territories of Canada, show the impression of what may be a stomach, an advanced feature that is not found in hagfishes and lampreys and suggests that thelodonts may lie on the lineage leading to jawed craniates. (Some paleontologists have even argued that thelodonts might be related to sharks and their relatives, because of detailed similarities in their scale structure.) The presence of both special pharyngeal denticles and a stomach suggests that these fishes could feed on large items that first required pharyngeal manipulation (utilizing a muscular pharynx, perhaps supported by an internal gill arch skeleton like that of jawed craniates) and subsequent enzymal digestion in the stomach. If thelodonts were capable of feeding on large prey items, they may have been the first fishy predators in the lineage leading to jaws.

PLATE 13
∾

Many *Phlebolepis* sp., a thelodont from the Late Silurian of Oesel, Latvia (about 410 million years old). Length 6cm.

ᯤ What Happened to All the Ostracoderms?

The oldest fossil lampreys and hagfishes are about 300 million years old, from the Late Carboniferous. The oldest sharks, and the ray-finned and lobe-finned fishes, are much older. They were contemporary with many groups of jawless ostracoderms during the Devonian and perhaps even earlier. All modern craniates probably evolved from ostracoderms, but modern hagfishes and lampreys probably arose from different ostracoderms than did the jawed craniates. If we choose to read the fossil record literally, all the major groups of living jawed craniates, from sharks to tetrapods, evolved long before the first lamprey-like fishes appeared. Of course, there may be a big gap in the fossil record, and lampreys could have been around even earlier, but it is equally likely that lamprey anatomy is actually more advanced than that of many primitive ostracoderms, and that lampreys evolved from a specialized group (anaspids, for example) that went on to lose the ability to synthesize a bony skeleton.

Did jawed craniates evolve from one group of ostracoderms or from more than one? Some ostracoderms, such as galeaspids, are thought to lie close to **gnathostome** (*jaw-mouthed*) origins, but it seems unlikely that either group gave rise directly to the first jawed fishes. It is just as unlikely that anaspids and thelodonts are direct ancestors of bony and sharklike jawed fishes. But if jawed craniates did not arise from among these groups, where did they come from? This question must remain unanswered, at least for now.

Only one thing is certain: just as the diversity of the mighty dinosaurs is gone, so also is the richness of the first fishes to colonize our planet. The fossil record is our only tangible link to that part of our history, and it is tantalizingly incomplete. Can we tie these first stages of craniate history in to a larger picture of global events? What was happening in the world that would have provided these early fishes with opportunities for success or failure?

The Ordovician was marked by a glacial episode of global dimensions, one of the most extensive the world has ever endured. Enough water would have been locked up in large ice sheets to lower the sea level globally by hundreds of meters, perhaps causing the withdrawal of the shallow seas that had previously covered large parts of the continents. Marginal marine habitats (especially in shallow waters) would have been reduced in extent, increasing competition for diminishing resources. Lowered sea levels may have provided temporary opportunities for more mobile ostracoderms to spread from the margins of one continent to another and to colonize new or vacant habitats.

This global shift in climate probably was not the only factor responsible for the initial success of ostracoderms. It does illustrate the point that the early success of ostracoderms may have been entirely serendipitous, rather than due to "better" anatomy. The timing of global events such as the Ordovician glaciation coincided fortuitously with the first appearance of craniates and may have provided them with opportunities that would, in the long run, change the course of life on Earth.

By the Silurian, the northern continent of Euramerica, the Old Red Continent, had a distinct endemic (native) fauna of fishes (particularly osteostracans, anaspids, and certain heterostracans) that it would retain throughout the Devonian. At about the same time, another distinctly endemic fauna developed in Asia, dominated by the galeaspids. Thelodonts were more cosmopolitan, perhaps because they were less restricted in habitat preference or were capable of roaming the oceans more readily than their more heavily armor-plated cousins.

Extinction certainly took its toll of these early fishes, although with such incomplete fossil records it is hard to pinpoint when extinction occurred. Until a few years ago, for example, it was assumed that anaspids were confined to the Silurian, but they have now been found in the Late Devonian. None of the original

Ordovician ostracoderms survived into the Silurian, but because the sample is so small it is uncertain whether their disappearance was related to a global extinction event that occurred at the end of the Ordovician.

Ostracoderm diversity increased throughout the Silurian with no major extinctions, but many ostracoderms disappeared in the Early Devonian, including most Asian galeaspids. It has been suggested that competition from jawed fishes (especially placoderms and osteichthyans) led to the demise of many ostracoderms, but another, more profound extinction took place toward the end of the Devonian and saw the demise of many families of jawed placoderms as well as all remaining armored ostracoderms and the thelodonts. There is no evidence that competition from new kinds of fishes was a factor in that extinction; ostracoderms did not become extinct through any inherent inferiority of their anatomy.

Then what was the cause? Probably there was increased competition generally for suitable shallow water habitats, for a dramatic decline in global sea levels occurred toward the end of the Devonian, after a lengthy period of gradual rising.

Caused perhaps by climatic shifts or by reconfiguration of the continents, lower sea levels may have resulted in the destruction of many habitats that were previously perched on continental shelves. Coincidental with this fall, the bottom waters of the world's oceans became increasingly **anoxic**, to such an extent that oxygen-depleted waters even spilled over the continental margins, rendering the deeper shelf seas uninhabitable by oxygen-dependent organisms. Shelf areas, populated by localized faunas of fishes and invertebrates during the earlier Devonian, were caught in an ever-tightening environmental squeeze, and these faunas suffered the greatest losses, among them the last of the bony ostracoderms. Freshwater and **pelagic** (open-ocean) fishes probably were less affected by this anoxic event than **benthic** (bottom-dwelling) shelf faunas, but the habitats of many non-marine ostracoderms may have simply dried up as continental climates became increasingly arid. As we will see in Chapter 10, one group of craniates found an emergency exit to the crisis, by experimenting with the land. The last of the ostracoderms witnessed the first of the tetrapods. ⌘

PREDATORS

*I*T IS HARD TO imagine life without jaws: giant killer sharks, carnivorous dinosaurs, saber-toothed tigers, and that talkative neighbor just would not be the same without them. The acquisition of jaws is perhaps the most profound and radical evolutionary step in craniate history, after the development of the head itself. [Plate 14] Jaws are not found in modern or fossil lampreys and hagfishes. Despite the fantastic variety of those armored fishes, the ostracoderms, none of them seems to have had movable internal jaw bones. In these jawless fishes the mouth was located either beneath the head or at its front, and in some forms there were bony oral plates, specialized to direct water currents into the pharynx. Some ostracoderms may have obtained food particles by filtering them from water during ram respiration, and others may have pumped watery sediment through the pharynx using muscles associated with their gills. Others had specialized pharyngeal scales, and may have been able to manipulate food items before swallowing them. None of the known ostracoderms, however, has movable mouthparts capable of seizing and subduing prey. Of course, the lack of jaws does not stop animals from effectively pursuing and consuming food. A variety of mechanisms have allowed jawless fishes to survive quite well for millions of years by catching and eating live or dead prey.

PLATE 14

Eastmanosteus, an arthrodire about 1m long, scatters a shoal of small primitive ray-finned fishes, *Moythomasia*, near a Late Devonian reef about 375 million years ago in north-western Australia. Ray-fins have survived to become the most abundant living fishes, but arthrodires and their relatives became extinct around the end of the Devonian.

PLATE 15
⤳

Model of the head of a modern hagfish,
showing its double row of tooth plates
used to rasp at its victim's flesh
(photograph No. 318382, courtesy Dept.
Library Services, American Museum of
Natural History)

Biting Without Jaws

Lack of jaws doesn't seem to be a problem
for modern **hagfishes**, which like to live
in thick mud on the seafloor. They have
paired, serrated **tooth plates**, one on
each side of a protrusible "tongue." [Plate
15] When the tongue-equivalent is protruded, these serrated plates separate and
then converge again in a pincerlike grip,
latching on to surface irregularities in the
prey (such as a dead or dying fish). The
slimy hagfish then literally ties itself in a
knot and moves the knot forward until it
is braced against the prey. Then the hagfish begins to tear pieces of flesh from its
victim. Slime hags sometimes eat only sufficient muscle flesh to make a hole in the
body cavity of their prey, then proceed to
feed off the soft internal organs.

Lampreys, which frequent fresh as
well as sea waters, have a somewhat
different feeding mechanism. Instead of
paired tooth plates they have many small
conical teeth arranged concentrically
around the mouth, and a "tongue" stud-
ded with similar teeth. After locating its
prey the lamprey uses its teeth to abrade
the skin, then secretes an anticoagulant
into the wound. Rather than continue
feeding, the lamprey then detaches itself
and waits for the prey to die. Lampreys
feed mainly on the body fluids of fishes,
although they have been observed feeding
on whales, and some swimmers in the
Great Lakes of North America have
reported lampreys attempting to attach
themselves. Versatile in their choice of
food, lampreys have survived for millions
of years without jaws.

Biters and Avoiders

The main adaptive advantage of jaws is
straightforward: larger prey can be seized
and subdued, and in water smaller prey
can be sucked into the pharynx (air is too
thin a medium for this to be feasible).
With jaws, food can be delicately nibbled
or crushed, and prey can be disabled by a
lightning-fast strike. Even filter feeding is
improved, because a large mouth supported by jaws can be adapted for

Gnathostomes
(jawed craniates)

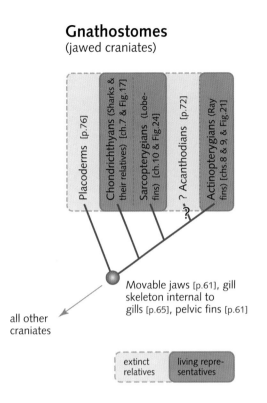

Movable jaws [p.61], gill skeleton internal to gills [p.65], pelvic fins [p.61]

all other craniates

extinct relatives | living representatives

FIGURE 12

Evolutionary relationships of living and extinct gnathostomes. Of five principal categories that evolved in the Paleozoic, two are now extinct (dashed boxes), so the diversity seen among modern gnathostomes does not reflect its full former extent. Living gnathostomes include chondrichthyans and osteichthyans, the latter being divided into sarcopterygians (lobe-finned fishes) and actinopterygians (ray-finned fishes).

directing the flow of water efficiently into the pharynx.

Improved predation, of course, makes improved predator avoidance an imperative. The development of an effective biting mechanism did not merely shorten the odds against jawless ostracoderms; it also put the new jawed fishes, known as **gnathostomes**, at risk. Fishes with jaws can themselves be eaten by other fishes with jaws. With new jaws on the feeding grounds, perception and mobility both had to improve so that animals could escape being eaten. Probably these traits were quickly developed by both predators and prey, so that not only were the earliest gnathostomes more effective hunters, they were also more effective avoiders. Jaws certainly opened up a new spectrum of feeding opportunities, but the adaptive advantages that evolved subsequently in different groups of fishes are as much concerned with predator avoidance as with prey capture, with more efficient jaws at one end and a more efficient propulsive device at the other!

How Old Are the Gnathostomes?
Living gnathostomes include all the sharks and rays, and all bony fishes (ray-fins and lobe-fins, including tetrapods). [Figure 12] The oldest identifiable gnathostome fossils are extremely scrappy, consisting of isolated scales and teeth. Because paleontologists find similar scales and teeth in more recent fossils that are complete enough to reveal the presence of jaws, it is inferred that the early fishes from which these bony fragments came also had jaws. Among the most ancient scraps are supposed shark scales from the Silurian of Mongolia and the Ordovician of the USA, thought to be about 420 and 450 million years old respectively, resembling the simple skin denticles (small toothlike scales) of modern sharks. Other scales, recently described from the Late Silurian of Russia and China, are thought to come from distant relatives of modern ray-finned bony fishes. Fragmentary bones, including a

shoulder girdle, scales, and teeth of a supposed ray-finned fish, have been found in Late Silurian strata of Estonia. The oldest fossil lobe-finned fishes are of Early Devonian age and have been found in present-day China, in Spitsbergen, Arctic Norway, and in Arctic Canada. Lobe-finned fishes remain the only group of still living gnathostomes *not* to have been found in Silurian strata.

There are also fossils of early jawed fishes that no longer survive (see Chapter 6). One group, known as the **acanthodians** (*thorny-skinned*), had sharp spines in front of the fins. These distinctive fishes are known from the Early Silurian to the Permian, and have even been reported from the Ordovician, although the oldest examples are represented only by isolated scales and spines. Another extinct group, the placoderms (*armor-skinned*), were abundant in the Devonian [Plate 16] and are also known from rare Silurian fossils.

What Are Jaws?
As far as jaws are concerned, the human condition, indeed the entire mammalian condition, is quite simple. We have a skull, to which is hinged a lower jaw or **mandible**, consisting of a pair of dentary bones. (In humans these two bones are fused into one.) Teeth sit in sockets around the biting edge of the mandible, and additional teeth are located in sockets along the lower margins of the skull. This condition is evolutionarily advanced, because mammals have lost or modified several additional bones that supplement the back of the jaw in other jawed craniates. As we move back down our evolutionary ladder, jaw structure becomes more instead of less complex, and in fishes the jaws are very elaborate indeed. In the fish world, perhaps the simplest jaws are seen in sharks, but even though shark jaws are frequently regarded as primitive (that is to say, resembling the supposed ancestral condition of gnathostomes), there is some evidence that they have become secondarily simplified, like mammal jaws, although in quite a

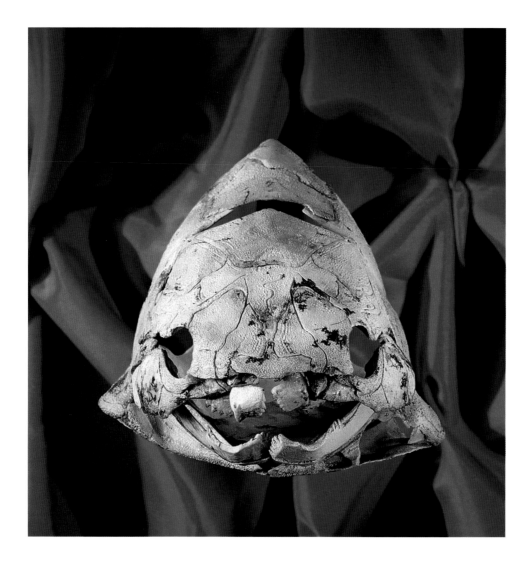

PLATE 16

Eastmanosteus calliaspis, an arthrodire, seen
from the front, Late Devonian, Western
Australia (about 375 million years old).
Length of armor 19cm; estimated body
length 45cm. Acid preparation by Robert
Evander, American Museum of Natural
History.

different direction, both anatomically and functionally.

For gnathostomes, the jawed fishes, the main internal structure of the jaw is provided by a pair of upper (palato-quadrate) and lower (mandibular or Meckelian) cartilages that form a mandibular arch around the mouth region. These cartilages represent the endoskeleton. The upper jaw in most fishes is separate from the braincase, but in humans and many other tetrapods, the upper jaw is fused to the braincase. Various dermal bones (formed in the skin) are attached to the jaws and may even enclose them. Teeth provide the jaws with an effective means of capturing, cutting, slicing, stabbing, crushing, grinding, and otherwise reducing food to appropriate dimensions for further processing internally.

In gnathostomes the upper and lower jaws meet at a strong, fluid-filled synovial mandibular joint, and biting is effected by powerful adductor (mouth closing muscles) that are attached to both upper and lower jaws. Many smaller muscles are also associated with the jaws and help fine-tune the biting mechanism. Strong ligaments hold the jaws together and bind them to the head, but in some fishes (notably among deep-sea advanced bony fishes) the jaws are highly movable and can be voluntarily disarticulated to accommodate prey much larger than the fish itself. (Some snakes have the same ability.)

Additional bracing for the jaw in fishes is provided by a second internal set of cartilages behind the first, known as the **hyoid arch**, with paired upper and lower cartilages that correspond to the upper and lower jaws of the mandibular arch. These cartilages are small and easily overlooked in humans—for example, the **hyomandibular** cartilage has become incorporated into the human ear as the stapes, or stirrup bone, and other parts of the hyoid arch are associated with the larynx, or voice box—but in fishes they usually play a major role in jaw support. Behind the mandibular and hyoid arches

in fishes there is a series of additional **gill arches** that forms the main internal support for the gills. These gill arches bear a striking resemblance to the jaws and hyoid arch. As we shall see, the similarity of the structures provides a key for unraveling the origin of the jaw.

The Evolution of Jaws

The jaws, the hyoid arch, and the gill arches are important features that help define a large and anatomically advanced group of craniates that evolved from a common ancestor in the distant past. These three features, along with many other features found only in jawed craniates, are derived in the embryo from the neural crest. This fact immediately confirms that our jaws are unique, for only animals with a neural crest are capable of developing them. But neural crest tissue is also present in craniates that lack jaws, such as lampreys, so we may well ask, Where *did* jaws, and the hyoid and gill arches, come from? Were they derived from some structure that was already present in primitive jawless craniates, or do they represent evolutionary novelties, without any counterpart in the jawless agnathans?

The obvious feeding advantage provided by jaws does not explain their origin. Some scientists have argued that jaws originally evolved to fill another role, such as respiration, as part of a series of internal skeletal supports for the gills. If this is true, the first jaws may have been quite unsuitable for feeding.

Carl Gegenbaur and Serial Homology

In the 1870's, German anatomist Carl Gegenbaur suggested that the jaws had evolved from an "ancestral" gill arch. Gegenbaur assumed the earliest gnathostomes first evolved a functional jaw that was not braced by the second (hyoid) arch. Instead, the jaw and hyoid arch were supposedly separated by a complete gill opening. Living rabbitfishes (the **chimaeroids**, relatives of sharks) came closest to this condition, for the hyoid is non–suspensory, but the required gill opening is absent. As it turned out, no modern fishes display the intermediate morphology predicted by the theory. It was widely hoped that this phase of fish evolution might be demonstrated by fossil evidence, and a spate of optimistic and ingenious interpretations of some fossil sharks and bony fishes ensued.

That phase of fish paleontology was particularly colorful and provides a wonderful example of how late 19th and early 20th century paleontologists thought that fossils would reveal the true course of evolution, thereby vindicating paleontology as the evolutionist's most powerful tool.

In fact, fossils have repeatedly failed to support the serial homology theory, this does not eliminate the possibility that jaws did in fact evolve from preexisting structures that filled some other function. Innovative suggestions have been put forward, among them the proposal that jaws evolved from the part of the pharynx that is represented in agnathans by a structure called the velum, which in hagfishes and larval lampreys is used to pump water through the pharynx when the animal is burrowing in sediment. One problem with this idea is that no structure comparable to a velum is recognized in fossil osteostracans or heterostracans, which suggests either that lampreys are more closely related to gnathostomes than are these fossils (a conclusion that is at odds with other anatomical data), or else that the ancestors of jawed fish evolved a velumlike structure independently of lampreys.

≡‖‖▷ The "New Mouth"
A modified proposal, made in the 1990s by American anatomist Jon Mallatt, is that the jaws originally lay some distance behind the mouth. Mallatt envisioned a "new mouth," dominated by the jaws as they evolved into much larger structures, and suggested that another "premandibular" skeletal arch lay in front of the jaws

and was later reduced to form the labial cartilages in sharks. [Figure 13]

According to Mallatt's theory, the mandibular and hyoid arches existed long before they became specialized for feeding. The hyoid arch would have been a respiratory structure first and foremost, and only later would it have evolved to help support the jaws. Feeding movements of the jaws in fishes support the idea that the jaws were primitively used in respiration, because prey capture involves opening the mouth and producing suction, as happens with forced inspiration of water, then the mouth closes as water is forced out, as in expiration. Mallatt has argued that feeding actions using jaws are essentially respiration movements taken to a new extreme. He further argues that these actions were superimposed on some other ancestral feeding mechanism, such as suction feeding. Thus, jaws may have offered the opportunity to open and close the mouth forcefully during respiration, and it was then but a small step to using them to clamp shut on prey. No longer was it necessary to pin the prey against something or wait for it to stop moving. Instead, strong suction could draw prey into the mouth, even as it attempted to escape. A new kind of predator was loose in the world, and it was very, very effective.

≡‖‖▷ Could Jaws Be Totally New?
After more than 150 years of study, we are only now beginning to unravel the connection between the evolution of fundamental craniate features, such as the braincase and jaws, and the way their formation is controlled by genes during embryonic development. In the mid–1970s, Bobb Schaeffer at the American Museum of Natural History pointed out that many new structures probably evolved in an ancestor of the gnathostomes as a consequence of altered developmental strategies in the embryo, the most profound of which are seen in the way the forebrain becomes greatly enlarged and angled downward with respect to the long axis of

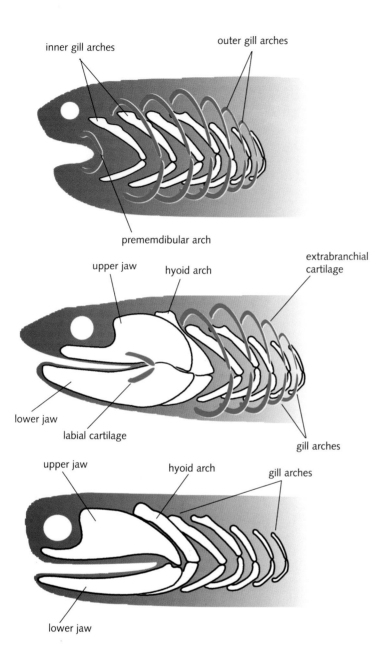

inner gill arches

outer gill arches

prememdibular arch

upper jaw

hyoid arch

extrabranchial cartilage

lower jaw

labial cartilage

gill arches

upper jaw

hyoid arch

gill arches

lower jaw

FIGURE 13

Hypothetical stages in the evolution of jaws: (top) ancestral condition in which no jaws are present; (middle) inner arches form jaws and hyoid arch, while outer arches form labial and extrabranchial cartilages, as in sharks; (bottom) only inner arches present, as in bony fishes.

the body. These changes, which do not occur in jawless fishes such as hagfishes or lampreys, have the effect of bringing together the special tissues generated by the neural crest that are crucial for the development of jaws. The reason why agnathans do not have jaws may be that they lack this requisite embryonic developmental strategy. And they may lack this strategy because they lack the necessary homeotic genes and regulatory pathways.

Did the first gnathostomes appear with fully evolved jaws, ready to consume everything within reach? For now, that idea must remain speculative, but hagfishes and lampreys may lack copies of homeotic genes responsible for generating the mosaic of gnathostome features, including jaws. The same modern advances in genetics that have shed so much light on the origins of craniates are beginning to have an impact on how we view gnathostome origins. Gnathostomes not only have jaws, they have a host of other unique anatomical features that set them apart from more primitive craniates. And they have new regulatory genes to put the whole together.

What Else Is New?

Unique to the anatomy of modern jawed fishes are paired pectoral and pelvic fins, with an internal skeleton and muscles to make them movable. Fins are stiffened and supported by collagen fibers, making them better for swimming. [Figure 14] Bone is deposited in the body behind the head, especially in the vertebral column and fins. The body muscles are divided into upper and lower regions, separated by a membrane (the horizontal septum). There is a third, horizontal semicircular canal in the ear labyrinth, providing increased awareness of lateral as well as vertical orientation, of equal value both to hunter and hunted. The pressure-sensitive lateral line is enclosed or supported by specialized scales. Everywhere inside the body, nerve fibers have a myelin sheath, providing them with improved insulation and message-carrying ability. There is a stomach, a spiral intestine, a spleen, and a pancreas; there are special blood vessels from the stomach to the liver; and there are separate male and female reproductive ducts, derived from different parts of the kidney tissue. This is but a partial listing of the features that first appeared in jawed craniates. [Figure 15]

This mosaic of new features raises the intriguing possibility that gnathostomes represent another level of genetic advancement within the craniate line, characterized by new copies of genes having regulatory functions that previously did not exist. These replicated genes may have taken on new roles in regulating the development of jaws and other new structures, such as paired fins in the embryos of ancestral gnathostomes.

Paired fins are lacking in lampreys, hagfishes, and lancelets. We do not yet have the complete genetic picture, but it appears that development in jawed crani-

ates is regulated by Hox genes that may be absent in lampreys. Some geneticists have recently suggested that a single genetic event, the acquisition of these regulatory genes, allowed gnathostomes to develop jaws and paired fins at the same time. The early fossil record of fishes suggests a more complex story, however, and helps define an area for future investigation by geneticists.

At present, we lack fossils to bridge the gap between chordates and craniates (apart from the enigmatic conodonts), but intermediate fossil links between primitive craniates and jawed fishes seem to exist. Curiously, however, these fossils seem to bridge the gap in features other than jaws. There are fossils of fishes lacking paired fins and jaws, and of jawless fishes with pectoral fins but no pelvic fins, and of fishes with jaws, pectoral fins, and pelvic fins. In other words, the fossil record shows a distinct distribution pattern of anatomical features in the fins, whose

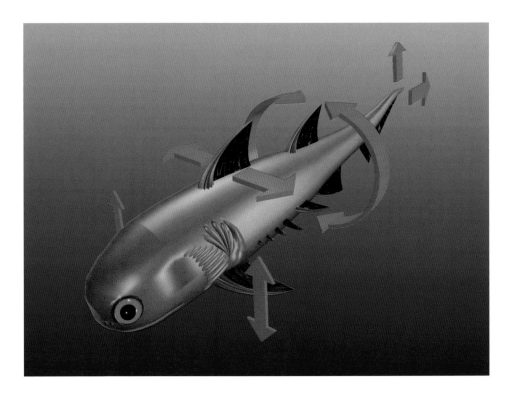

FIGURE 14
⊙ᕫ⊙

Swimming and stability in a gnathostome such as an acanthodian. The full complement of paired and median fins generates lift and enhances stability and directional control in three-dimensional space.

development seems to be regulated by new genes in modern fishes. Could the same be true for the jaws? Fossils are unlikely to yield actual genetic material, and there is little hope that we will ever be able to map the distribution of homeotic genes among extinct jawless fishes, but we can at least begin to understand the underlying genetic cause of the evolution of the jaw and the mosaic of attendant features we observe in these fossils.

Even the oldest fossil lampreys and hagfishes do not have any paired fins, so it is unlikely that they had the appropriate Hox genes or regulatory pathway for these structures, although we will never know for certain. But extinct ostracoderms hint that the genetic difference between modern lampreys and jawed fishes involves more than a single-step acquisition of the Hox genes responsible for paired fin development. Maybe the genes controlling paired fin development were expressed only at the front of the body in these advanced ostracoderms, and in the ancestors of gnathostomes the pattern of gene expression was manifested differently, in the additional development of paired pelvic fins farther back on the body. The first step (evolution of pectoral fins) evidently occurred in fishes before jaws had evolved. The second step (evolution of pelvic fins) was confined to jawed craniates.

Stasis in Craniate Evolution

Lampreys and hagfishes attained essentially their modern form at least 300 million years ago. Among the gnathostomes, sharks, coelacanths, lungfishes, and ray-finned fishes all became established at least 400 million years ago, and perhaps earlier. Since that time, all these groups of fishes have experienced evolutionary change, and some groups—the ray-finned bony fishes, for example—display spectacular diversity, but their primitive gnathostome (and craniate) features remain

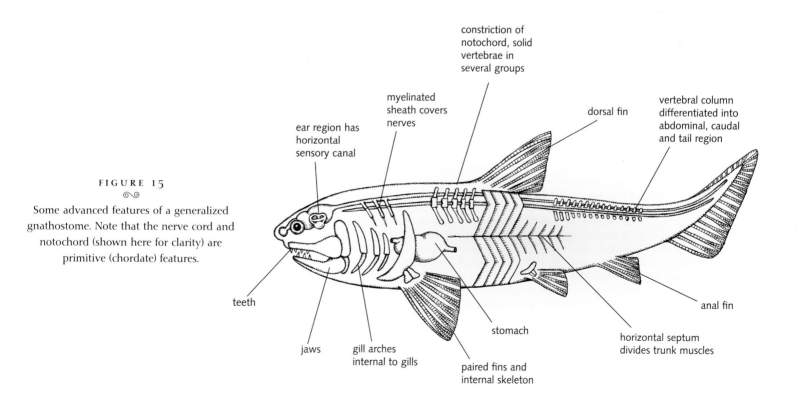

FIGURE 15

Some advanced features of a generalized gnathostome. Note that the nerve cord and notochord (shown here for clarity) are primitive (chordate) features.

constriction of notochord, solid vertebrae in several groups

myelinated sheath covers nerves

ear region has horizontal sensory canal

dorsal fin

vertebral column differentiated into abdominal, caudal and tail region

teeth

jaws

gill arches internal to gills

paired fins and internal skeleton

stomach

horizontal septum divides trunk muscles

anal fin

virtually untouched, providing a magnificent example of evolutionary stasis.

The anatomical and genetic differences between gnathostomes and lampreys, their closest living agnathan relatives, seem to be almost as profound as those between craniates and other chordates. The basic craniate pattern, which evolved in the Ordovician or even in the Cambrian, has remained unchanged for some 450 to 500 million years. The developmental and anatomical complexity attained by gnathostomes has been relatively stable at least since the Silurian. We can view the rise of the gnathostomes as a second punctuated event, followed by more than 400 million years of relative stasis.

It is quite remarkable that the basic diversity of jawed craniates became fixed so early in their evolution. Sharks, ray-finned fishes, and lobe-finned fishes all appeared about 400 million years ago and have survived to the present day. Conservatism of design is striking, for example, between Devonian coelacanths and *Latimeria*, or between Devonian and a modern ray-finned fishes. But in other cases evolutionary progress has been dramatic–for

example, among modern advanced bony fishes, and in the lineage that includes the tetrapods.

It would be a serious error to regard the **conserved** morphology of fishes as "unevolved," just as it would be erroneous to regard tetrapods as unevolved because they, too, have conserved craniate and gnathostome features. Fishes are as highly evolved as mammals and birds, but in a completely different direction. Fishes have come to dominate the water, which happens to be the primitive environment of craniates. Their conserved features are precisely those with which the first aquatic craniates and gnathostomes were endowed, and fishes have simply taken further advantage of these attributes. Tetrapod success on land is different from, not intrinsically better than, fishes' success in water. In fact, the evolutionary richness of fishes is so dramatic that it is impossible to document in a book of this size. The following chapters provide some thumbnail sketches of the major evolutionary patterns seen among fishes in the last 450 million years, in an attempt to measure that elusive concept, evolutionary success.

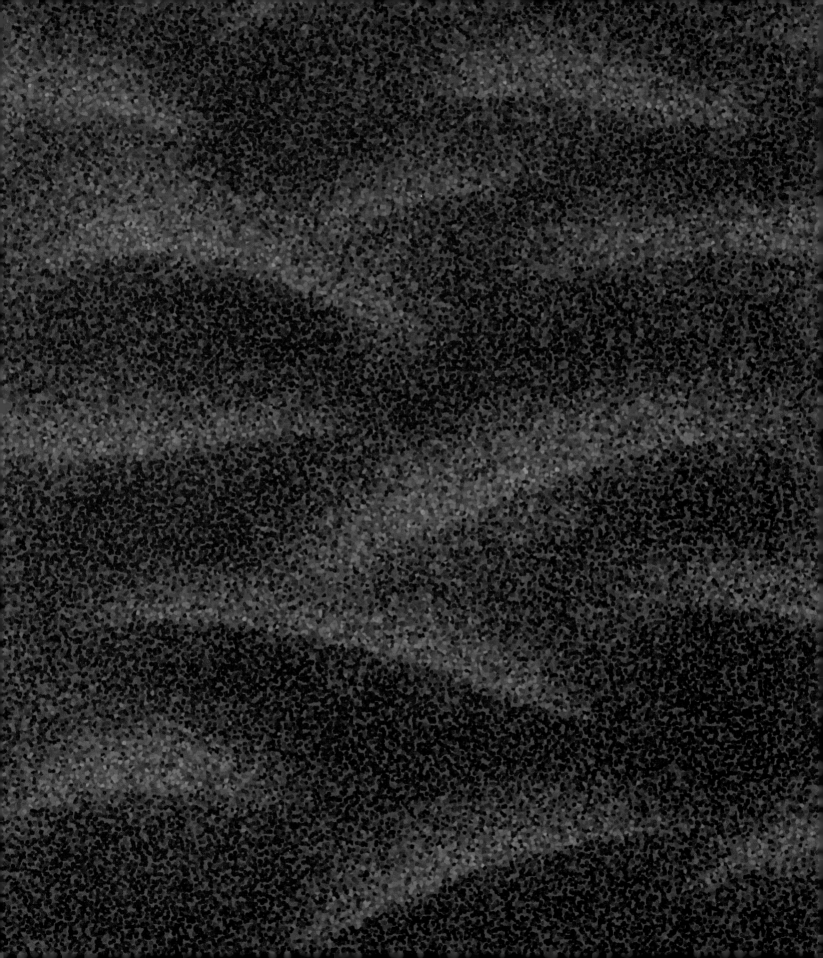

MODERN FISHES

⋙ Devonian Diversity

*I*F *WE COULD* dive into the sea and swim back in time about 375 million years, to the Late Devonian, we would be greeted by a bizarre variety of fishes. Some would have a familiar yet odd appearance—the sharks, ray-finned fishes, and distant relatives of modern coelacanths and lungfishes (yes, even in the sea!). The basic patterns of modern fish diversity were already established as far back as the Paleozoic era, that time of so-called "Ancient Life." Geological time is customarily divided into the three great eras of "Ancient Life" (Paleozoic), "Middle Life" (Mesozoic), and "Recent Life" (Cenozoic). (See Figure 2) Such a division may be convenient, but it overly emphasizes the *differences* between ancient and modern life forms and detracts attention from their underlying *similarities* of form. The fundamental patterns of animal and plant life that surround us today were established in the distant past, and fishes are no exception. Modern gnathostomes, the craniate animals with jaws, include the sharks and their allies (**chondrichthyans**), and the **bony fishes (osteichthyans)**, which are further subdivided into **ray-finned** and **lobe-finned fishes**. All these groups are represented by fossils in the Devonian.

Our Devonian scuba dive nevertheless reveals significant differences from the modern pattern of fish diversity. Of course, all of the species and even the families are different, for these have far shorter temporal

PLATE 17
☙

Gemuendina, a specialized rhenanid placoderm up to 25cm long, swimming slowly above the bottom of a sea that covered central Germany in the Early Devonian, about 400 million years ago. (See Plate 25)

durations that are usually measured in tens, not hundreds, of millions of years. Furthermore we do not see comparable levels of variety among groups such as sharks or ray-finned fishes; their range of anatomical diversity is in fact quite small. More fundamentally, however, we would discover jawed fishes whose basic anatomical design is completely unfamiliar, swimming with evident success among the more familiar sharks and other fishes. The fossil record, where our swim is actually taking place, shows us that *gnathostomes were much more diverse in the Devonian period than they are today.* The extinction of so many unfamiliar creatures has robbed us of the opportunity to see them in the flesh; a few fossilized bones are the only testament to their having existed.

⇒⫙⫙⪢ Spines and Armor

One such group, known only from fossils, is represented by bizarre armored fishes known as placoderms (*armor-skinned*). Bony armor plates thickly encased not only their heads, but a large part of their bodies as well. Placoderms were successful throughout the Devonian period, evolving new species and filling the seas; and some were *really* big, posing a worrisome threat to smaller fishes.

If we were to pick a Late Devonian lake rather than sea for our dive, we would notice even fewer familiar fishes than in the sea and a greater proportion of bizarre armored placoderms, some gently nosing about in the bottom muds, some cruising silently or swimming against fast-moving currents, others peering shyly from beneath stones.

Among the heavily armored placoderms we might also notice smaller and more graceful fishes, their bodies glistening with tiny diamond-shaped scales, their fins armed with sharp spines that seem to project in every direction. Unrelated to placoderms, these odd and unfamiliar little jawed fishes (called **acanthodians** from the Greek word for spine) appeared in the Silurian and became extinct in the Early Permian.

Until fossil placoderms and acanthodians were discovered, early in the 19th century, we had no idea that these fantastic creatures ever existed. In fact, the fossil record reveals that placoderms and acanthodians each had noteworthy histories, and each group was successful in its own way. But their histories could hardly be more different. Whereas placoderms were highly diverse, as a group they were short-lived; their entire fossil record is confined to an interval lasting only about 50 million years, but many different families flourished across the world, and some placoderms became the largest predators of their day. The recorded span of acanthodian success is longer, approximately three times that of the placoderms, but from that interval less than half a dozen acanthodian lineages are known.

When we study the oldest fossil sharks, ray-finned fishes, or lungfishes, we have some living species for comparison. Coelacanths were known for more than a century only from fossils, so the discovery of a living species in the 1930s gave a tremendous boost to our understanding of their anatomy. But we don't have a single living placoderm or acanthodian to examine. We know little about their anatomy, and our knowledge is biased toward the skeleton: their soft parts, cells, and genes are gone forever. It isn't easy to say anything meaningful about an organism that lived hundreds of millions of years ago, left only a fragmentary fossil record, and has no living direct descendant.

⇒⫙⫙⪢ The Acanthodian Pattern: A Thorny Problem

Among the earliest fossil fishes with jaws are the acanthodians (Plate 18) Until very recently, the oldest acanthodian fossils came from the Early Silurian, 440 million years ago. In 1996 a team of scientists reported finding scraps of acanthodian-like fossils in the Late Ordovician Harding Sandstone of the usa (about 450 million years old). The youngest acanthodians are from the Early Permian (about 290 million years old), giving them a geological time span of about 160 million years.

Acanthodian diversity was greatest during the Early Devonian. Details of their internal skeleton are known only in *Acanthodes*, a long-lived genus that included the last known acanthodians from the Early Permian. Most other acanthodians are represented only by isolated spines and shadowy impressions in the rocks. The oldest acanthodian fossils have been found in marine strata, suggesting that the group first evolved in the sea, but from the Devonian onward the majority of acanthodian fossils are from strata deposited in fresh water.

Acanthodians do have peculiarities all their own, and consequently paleontologists are convinced they represent a distinct group of bony fishes that had a common ancestor in the Silurian or Ordovician. The most striking acanthodian feature is that they bristled with bony spines. Paired spines projected in front of the pectoral and pelvic fins, and median spines projected in front of the dorsal and anal fins. Additionally, in some acanthodians extra paired spines projected from the belly region between the paired fins. The only fin that lacked spines was the tail, which resembled a shark's tail.

Acanthodians are all rather similar, with little anatomical diversity to show for their 160-million years of existence on Earth; only four or five families are recognized. Some of the earliest acanthodians are referred to a large group known as climatiids (*sloping spine*). These had two dorsal fins and many pairs of intermediate spines. All the spines were short and stout. The head and shoulder girdle were partly covered with large dermal plates. Silurian climatiids were marine, but during the Early and Middle Devonian, both marine and non-marine forms existed.

Members of a second acanthodian group, the diplacanthids (*double spine*), are similar to climatiids but had much longer fin spines and only two pairs of intermediate spines. [Plates 18 and 19] They ranged from the Early to Late Devonian,

and their fossils are found mostly in freshwater deposits. The gyracanthids (*curved spine*) represent a third, poorly known group that is found in the Early Devonian to the Late Carboniferous, in both freshwater and seawater deposits. Gyracanthid fossils are all fragmentary, but we know that they included the largest acanthodians, which may have reached lengths of several meters.

All remaining acanthodians have been classified into two groups. The ischnacanthids (*thin spine*), found in Late Silurian to Late Carboniferous strata, in marine and freshwater deposits, had two dorsal fins, either a single pair of intermediate spines or else none, small dermal bones on the head but none in the shoulder girdle, and strong dermal jaw bones to which large teeth were fused. Acanthodids, found in Early Devonian to Early Permian strata, are mostly freshwater, but some apparently could enter salt water. They had only one dorsal fin and spine, sometimes a single pair of intermediate spines but usually none at all, and no large dermal bones covering the head or shoulder girdle.

⇒⦙⦙⦙⊳ Finding a Place in the Pattern of Life

How do we determine the evolutionary relationships of extinct creatures such as acanthodians to living forms? They didn't evolve in a vacuum, and acanthodian anatomy reveals many general similarities to modern jawed fishes. The question is whether these similarities merely represent primitive gnathostome features or whether some of them place acanthodians closer to one modern group than to another.

Historically, acanthodians were first classified, along with some ray-finned fishes, as "ganoids" (*lustrous scale*) by Swiss ichthyologist Louis Agassiz in the early 19th century, because of their close-fitting rectangular scales covered with a shiny outer layer. Much later, the British paleontologist Roger Miles found many similarities in the head and gill arches of

PLATE 18
ري

Diplacanthus, an Middle Devonian fresh
water acanthodian from Scotland, about
380 million years old. Length up to 20cm.

PLATE 19
ري

Diplacanthus longispinus, an acanthodian
from the Middle Devonian of Banffshire,
Scotland (about 380 million years old).
Length 15cm.

acanthodians and ray-finned fishes to support the hypothesis that they shared a common ancestor.

Acanthodians have been nicknamed "spiny sharks," and between the 1930s and 1970s many anatomical similarities between acanthodians and sharks were recognized in the shoulder girdle, fin skeleton, and separate gill openings, particularly by Scandinavian anatomists Eric Stensiö, Niels Holmgren, and Erik Jarvik.

Unfortunately both arguments, whether for a relationship with sharks or ray-finned fishes, were supported by features that cannot be compared in lampreys, the closest living relatives of jawed craniates. Thus there was no way to determine if similarity A in acanthodians and sharks, or similarity B in acanthodians and bony fishes, is primitive or advanced relative to the condition in lampreys. We needed some features that could also be studied in a lamprey, to determine the advanced and primitive condition and thereby provide polarity (evolutionary direction). If a feature has one condition in a lamprey and a shark, and another condition in acanthodians and ray-finned fishes, for example, we are in a much stronger position to argue that the latter condition represents an evolutionary advance, and that acanthodians and ray-finned fishes share a common ancestor.

Such a feature finally came to light in the recent rediscovery of engravings published in 1895 by a European paleontologist, Anton Fritsch, in a monograph about vertebrate fossils from the Permian of Bohemia. He illustrated two *Acanthodes* specimens in which parts of the soft gills were amazingly well preserved. From these renderings their structure was exactly that of a ray-finned fish. In particular the paired, fleshy respiratory surfaces (gill lamellae) on each gill are separate, whereas in a shark, lungfish, coelacanth, and—most important—in larval lampreys, they are fixed back-to-back to a gill septum. Fritsch's illustrations offer an important clue about the relationships of acanthodians, even though the original

specimens on which they were based are now lost.

A second feature shared by acanthodians and ray-finned fishes is the presence of three pairs of ear stones (otoliths) in the labyrinth region. Preservation of these microscopic structures is rare in such ancient fossils, but they are known in several different species. Among living craniates, only ray-finned fishes have three pairs of otoliths.

Evolution of the Unknown

Acanthodians provide a good example of the kinds of dilemmas faced by paleontologists when the fossil record is slim and evolutionary relationships are tenuous. How should this minimum evidence be interpreted, and which aspects of it are more informative? Which is preferable— an evolutionary scenario that is congruent with geological time but makes some assumptions about anatomy, or a scenario that is founded on morphological comparison with other organisms but is incongruent with geological data? From what kind of primitive craniate did acanthodians evolve, and what are their closest living relatives? Were they primitively marine, as suggested by the earliest fossils, and could later forms move between fresh and salt water? Arguments over the evolutionary relationships, habitat, and behavior of these enigmatic fishes have raged since the mid-19th century, but progress in understanding acanthodians has been slow.

There is a legitimate difference of opinion among scientists about geological (time-dependant) versus phylogenetic (anatomy-dependant) analysis of fossils, and nowhere is this dichotomy greater than where extinct groups are concerned. Geological analysis seeks to identify changes in the abundance, diversity, and distribution of organisms through time. **Phylogenetic analysis** maps patterns of diversity among organisms. Scientists in each school find shortcomings in the other, but both approaches provide empirical data, although they may lead to different conclusions.

FIGURE 16
∽

A common paleontological dilemma; what evidence to believe? Two alternative versions of acanthodian relationships; one suggested by (A) anatomical comparison with other fishes; (B) the other suggested by geologic data and 19th-century ideas about fin evolution.

≋◗ Acanthodians through Time

First, let's look at the geological data. In their 160 million years of documented history, acanthodians were remarkably conservative, and the tempo of evolutionary change was extremely slow. To date only 56 acanthodian genera have been described, and that number includes 18 genera based on fragments about which nobody really can be sure. This works out to about one new genus appearing every 2.16 million years. It is likely, however, that many types thrived at the same time, and we know that many genera were remarkably persistent over long periods of time. For example, the genus *Acanthodes* is known from fossils throughout the Carboniferous 360 million years ago and Early Permian 440 million years ago, a span of some 80 million years.

We could array acanthodians into an evolutionary sequence based on geological occurrences [Figure 16A]. Climatiids, the oldest (Silurian to Middle Devonian) and by far the prickliest (with lots of intermediate spines), were deemed to be the most primitive. Ischnacanthids and acanthodiids, which survived until the Late Carboniferous and Early Permian respectively, are among the least spiny (either one pair of intermediate spines, or none), and have been regarded evolutionarily as the most advanced acanthodians. Diplacanthids and gyracanthids appear in the fossil record after climatiids, and disappear before the acanthodiids, and thus could be interpreted as intermediate forms. This time–based evolutionary scenario is all very well, but is not the only possibility.

≋◗ Acanthodians and anatomy

Anatomical rather than geological comparison of acanthodians may lead us to virtually opposite conclusions about their evolution. When we survey all the different kinds of jawed fishes (including sharks, ray–finned and lobe–finned osteichthyans, and even the extinct placoderms), paired intermediate spines occur

A. Acanthodian evolution based on geological evidence

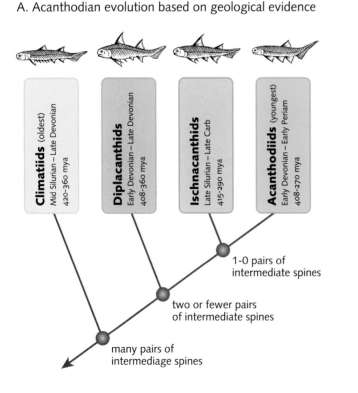

B. Acanthodian evolution based on anatomical comparison with other fishes

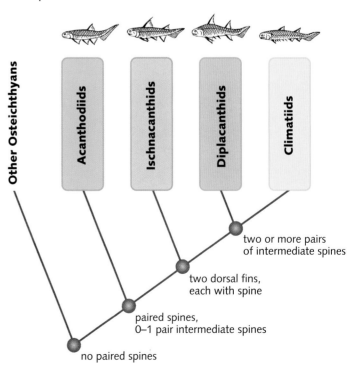

nowhere but in acanthodians. The presence of these structures therefore may be interpreted as an advanced feature that evolved in the common ancestor of acanthodians. Furthermore ray–finned fishes primitively have only one dorsal fin. If acanthodians are closely related to this still–living group, those with a single dorsal fin may be viewed as primitive, and the presence of two fins would be a secondary condition.

Comparison of acanthodians with other jawed fishes in general, and ray–finned fishes in particular, thus leads to the following evolutionary scenario. Acanthodiids, with a single dorsal fin, may be the most primitive acanthodians, for in all the other acanthodian groups there are two dorsal fins. Among the acanthodiids, those with no intermediate spines may be the most primitive of all. Ischnacanthids have two dorsal fins and some have one pair of intermediate spines while others have none, but only diplacanthid and climatiid acanthodians have two or more pairs of intermediate spines.

According to this evolutionary scenario, the number of intermediate spines increased rather than decreased during acanthodian evolution—just the opposite of what was predicted from the temporal sequence of the fossils. [Figure 16B] Furthermore, our geological intuition that acanthodians evolved in the sea must now be questioned because, according to our analysis, only the most advanced ones (climatiids) are marine.

≕⫷ Placoderms: An Armor–Plated Paradigm

Another example of an extinct pattern of bodily organization is found in placoderms. These jawed fishes were hugely successful in seas and fresh waters all over the world, but almost their entire evolutionary history was crammed into a single geological period, the Devonian. The contrast with acanthodians is reminiscent of an old television advertisement for electric light bulbs: acanthodians are like the dim ones that lasted for ages, and placoderms are like the flashy ones that soon burned out.

Placoderm anatomy clearly represents a variation on the basic gnathostome pattern, for there are powerful jaws encased in bone; indeed, most of the head is encased in bone, as it was in the ostracoderms. The arrangement of bones in the head is unlike that in any other craniates, however, and several unique patterns are found within placoderms. In most of these fishes there is a bony joint between the head and trunk armor, unlike anything seen in other jawed fishes or the ostracoderms. This feature, once established, remained with placoderms until their extinction about 360 million years ago.

Placoderms provide us with many paleontological enigmas. How could such bizarre creatures become so abundant and diverse? What led to the virtually world–wide success of placoderms in such a short span of geological time? And what caused the placoderms to disappear after only 50 or so million years of dazzling success?

≕⫷ Antiarchs: Bug–Eyed Swimming Boxes

Antiarchs were one of the two most abundant and widely distributed placoderm groups, but it is hard to imagine more bizarre or unlikely creatures. The back end of an antiarch looks completely normal, with a tapered muscular body, elongate dorsal fin, a pair of pelvic fins, and a slender, sharklike tail. It's the front end that's all wrong! The body was encased in a bony box that had flat sides and bottom and an angled roof. Toward the front of this box, and sticking out from each side, was a pair of bone-covered appendages that looked like crab legs, with a bony joint where they met the body. At the front of the box was a bony helmet with a central opening that contained both eyes, which protruded like those of a frog. A joint between the head and trunk armor was formed by a pair of rounded processes on the head shield and corresponding sockets on the trunk armor.

PLATE 20
∽

Bothriolepis, a Late Devonian antiarch (age;
about 375 million years) about 25cm long,
is known from every continent of the
world. Most of its 100 or so species lived in
fresh water, but some were probably salt–
tolerant, helping to explain its widespread
distribution.

These unlikely fossils caused consternation when they were discovered back in the 1830s. They fascinated the late-19th-century American paleontologist William Patten, who thought that antiarchs and ostracoderms provided a link with the arthropods. Edward D. Cope, another 19th-century American paleontologist, thought antiarchs were allied to the tunicates, especially armor-plated ones like the living *Chelysoma* In these odd creatures, the mouth and the anus both lie on top of the body. Cope coined the name antiarch, meaning "opposite anus," because the opening he thought was the mouth (actually it was the eye-hole!) was not on the same side of the body as the anus.

These bug-eyed antiarchs, boxes with arms, swam all over the world, and their fossils have been found on every continent, including Antarctica. At first, their distribution seemed almost as odd as their appearance, because they were found most abundantly in strata deposited in fresh waters, but subsequent discoveries showed that

PLATE 21
ༀ
Many *Bothriolepis canadensis*, an antiarch from the Late Devonian of Escuminac Bay, Quebec, Canada (about 375 million years old). Length of armor 12cm; length with tail 25cm.

antiarchs probably originated in the sea. Antiarchs are one of the oldest placoderm groups, with a fossil record extending back to the Silurian of China 440 million years ago. *Yunnanolepis*, for example, is a primitive antiarch in which the armored pectoral appendages were short, unsegmented, and lacked a shoulder joint with the body armor. Even so, these fishes had clearly evolved far in the antiarch direction, which suggests that the group had an extensive but unknown prior history.

Sinolepids and bothriolepids are considered by many paleontologists to be the most advanced antiarchs. Sinolepid fossils are found only in parts of China (*Sinolepis*) and Australia (*Grenfellaspis*), which suggests that these regions were much closer together in the Late Devonian than they are today. Bothriolepids were much more widespread, particularly *Bothriolepis* itself, which has been found on every continent. [Plates 20 and 21] Most *Bothriolepis* specimens have been found in freshwater deposits, but a few are from marine strata.

It was once suggested that *Bothriolepis* was able to leave the water and crawl around on land, which may explain the bug-eyes, boxy armor (perhaps necessary to support the body out of water), stiff pectoral appendages (to drag the fish along), and the strong shoulder joint. In the 1940s American paleontologist Robert Denison sliced up several well-preserved specimens of *Bothriolepis*. Inside he discovered evidence of two sacs that apparently arose on either side of the pharynx and extended back as far as the intestine. He interpreted these as lungs, and suggested that *Bothriolepis* was a facultative air-breathing fish. *Bothriolepis* fossils are commonly associated with those of Devonian lungfishes, and they evidently shared the same habitats. Unfortunately the evidence (different kinds of sediment inside the body where the supposed lungs would be) is

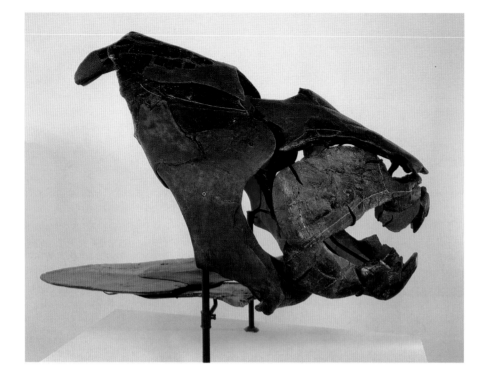

PLATE 22
∽

Dunkleosteus terrelli, head and trunk armor of a giant arthrodire in side view from the Late Devonian of Ohio, USA (about 375 million years old). Length of armor 135cm; estimated body length 4m.

PLATE 23
∽

Dunkleosteus is a giant Late Devonian arthrodire, reaching lengths of five or six meters, that lived in shallow seas covering the interior of North America some 375 million years ago. Its armor plates are over 5cm thick in places, and its massive bony jaws were armed with sharp shearing sur–faces, making it an awesome predator.

equivocal, and Denison's colorful interpretation has not recieved widespread acceptance, although nobody has yet offered an alternative interpretation of the structures he described.

Anatomy of an Arthrodire

Almost two thirds of placoderms are classified in a single group known as **arthrodires** (*jointed-neck*). In all but the most primitive arthrodires, the bony head shield was hinged on each side to the armor protecting the front part of the body, unlike any modern fish. The name "arthrodire" is not altogether appropriate, because other placoderms (antiarchs, for example) also had a neck joint, and it is therefore an ambiguous feature with which to define the group. The eyes were large and usually were protected and supported by a ring of sclerotic bones. Behind each eye, the bony covering of the cheek region was hinged against the head shield and was able to swing laterally and expand the size of the mouth cavity. When the first arthrodire fossils were found, early in the 19th century, nobody understood the anatomy of this joint. Hugh Miller, a Scottish writer and amateur paleontologist at that time, thought that these fossils had a mouth at the back of the head, behind the eyes!

Apparently arthrodires were efficient predators. The neck joint (reversed from the condition seen in antiarchs, which had sockets on the head shield) probably enabled the head to be raised as the mouth opened, increasing the gape. Arthrodires had two pairs of upper jaw tooth plates in the mouth (all other placoderms have a single pair). Upper and lower jaw tooth plates had well-developed cusps and serrations, arranged so that the upper and lower cusps interlocked and sliced past each other. The upper jaw cartilage was attached to the inside of the cheekbones, and a strong hinge joint connected it with the lower jaw. Adductor (mouth-closing) muscles were attached both to the upper jaw and inside the cheek region, providing a powerful shearing bite. The cutting edges were kept sharp by abrasion between tooth plates as they occluded. This abrasion was closely matched by growth on the opposite side of the tooth plate, thereby maintaining a sharp cutting surface throughout the life of the fish, and up to several centimeters of bone was lost to self-sharpening.

Arthrodire aggression

Some of the largest bony plates from arthrodires in the American Museum of Natural History belong to *Dunkleosteus*, a giant dinichthyid from the Late Devonian. Its body length is estimated to have been about 6 meters, of which about 1.5 meters was armored. [Plates 22 and 23] Interestingly, many *Dunkleosteus* bones display puncture wounds and deep gouges that seem to correspond in size to cusps on the tooth plates. In one or two cases there are paired puncture wounds, spaced as far apart as the two principal fangs of a large *Dunkleosteus*. These wounds, some of which show evidence of repair, offer compelling evidence for the voracious habits of *Dunkleosteus* and its relatives. Large modern open-water marine sharks such as the great white frequently are scarred by encounters with others of the same species, either when feeding, or in displays of aggression, or when mating. Scrapes and scars on *Dunkleosteus* bones may be Paleozoic love bites, but puncture wounds, especially unhealed ones, tell a darker tale.

Other Placoderms

Besides arthrodires and antiarchs, there are several lesser groups of placoderms. A few will be mentioned to give a general idea of their diversity.

Phyllolepids (*leaf-scaled*) were flattened freshwater placoderms with an extremely large central bone in the head shield. They may be related to arthrodires, or to both arthrodires and antiarchs, but the exact association remains uncertain. Eyes were probably absent (or internal), because there is no indication of an orbital opening or of circumorbital bones. The mouth

PLATE 24

Lunaspis, a petalichthyid placoderm with long, sharp spines projecting from its trunk armor, swims into the shallows of an Early Devonian sea that covered Germany some 400 million years ago.

EXTINCT RELATIVES OF MODERN FISHES

Gemuendina stuertzi, a rhenanid placoderm
from the Early Devonian of
Hunsruck, Budenbach, Germany (cast),
about 400 million years old. Length 15cm.
Plate 17 shows what *Gemuendina* may have
looked like in Life.

was wide and situated right at the front of
the head.

Petalichthyids (*plate fish*) were distinctive sea-going placoderms. Their dermal bones were strongly ornamented with
concentric rings, and they had long spines
projecting in front of their pectoral fins.
[Plate 24]

Ptyctodontids (*beak-toothed*) had strong
tooth plates suited for crushing food. They
had elongate bodies with a whiplike tail
and were sea dwellers. Their body shape
and tooth plates are reminiscent of modern
chimaeroids, which are relatives of sharks,
and it has been suggested that ptyctodontids are a link between placoderms and
sharks because clasperlike reproductive
structures have been described in the
ptyctodontid *Rhamphodopsis*. On the other
hand, ptyctodontids lack any other features
unique to sharks and chimaeroids and
anatomically are more like other placoderms, especially arthrodires.

Rhenanids (Rhenish [fish]) were the
placoderm equivalent of rays. [Plate 25;
and see Plate 17] Some had an expanded
disk formed by the pectoral fins, a flattened body, and eyes on top of the head.
They were all marine and formerly were
known only from the Early Devonian of
Germany and North America, but
rhenanids have now been found in the
Middle Devonian of Bolivia and the Early
Devonian of Africa.

Besides these groups, there are some
obscure and poorly preserved fossils (for
example, *Pseudopetalichthys, Stensioella*) that
are classified as placoderms, although it is
not altogether clear why. These fossils lack
most of the features uniting other placoderms, and for that reason they are usually written off as primitive placoderms of
uncertain affinity.

⫸ Early Success and Failure

Few Silurian placoderms are known, apart
from some antiarchs and indeterminate
arthrodires from China, but they show
that placoderm diversity originated long
before the Devonian. Antiarchs and
arthrodires are anatomically advanced

placoderms, so the origins of more primitive groups presumably also lay in the Silurian or earlier. Silurian antiarch and arthrodire groups survived until the end of the Early Devonian but then became extinct, along with many jawless ostracoderms in China and Euramerica. Some jawed fishes, particularly primitive relatives of lungfishes, also died out at that time.

This extinction at the end of the Early Devonian coincided with a dramatic rise in the abundance and diversity of advanced antiarchs. It has been suggested that these bizarre fishes locally displaced bottom–dwelling ostracoderms and perhaps more primitive antiarchs from sandy bottom environments in early Middle Devonian times. We know that, in Euramerica, the Early Devonian marked the final closing of the ancient Sea of Iapetus that had previously existed between parts of Europe and North America, eliminating continental margins in many parts of the world and presumably heightening competition for this diminishing habitat. At the same time, global sea levels fell appreciably. Just when local benthic real estate was at a critical premium for filter-feeding ostracoderms, along came the advanced antiarchs. During the Middle Devonian, global sea levels temporarily rose again, flooding more of the continental margins, but as far as many ostracoderms were concerned, the damage was done. Antiarchs, not ostracoderms, took advantage of the increased availability of shallow benthic environments in parts of Euramerica and Asia.

The mid-Devonian extinction of so many ostracoderms and primitive placoderms certainly was not part of a global mass extinction. Most invertebrates were unaffected, and although some faunal changes can be detected (several coral families became extinct and some new ones appeared at around that time, for example), there is no evident link with what was happening among fishes. If loss of benthic environments was a significant factor in the extinction of ostracoderms,

why did it not have greater impact on the invertebrate fossil record? We simply don't know the answer. The dispersal of advanced antiarchs during the Middle and Late Devonian was certainly global, but its apparent impact, measured by extinctions of other benthic fishes, was localized, affecting the northern land masses of Euramerica and China more than the southern continent, Gondwana.

Taking the Plunge

The Middle Devonian also marked the rise of many new pelagic placoderms, notably the predaceous arthrodires. Again, there is little to suggest this was part of a major faunal turnover, and it is possible that these free swimmers were moving into previously unoccupied marine habitats. We can draw an analogy with later pterosaurs and birds, which were able to "conquer" the previously almost empty skies in the Mesozoic. Besides placoderms, many other groups of pelagic jawed fishes became abundant during the Middle Devonian, including sharks and osteichthyans. The Middle Devonian may therefore represent a time when fishes "conquered" the open oceans.

Why Were Placoderms Excluded from South America?

Despite their global distribution, placoderms are virtually absent from the Devonian of South America. There is no shortage of Devonian strata with fossils, but sites with placoderms are virtually nonexistent. In the Lower and Middle Devonian, the circumpolar seas of western Gondwana (including much of present-day Brazil and Bolivia, South Africa, and the Falkland Islands) were cold. This region, known to geologists as the Malvinokaffric Province, was populated by a sparse but distinctive marine fauna of trilobite arthropods and shelled invertebrates known as brachiopods. The only Malvinokaffric placoderm is *Bolivosteus*, a lightly armored rhenanid from Bolivia, whose closest relatives are from the Early

Devonian of Germany and North America. Other Malvinokaffric fishes include rare sharks (*Antarctilamna*) and acanthodians. By the end of the Middle Devonian the Malvinokaffric fauna disappeared as warmer conditions prevailed and organisms from Euramerica began to enter the region, including marine "Appalachian" trilobites and freshwater *Bothriolepis* in Venezuela.

Cold, stormy waters associated with the polar position of western Gondwana may explain the paucity of Early Devonian invertebrates as well as the virtual absence of placoderms in what is today South America. The global ingress of anoxic seawater into marginal shelf seas would also have had an impact. None of the abundant and diverse Lower and Middle Devonian placoderms of tropical eastern Gondwana (including present-day Australia and Antarctica) seem to have lived farther westward. A strong circumpolar current, the austral gyre, may have isolated the southern continent from outside invasion. Only after Euramerica came into close proximity with Gondwana was this current possibly disrupted, allowing faunal interchanges to occur—an event that might be linked to the global oceanic oxygen crisis of the Late Devonian.

⟩⟩⟩ Placoderms in Crisis

A massive extinction event, regarded as one of the five most profound in the past half-billion years of Earth's history, occurred about 5 million years before the end of the Devonian. It has been estimated that 35 out of 46 families of fishes became extinct at that time, about 365 million years ago. This global event took out the last of the ostracoderms, virtually all the placoderms, and ten families of lobe-finned fishes. Some sharks and primitive ray-finned fishes were also affected. Unlike the previous mid-Devonian extinction, this time many invertebrate groups were also hit hard. It has been estimated that over 20% of all marine animal families became extinct at that time.

The shelly invertebrate fossils called brachiopods were common sea creatures, and their history through the crisis reveals an interesting phenomenon. The maximum extinction rate among these brachiopods occurred about 2 million years before this massive extinction event but was associated with relatively high rates of new brachiopod appearances. The sum total of diversity among brachiopods thus remained high until 365 million years ago when diversity dropped dramatically. Few new forms appeared, but the extinction rate was actually lower than it was 2 million years earlier.

The fossil fish record is less revealing, and in placoderms we cannot resolve a similar picture of rapid extinction and diversification followed by slowed extinction and a decline in diversification. Nevertheless we can obtain a general impression of the placoderm demise. Before 365 million years ago, during the Late Devonian, approximately 22 placoderm families existed, but only nine survived after that date. Of these nine, four families had a worldwide distribution both before and after the crisis (bothriolepid and asterolepid antiarchs, plus two families of arthrodires), two were cosmopolitan before the crisis and apparently were more restricted (to Euramerica) afterward (ptyctodontids and one family of arthrodires), one arthrodire family was restricted to Euramerica before and after the event, and two families (phyllolepids and sinolepid antiarchs) actually became more widespread after the crisis. Among the families that did not survive, only three were widespread before the crisis, whereas 12 localized families became extinct. Most of the extinct families were marine, but freshwater placoderms were also affected.

The extinction of so many localized, and presumably more specialized, groups may provide clues to what happened. Global sea levels rose throughout most of the Late Devonian, flooding more and more of the continental margins and creating new environments for fishes and invertebrates, while at the same time destroying freshwater habitats in lower-lying areas. Inundation also tended to break down barriers between originally separate areas, resulting in opportunities for invasion of habitats by hardy, generalized species. Fishes that were physiologically tolerant of a wide range of salinity (bothriolepids seem to have been such a group) could disperse via shallow seaways. More specialized freshwater fishes that were not so salt tolerant may simply have died.

Major changes in global climates also occurred at that time and have been associated with a worldwide decline in the circulation of water within the ocean basins. Reduced circulation led to the build-up of bottom waters low in oxygen, which eventually accumulated to such an extent that their upper regions spilled over into the shallow seas surrounding the continents. As these shallow environments went into prolonged oxygen crisis over several million years, their faunas and floras suffered massive extinctions.

As we saw earlier, there is evidence that a dramatic decline in global sea levels occurred toward the end of the Devonian, after a lengthy period of gradual rising. The loss of shallow shelf environments was further exacerbated by elevated levels of anoxic waters during the oxygen crisis, because the marginal belt of habitable oxygenated seas would have been narrowed further. Many placoderms, as well as the last bony ostracoderms, may have been caught in the squeeze between advancing shorelines and lifeless deeper waters.

It has also been suggested that continental drift played an important part in Late Devonian extinctions, but scientific opinion is divided about the relative positions of the northern and southern continents. Some paleogeographic reconstructions have them far apart, separated by a wide ocean in the Late Devonian, but the distribution of certain fishes, invertebrates, and plant spore fossils, together with other paleoclimatic data, suggests

that the two continents moved much closer together, closing off part of the southern ocean and dramatically changing its circulation patterns. There is evidence of extensive glaciation in parts of today's southern continents, probably related to this altered geography, and the end of the Devonian may have been a time of global cooling.

Stragglers

The closing bell for the placoderms—and for some primitive sharks and certain groups of ray-finned and lobe-finned bony fishes—came at the very end of the Devonian 360 million years ago. This extinction event differed from the massive one that took place five million years earlier, in three important respects. First, fewer families of fishes actually became extinct in the second event, so in this respect the scale was smaller. Second, few new fishes appeared following the earlier extinction event, whereas the terminal Devonian extinction was accompanied by the appearance of many new fishes, so that the overall diversity was hardly changed (paralleling what happened earlier to brachiopods in the Devonian). And third, this extinction was not accompanied by a corresponding crisis among invertebrates.

Sharks and ray-finned fishes became even more abundant and diverse at the end of the Devonian, it has been suggested that the last placoderms were unable to compete with them. Placoderms were depicted in the past as rather inefficient fishes, with heavy bodies best suited to a sluggish, benthic existence and jaws that lacked the mobility seen in higher fishes. But in Australia scientists have discovered slender, streamlined pelagic arthrodires that probably were capable of high swimming speeds. Fossils of the largest placoderm predators, including the dinichthyid *Dunkleosteus* and its relatives, are found in many parts of the world, attesting to the ability of those fishes to traverse open oceans that lay between Euramerica and Gondwana. Even the bizarre and specialized bottom–living bothriolepids became widespread in fresh and sea waters throughout the world. Collectively, placoderms display far greater anatomical variety than any group of Devonian fishes except possibly for the lobe-fins, among which were the earliest tetrapods. With such an array of anatomical diversity and specializations, it is impossible to continue viewing placoderms as inferior to their contemporaries.

It is certainly possible to identify cases of possible competition between placoderm stragglers and other fishes at a local level, but these do not offer satisfactory explanations for the global extinction of placoderms. For example, Middle and Late Devonian lobe–finned fishes, some of which were large predators, may have displaced some of the last pelagic placoderms in parts of Gondwana. Elsewhere, the earliest tetrapods, which were not yet terrestrial animals, may have ousted some placoderm stragglers, for we find their bones together in Late Devonian freshwater strata of modern–day North America and Greenland. But there may be no single cause of placoderm extinction. Instead, each group of stragglers may have met its own end independently of the others.

As the last placoderm died, however, all placoderms went extinct. After a phenomenal rise to success and a serious setback in the early part of the Late Devonian, they quietly left the stage.

The stories told by placoderms and acanthodians are very different, yet both provide fascinating insights into the early evolution of fishes, insights that cannot be gotten by studying living species. They reveal that patterns of anatomical diversity among living creatures are not the only ones possible, and that different patterns existed in the past. Equally important, they show that even those anatomical patterns that are now extinct were governed by the same kinds of developmental constraints that exist today, and therefore we can interpret the fossils in the light of present-day developmental and anatomical studies. Placoderms and acanthodians had dermal skeletons and endoskeletons, jaws, paired sensory structures, and a fin arrangement just like that of modern fishes. These fundamental similarities in their body plan are possible only if they shared the same developmental and genetic processes. The more we come to understand these processes today, the more we may come to understand these fossils in the future.

THE LORDS OF TIME

⇒〜〜▶ Finding the First Sharks

PLATE 26
〜〜

This almost surrealistic collage of sharks from the Miocene (some 15 million years old) is dominated by the gigantic extinct great white (*Carcharodon megalodon*), which is estimated to have exceeded lengths of 12m (twice that of the modern white shark). Although *megalodon* dwarfs other Miocene sharks, they too were usually larger than their modern counterparts.

*I*F *RECENT DISCOVERIES* are correct, sharks are the oldest group of jawed fishes existing today, with a fossil record extending back about 450 million years into the Late Ordovician.

Given the well-known fact that modern sharks can produce thousands of teeth in their lifetime, we might expect the earliest traces of fossil sharks to be their teeth, but we would be disappointed. Currently the oldest known shark tooth fossils are from the Lower Devonian of Spain, about 400 million years old. The oldest fossils classified as **chondrichthyans** (*cartilage fish*; sharks and their relatives) are from the Early Silurian, and Late Ordovician, but these consist only of isolated, microscopic scales, fragments of their dermal (skin) skeleton. In living chondrichthyans these small scales (dermal denticles) are embedded close together in the skin. They are streamlined, with fluted crowns that help maintain laminar flow over the body, assisted by mucous secretions from cells in the skin. After the shark died these scales became detached and were readily scattered by currents. Although fossil shark scales are common, they are hardly noticeable except with a keen eye and a good microscope!

The fragile internal skeleton of chondrichthyans does not lend itself to fossilization either! Many people incorrectly think of the shark's endoskeleton as soft and cartilaginous, but there is usually a hard superficial layer made of the same mineral (hydroxyapatite) as bone. Unlike bone, this hard layer consists of thousands of tiny prisms, usually less than 1 mm in diameter, each one attached to the next by collagen fibers. After death, unless the skeleton is buried rapidly and in very quiet conditions, the collagen decays and the prisms are scattered by currents and scavengers.

The prismatic layer is found in all chondrichthyan fossils from the Devonian onward, and is the most diagnostic chondrichthyan characteristic. Earlier chondrichthyans either lacked these prisms, or else they have gone unnoticed in the fossil record.

Rarer than gold, fossil shark skeletons are difficult to find and collect because their denticles, teeth and prisms tend to fall apart very easily. The anatomy of Devonian sharks is known only from a handful of exceptionally well-preserved fossils, mainly from North America, plus a few more from Europe, Australia, and Antarctica – a limited assortment that probably does not reflect the range of morphological diversity originally present.

The Tooth Factory

We cannot determine much about shark anatomy just from their teeth, but they make up the bulk of the chondrichthyan fossil record and are, in fact, the most commonly collected craniate fossils. The first shark teeth may have resembled skin denticles, making it hard for us to distinguish them. Shark teeth and skin denticles are both made of dentine, the same kind of hard tissue found in teeth generally.

By the time shark teeth show up in the fossil record, they are already quite distinctive. They are rare in Early and Middle Devonian strata, but are more common in the Late Devonian. They increase in abundance in the Early

PLATE 27

Carcharodon megalodon, tooth of an extinct great white shark, from the Miocene of South Carolina, USA (between 5–23 million years old). Height of tooth from tip to "gumline" 16cm; estimated length of shark 12m.

Carboniferous (about 360 million years ago), increase again in the Middle Cretaceous (about 90 million years ago), and attain a modern level of diversity in the Miocene (between 5 and 25 million years ago). [Plate 27; and see Figure 18] To some extent this trend may be skewed artificially by the erosion of older strata and the fossils embedded in them, but, as anybody who has gone fossil hunting will attest, it is a lot easier to find shark teeth in shallow-water marine deposits of Tertiary or Cretaceous age than in corresponding Jurassic or Carboniferous strata. The teeth simply aren't there in such numbers, either because sharks were far less abundant or because they were not producing new teeth at such prodigious rates.

Shark teeth are produced on a conveyer belt of gum tissue that lines the inside surface of the upper and lower jaws. New teeth are formed within this gum tissue and are carried into a functional position closer to the edge of the mouth. Depending on the kind of shark and position in the mouth, each tooth is functional for a few days or weeks before its nutrient supply is cut off, the gum tissue holding it dies, and the tooth falls out. Estimates vary, but it is said that a small lemon shark may go through 10,000 teeth in a 10-year life span. Maybe larger sharks, such as the great white, have slower rates of tooth replacement (nobody has yet been sufficiently brave or foolish to try and count them!), and replacement rates in sharks may decline as the shark ages, but the message is clear: sharks have no equal when it comes to making teeth! Because shark teeth are dense and tough, and composed of relatively stable calcium phosphate, their potential for fossilization is high. Multiply the possible number of teeth by the number of sharks that lived over millions of years, and you have a lot of fossilized shark teeth.

⇒⫸ Evolution of a Consumer Society

There is good evidence that tooth replacement was slow in many early sharks. Not only are Devonian and Carboniferous

shark teeth rare, many also show signs of considerable wear and abrasion. We see this today only in those sharks and rays that have slow tooth replacement, usually bottom-dwelling species with crushing dentitions, not in sharks with pointed teeth that are still sharp when they fall out. Further evidence of slow tooth replacement is found in some complete Devonian shark fossils, whose outer teeth, formed when the shark was younger, are much smaller than the inner (replacement) ones. In modern sharks the replacement teeth are about the same size as those preceding them, because the shark grows only a little in the few days needed to grow a new tooth row. The different size of inner and outer teeth in some Devonian sharks suggests that they took months or even years to form new ones. Some ancient sharks conserved their teeth until they were worn to a stub.

Many other sharks, including some from the Devonian, replaced and discarded their teeth with greater abandon. Shark tooth production must rank as one of the most efficient organic methods of removing phosphate from the biological environment and burying it in sediment. There probably is more phosphate in a single 15-centimeter Miocene fossil white shark tooth than was used during the whole life of a meter-long Devonian shark. Fossil teeth provide dramatic testimony of increasing phosphate consumption during the evolution of sharks.

It is erroneous to think that sharks expend so much metabolic effort growing teeth that they have sacrificed a bony internal skeleton. Sharks certainly possess the hormonal pathway necessary for bone production, and their internal skeleton is mineralized with calcium phosphate. When scientists say that sharks lack bone, their intended meaning is that sharks typically lack a particular kind of hard tissue with certain properties. Human bone is full of microscopic spaces, occupied in life by cells (osteocytes) responsible for depositing phosphate. The dentine of teeth typically lacks these spaces, as it is formed by cells that migrate as they deposit phosphate

PLATE 28

Cladoselache, a meter–long shark from the Late Devonian of North America (about 375 million years old) probably ate small ray–finned fishes, but was wary of gigantic arthrodires such as *Dunkleosteus*. *Cladoselache* is recognizably sharklike in form, but has none of the more advanced features of modern sharks.

PLATE 29

Cladoselache fyleri, a shark from the Late
Devonian of Ohio, USA (about 375 million
years old). Length 76cm.

and so do not become caught up in the hard tissue. Scientists have occasionally noted the presence of osteocyte spaces in the teeth and vertebrae of living sharks, and similar cell spaces occur in fossil sharks.

So we cannot correlate toothiness and bonelessness. Solid bones are absent even in early sharks with slow tooth replacement. Prismatic calcification of their internal cartilage skeleton undoubtedly represents an evolutionarily advanced state that probably evolved independently of the ability to grow innumerable replacement teeth.

What Were the First Sharks Like?

The most anatomically primitive shark fossils, such as *Cladoselache*, are of Late Devonian age (about 370 million years old). [Plates 28 and 29] Despite their great antiquity, these sharks are undeniably similar to living ones in many features, with an elongate body and large triangular fins supported by stiff rods of cartilage. The tail was sharply upturned and had a large lower lobe, like many fast-swimming fishes today. Its mouth was full of tooth rows, just like a modern shark's mouth, but in well-preserved fossils we can see that the teeth in each replacement series (called a tooth family) differ in size, and probably were replaced slowly. The teeth do not look quite like modern ones, having a flat, semicircular base supporting several pointed cusps, the central one being the largest. Unlike the tooth array in modern sharks, the base of each tooth overlapped the one behind, with small bumps of tooth tissue acting as spacers. This kind of shark tooth is known as cladodont, and sharks with these teeth used to be classified together as cladodonts. The cladodont tooth pattern is very ancient, and was retained in an almost unmodified form by many later sharks, including extinct relatives of modern sharks, such as *Palaeospinax* and *Synechodus* of the Jurassic and Cretaceous. [Figure 17]

The jaw joint of modern sharks and their relatives is very strong, but that of *Cladoselache* was weak and poorly developed. Its adductor muscles for closing the mouth were nevertheless large (fossilized muscles frequently are well preserved in these sharks), and *Cladoselache* fossils found with other fishes in the stomach show that it certainly was capable of catching large prey. The upper jaw was attached to the braincase at a joint just behind the eye and by ligaments beneath the snout, and probably could not be moved very much. The jaw was also supported by the hyoid. A similar arrangement occurs in acanthodians, and probably represents a primitive condition among all gnathostomes (See page 65).

⋙ Clues to Bony Ancestry

In *Cladoselache* two dorsal fins were present, and in front of the first one was a bony spine, mostly buried inside the

FIGURE 17
⚭

Evolutionary relationships of some living and extinct chondrichthyans. Living chondrichthyans include chimaeroids (rabbit-fishes) and neoselachians (sharks and rays).

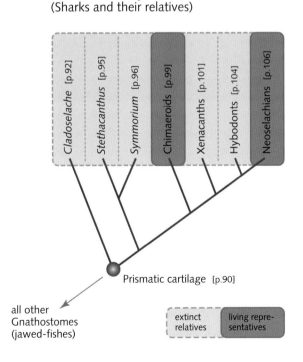

Chondrichthyans
(Sharks and their relatives)

Cladoselache [p.92]
Stethacanthus [p.95]
Symmorium [p.96]
Chimaeroids [p.99]
Xenacanths [p.101]
Hybodonts [p.104]
Neoselachians [p.106]

Prismatic cartilage [p.90]

all other
Gnathostomes
(jawed-fishes)

extinct relatives | living representatives

body. When thin sections of these spines are examined under a microscope, their bony structure becomes apparent, with many small spaces for osteocytes. Other sharks also had dorsal spines, but, like teeth, these were usually made of dentine, not bone. *Cladoselache* shows that bone was well developed in some parts of the dermal skeleton in primitive chondrichthyans. Teeth are made of dentine instead of bone in all jawed craniates (evidently representing an early evolutionary step). In chondrichthyans, the switch from bone to dentine in other parts of the dermal skeleton occurred after they diverged from other jawed fishes.

Sharks and Sex

The males of modern sharks and their relatives, the rays and rabbitfishes, are all characterized by the presence of paired penislike structures, called claspers, that form extensions to the paired pelvic fins and are used in internal fertilization. This mode of reproduction evolved early in chondrichthyan history, and many fossil sharks can be sexed according to whether or not they have claspers. Curiously, despite the discovery of many specimens of *Cladoselache*, not one has been found with claspers, leading to all kinds of speculation. Did *Cladoselache* employ external fertilization, as most other fishes do? If so, was this a derived attribute of *Cladoselache*, or did internal fertilization arise later in shark evolution? Or are all known *Cladoselache* fossils female? Unfortunately, there is no known alternative way to distinguish between the sexes in these fossils. But in some other extinct sharks we can tell the difference in a variety of ways.

Other Late Devonian sharks such as stethacanthids (*chest spine*) were apparently more advanced than *Cladoselache* in that the males certainly had claspers. [Plate 30] One remarkable feature of *Stethacanthus* was the presence of a curious forward-curving spine that projected from the body in the same region as the largely internal spine of *Cladoselache*. There is no fin associated with this spine in *Stethacanthus*, but there is a brushlike array of enlarged skin denticles and fin rays, suggesting that the fin was highly modified. [Plate 31] Other relatives of *Stethacanthus*, that lived in the interval between the Early Carboniferous and Early Permian (about 350 to 275 million years ago), display a curious variety of ornamented spines and "brushes," and there is mounting evidence that these structures represent secondary sexual features of different species; if so, these were effective reproductive signaling devices for more than 100 million years. Fossil sharks similar to *Stethacanthus*, but lacking a spine and brush, have been classified separately but could represent female stethacanthids (for example *Symmorium*). [Plates 32 and 33] The corroborative test—finding a spineless specimen with claspers—has yet to be fulfilled. Published reconstructions showing such a specimen are composite reconstructions, and there is no guarantee that the male claspers illustrated in them went with the rest of the fish.

Among chondrichthyans, secondary sexual features are not restricted to stethacanthids. In the extinct hybodont (*lump tooth*) sharks (from the Late Pennsylvanian to the Late Cretaceous, 300 to 65 million years ago), for example, males possessed hooklike spines on each side of the head. Today, no sharks or rays have externally distinctive sex-linked features other than claspers, although there are slight differences in the teeth of males and females in some species. Rabbitfishes (chimaeroids) display secondary sexual features in the head region.

Other Early Sharks

Two other Devonian sharks deserve mention here, for each in its own way sheds some light on the early evolution of these fascinating creatures. One of these, called *Ctenacanthus*, is known from many localities around the world. The other, called *Antarctilamna*, apparently was restricted to the Southern Hemisphere. Both were probably more advanced than

PLATE 30
෴

Stethacanthus from the Late Devonian of
North America (approximately 375 million
years old) had a curious spine and brush–
like structure in place of the first dorsal fin.
This may have been a visual signal in
males of different species, enabling them to
locate an appropriate mate. These sharks
were a little over one meter long.

PLATE 31
෴

Stethacanthus tumidus, spine and "brush"
from the back of a shark, from the Early
Carboniferous of Ohio, USA (cast), about
340 million years old. Length of spine
22cm; estimated length of shark 150cm

PLATE 32
⟋⟍

Symmorium from the Late Carboniferous of
North America (about 300–310 million years
old) was anatomically similar to
Stethacanthus, but lacked the elaborate spine
and brush complex. There is controversy
over whether spineless forms represent
female stethacanthids or a distinct lineage
of sharks.

PLATE 33
⟋⟍

Symmorium reniforme, a shark from the Late
Carboniferous of Indiana, USA (cast), about
310 million years old. Length 122cm.

Cladoselache and stethacanthids, but it is not clear whether they were closely related to each other.

Ctenacanths (*comb spine*) had a strong jaw joint like that of modern sharks, but, based on the relative size and arrangement of teeth across the jaws, tooth replacement still was apparently slow. Instead of a single spine, two spines were embedded deep in the body and projected immediately in front of each dorsal fin. Instead of being platelike, these spines were cylindrical and pointed, and the projecting part of the spine was ornamented with rows of small denticles or tubercles. Although most living sharks lack fin spines like these, they are present in a few forms such as the Port Jackson shark (*Heterodontus*) and the pickerels, spurdogs, and cookie-cutter sharks (*Squalus* and its relatives). Similar spines occur in many extinct sharks from the Mesozoic, such as *Hybodus*, and signify that all these sharks share a common ancestor with *Ctenacanthus* and its Devonian relatives. These sharks also share some other advanced features in the arrangement of cartilages inside the paired fins, and in the structure of the gill arches. The structure of the pectoral fin is particularly important, because it has three large basal cartilages that are constricted together where they meet the shoulder girdle, allowing greater freedom of movement for maneuvering and stability. The ancestry of sharks can therefore be traced to the Ordorician, although no modern families extend farther back in time than the Early Jurassic (about 200 to 180 million years).

Antarctilamna, a slightly older shark from the Middle Devonian (380 million years ago) of Australia and Antarctica, had two dorsal spines ornamented like those of *Ctenacanthus*, although they were not so deeply embedded beneath the skin. Its teeth were remarkably different, however, with two main cusps instead of one. The oldest known shark teeth, from the Early Devonian of Spain (400 million years ago), are also this shape, and similar bicuspid teeth occurred in a group of extinct eel-like sharks known as xenacanths (See page. 101) that appeared in the Devonian and became extinct in the Early Triassic (about 250 million years ago). It is not clear at the moment whether the bicuspid tooth pattern is more primitive than the cladodont one (suggested by its greater antiquity), or if *Antarctilamna* is a primitive xenacanth (suggested by anatomical similarities of its teeth). This is one more instance of a disparity between geological and anatomical evidence (See page 77).

Ecology and Distribution of Early Sharks

Until recently, the earliest traces of sharks were from the Silurian of Asia and other localities that originally lay in the southern continent of Gondwana, and it had been suggested that sharks first arose there 420 million years ago. Now, however, some shark like scales from the Late Ordovician of North America seem to push the origins of sharks back another 30 million years, and suggest they were already widespread by the Silurian From the Late Devonian 375 million years ago onward, sharks were in seas everywhere, and they also invaded fresh waters to a greater extent than we see today.

The famous Cleveland Shale strata of Ohio provide a glimpse of a Late Devonian shallow-water marine community populated by many sharks, including *Cladoselache*, *Stethacanthus*, and *Ctenacanthus*. The community is unusual for its time in having so many sharks among its fishes, which also included giant arthrodires such as *Titanichthys* and *Dunkleosteus*, and primitive ray-finned fishes. Here, the Devonian shark *Cladoselache* preyed on ray-finned fishes, which it sometimes swallowed tail-first, suggesting high swimming speeds and an ability to overtake its prey. *Cladoselache* also fed on shrimplike crustaceans and conodont animals, as revealed by fossilized stomach contents. We do not have direct evidence that sharks were preyed on by placoderms, but it seems probable that arthrodires such as *Dunkleosteus* preyed on them.

Explosions and Extinctions

Between 360 and 325 million years ago, during the Early Carboniferous, large parts of present-day northwestern Europe and North America were covered by warm, shallow seas in which thick deposits of calcareous (containing calcium carbonate) muds were deposited. Eventually these sediments hardened into great limestone shelves, thousands of meters thick. Today these limestones are exposed in northern England and Belgium, and in North America they form a continuous sheet running from Iowa into central Kentucky.

Conditions in these shallow seas were ideal for fishes of all kinds, but especially for sharks and their relatives, which apparently underwent rapid diversification in a short space of geologic time. Of about ten Devonian chondrichthyan families, less than half of which are known from complete skeletons, eight made it into the Early Carboniferous, where they were joined by at least three new families. A few million years later, at least nine additional families were present, almost double the number found at the beginning of the Carboniferous. By about 320 million years ago, a few families had disappeared and a couple more had been added, for a total of about 19 chondrichthyan lineages.

Another explosion of chondrichthyan diversity took place around the time of the Late Carboniferous (about 300 million years ago), with several new groups bringing the total to about two dozen families. Chondrichthyan fishes would not be as diverse again until the Tertiary, more than 230 million years later. The number of chondrichthyan families declined through the remainder of the Carboniferous, and by its close little more than half remained, but their decline seems to have been gradual rather than catastrophic. Corresponding drops in invertebrate diversity occurred during that time, and on land several families of primitive tetrapods also became extinct.

Ghosts from the Past

We see a shadow of that Carboniferous diversity today in the strange living relatives of sharks known as chimaeroids, rabbitfishes, or ghost fishes. Their name is derived from the Greek *Chimaera*, fantastic animal, which these fishes truly are. When they swim, their ribbonlike tails and metallic coloration give these fishes a ghostly, ephemeral quality. How appropriate their name is! In the Carboniferous, distant relatives of modern-day chimaeroids known as the holocephalans, or *entire-headed*, in reference to jaw fusion, first became diverse and abundant.

Few holocephalans are known from complete fossils, but we can see the beginnings of chimaeroids in forms such as *Helodus*. Its upper jaw was fused to its braincase, and it had a sharklike dentition of separate teeth. Later holocephalan fossils evolved tooth plates, which must have involved developmental changes so that individual teeth were no longer formed. A fantastic variety of differently shaped tooth plates is found in these fishes.

Some of these holocephalans also did a most unsharklike thing: they developed armor plates and spines in the skin covering their head. Unlike the armor of placoderm fishes, these plates and spines were not made of bone but of dentine, the same material of which teeth and shark fin spines are made. Perhaps the most heavily armored holocephalans were the menaspoids (*moon shield*), which had a "bony" shield covering the head and many paired spines projecting from the sides of the mouth.

Much of this holocephalan **radiation** was short-lived, and many groups disappeared in the Carboniferous and succeeding Permian period. There are real chimaeroid ghosts, for now there is a gap in the fossil record. A few holocephalans survived into the Triassic and Jurassic, where they are represented by a group called myriacanthoids (*numberless spine*). Some of these had small armor plates on the head. Close relatives of modern ghost fishes are known from the Jurassic, such

PLATE 34
༄

Ischyodus is a meter–long relative of modern
rabbitfishes (chimaeroids) from the Late Jurassic
of Germany (150 million years old), and shares
many evident specialisations with them, such
as a ribbon–like tail, erectile dorsal fin with a
spine, and curious "head–clasper" consisting of
cartilage covered by sharp scaly denticles. All
chimaeroids, living or extinct, are marine.

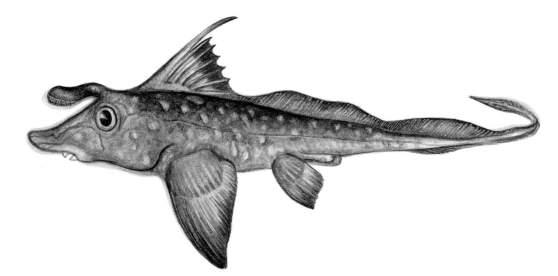

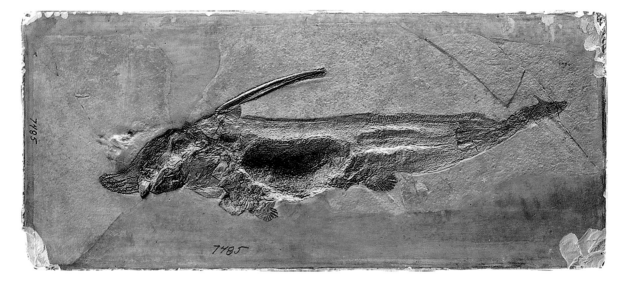

PLATE 35
༄

Ischyodus avitus, a chimaeroid (rabbitfish)
from the Late Jurassic of Solnhofen,
Germany (about 150 million years old).
Length 84cm.

as *Ischyodus*. [Plates 34 and 35] Modern chimaeroids probably arose from a ghostly common ancestor in the Late Cretaceous.

⌇⌇⌇ Getting Fresh with a Shark

Although ostracoderms and placoderms colonized many freshwater habitats in the Devonian, we rarely find evidence that sharks lived alongside them. Despite their rarity in fresh waters during the Devonian, however, a few sharks successfully managed to adjust their osmotic requirements to penetrate these environments.

Modern freshwater **stingrays**, sawfishes, and even some bull sharks are perfectly happy swimming in fresh waters, and several families of sharks and rays include species that can tolerate estuarine conditions with low salinity. In general, however, sharks have not adjusted well to freshwater habitats, and holocephalans apparently never entered them at all. To understand why, we need to look at how sharks regulate and balance their salt and water levels.

In sharks that live in the sea, salt concentration is overcome in two ways: first, sharks have a rectal gland that removes a lot of sodium chloride from the body, and second, they have evolved a physiological mechanism for retaining nitrogenous waste (as urea) in their bloodstream. This is a fine arrangement for saltwater sharks, but it doesn't work in fresh water. In order to survive there, some shallow-water marine species retain less urea in the blood, reduce the level of rectal gland activity, and compensate for a massive uptake of water by copious urine production (the bull sharks and sawfishes of Lake Nicaragua are good examples). Truly freshwater species, such as South American stingrays, have lost the ability to concentrate urea, and their rectal gland is nonfunctional. They cannot revert to salt water and will die if transferred to water containing more than 14 parts per thousand salt.

The physiological limitations of urea retention, salt removal, and water uptake thus prevent most sharks from entering fresh waters. Temporary incursions are possible only at high cost, and the permanent occupation of fresh water seems to be a one-way street: having invaded rivers and lakes in South America, freshwater stingrays are unable to escape. The same physiological constraints probably affected prehistoric sharks, and only those possessing some ability to juggle their osmotic balance stood any chance of survival in fresh waters. After the Devonian, only two groups of extinct sharks seem to have colonized fresh waters successfully, and after doing so they both proved remarkably resilient.

⌇⌇⌇ Creatures of the Black Lagoon

The earliest group of sharks to enter fresh water are known as xenacanths (*strange spine*). Their peculiar double-cusped teeth are abundant in freshwater strata deposited in coal swamps of Late Carboniferous age, and from lagoonal and bayou deposits from the Permian. Some of the oldest fossil shark teeth resemble those of xenacanths, such as those of *Antarctilamna* from Middle Devonian freshwater deposits of Antarctica, and teeth from the Early Devonian of Spain. The last recorded xenacanths lived in the Triassic period, so if we include the Devonian fossils the history of these sharks spanned at least 200 million years.

Although some xenacanth fossils occur in marine strata, it was in fresh waters that xenacanths were most abundant and diverse. There they lost their primitive shark shape and evolved toward an eel-like form, with a long, slender body, tapered tail, and elongate dorsal fin. One anatomically primitive xenacanth (although geologically it is too late to be regarded as ancestral) is *Diplodoselache*. This Early Carboniferous form still had a shark-like tail and two dorsal fins.

Orthacanthus, from the Permian of Europe and North America, had an elongate body and slender tail. [Plates 36 and 37] It grew to over 3 meters in length, and it must have been a formidable predator of Permian lakes and swamps. The idea of

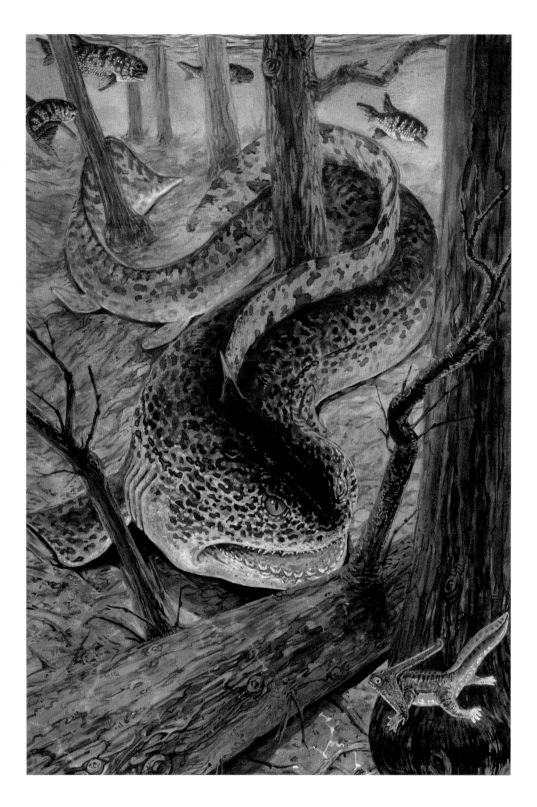

PLATE 36

Permian fresh water swamps and bayous of Europe and North America, 260 million years ago had no alligators, but were full of eel-like xenacanth sharks such as *Orthacanthus*, which reached lengths over three meters. Its double-fanged teeth and massive jaws could have made swift meals out of unsuspecting prey such as the small amphibian *Diplocaulus* (lower right).

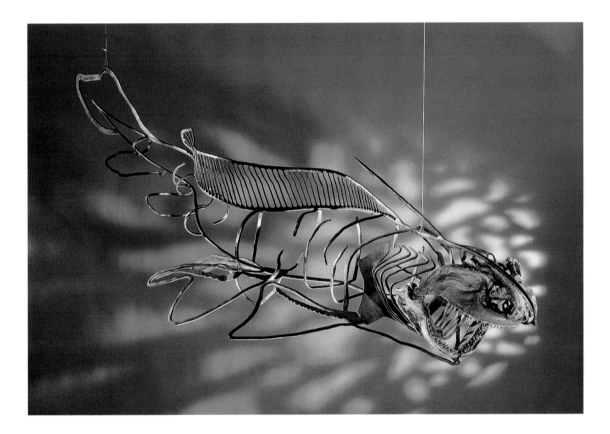

PLATE 37
〜

Orthacanthus sp., braincase and jaws of a
xenacanth shark, from Texas, USA (about
260 million years old). Length of braincase
33cm; estimated length of shark 3m.
Restoration in metal by Richard Weber,
American Museum of Natural History.

such a monster is quite frightening—its mouth bristling with double-loaded teeth, its slimy, scaleless body entwined around a submerged tree trunk, waiting for some unsuspecting fish or amphibian. At 260 million years ago, there really *were* creatures of the black lagoon!

What caused the demise of xenacanths toward the end of the Triassic is still a mystery. Their disappearance coincides approximately with extinctions of several reptile groups, including some marine reptiles, and also coincides with the extinction of many primitive ray-finned fishes. On land, many primitive mammal-like reptiles disappeared, pterosaurs appeared, and dinosaurs began a two-phased increase, once in the Late Triassic and again in the Early Jurassic. If the extinction of xenacanths was linked to any of these changes, it cannot be detected. But the demise of xenacanths may be connected to the rise of freshwater hybodont sharks. In Permian and Triassic freshwater deposits of North America the relative abundance of xenacanth teeth declines with time, whereas the abundance of hybodont fossils increases.

⇒ Sharks in the Age of Dinosaurs

Hybodonts (*hump tooth*) included the largest and most common marine sharks during the Age of Dinosaurs (Triassic, Jurassic, and Cretaceous periods, 245 to 65 million years ago). Unlike the xenacanths, hybodont sharks were predominantly marine, with specialized freshwater lineages that diverged from them. [Plate 38] First appearing in the Triassic of Africa, freshwater hybodonts became abundant in the Early Cretaceous and survived until the Late Cretaceous, apparently outliving their sea-going relatives by several million years.

Teeth and fin spines remarkably like those of Mesozoic hybodonts can be recognized among Devonian and Early Carboniferous fish debris. One of the oldest known complete hybodonts is *Hamiltonichthys*, from the Late Carboniferous of Kansas. Interestingly, the environment of

these fishes may have been brackish or freshwater, and they are associated with xenacanths, lungfishes, acanthodian fishes, and terrestrial vertebrates.

Anatomically, hybodonts looked a lot like ctenacanth sharks from the Devonian and Early Carboniferous, and they probably evolved from similar sharks. Early hybodonts had a curious feature linking them to later members of the group: males had large paired spines on each side of the head, with a curved base and one or more sharp cusps. Sometimes more than a single pair was present. In the primitive *Hamiltonichthys* the head spines resemble "cladodont" shark teeth, and some Devonian and Early Carboniferous fossils originally identified as teeth may actually be early examples of these secondary sexual devices. Head spines may have been periodically shed and replaced, but their rarity suggests that this was infrequent. Their sex-linked distribution suggests some function linked to reproduction, possibly to injure other males or to coax an unwilling female!

Hybodonts were more advanced than many Paleozoic sharks in their jaw suspension. Limited protrusibility of the jaws seems possible, with the upper jaw gliding forward beneath the braincase as the mouth opened. Primitively the jaws passed all the way to the front of the head, but in some hybodonts the jaws were shorter and more transverse, giving them a remarkably modern appearance. The early Cretaceous hybodont *Tribodus*, from Brazil, had transverse jaws that did not extend to the front of the snout, and a flattened pavement of teeth that are remarkably similar to those of some modern rays. Stomach contents reveal that this highly specialized hybodont was able to feed on small shrimps and other shellfish on the seafloor.

Despite these similarities to modern sharks and rays, other features suggest that there was no immediate relationship between hybodonts and modern species. In the past, it was thought that the modern Port Jackson sharks, *Heterodontus*, of the

PLATE 38

Hybodus was one of the most common
sharks of the Mesozoic era. This two-meter
long example from the Early Jurassic
(about 180 million years old), is chasing
after squidlike belemnites (found as fossilized stomach contents). It shared the
oceans with some of the first neoselachian
sharks, such as the half-meter *Palaeospinax*
(left). All modern sharks and rays are
descended from neoselachian ancestors.

Pacific Ocean were living descendants of the hybodonts, but they share only primitive features (such as fin spines) that were widespread among many ancient sharks. Hybodonts possess none of the advanced anatomical features that unite *Heterodontus* with other modern sharks, and are only distantly related to them.

The occurrence of *Hybodus* fossils in both freshwater and marine strata suggests that some species may have been euryhaline, able to move in and out of fresh waters with ease, rather like the modern bull shark, *Carcharhinus*. Other hybodonts apparently were more restricted. Many of those with flat, crushing teeth, such as *Acrodus* and *Asteracanthus*, tended to favor marine over brackish environments. Freshwater hybodonts tended to be extremely small; for example, *Lissodus* from the Permian of Africa (about 275 million years old) was less than 15 centimeters long at maturity. These are the smallest known sharks. (The modern cookie-cutter shark, *Etmopterus*, has the distinction of being the smallest living shark, but it is still twice the size of *Lissodus*.) These freshwater hybodonts had distinctive teeth, with a low crest and a peculiar central bump. It is hard to see how such puny little sharks could have muscled in on xenacanth territory back in the Triassic, displacing, as they did, such giants as *Orthacanthus*.

Sharks Get a Backbone

Anybody who is unfamiliar with the evolution of fishes could be forgiven for thinking that bony vertebrae represent a primitive feature. We take these structures for granted in our own skeletons, and most people are not aware that bone is primitively absent from the backbone in fishes. From the geological perspective, in sharks we do not find fossilized shark vertebrae until the Triassic and Early Jurassic periods (about 200 million years ago). From an evolutionary perspective, solid vertebrae represent an advanced feature that arose in the ancestors of all living sharks and rays (neoselachiano;

new sharks). More primitive chondrichthyans have a continuous notochord that is not surrounded or constricted by solid vertebrae, just as do coelacanths and primitive ray-finned fishes (discussed separately in following chapters), and extinct acanthodians and placoderms. Neoselachians are characterized by several features in their dermal and internal skeletons, but one of the most obvious is the presence of solid vertebrae. [Plate 39]

A string of non-compressible bony vertebrae might have some selective advantage in enabling higher swimming speeds and greater maneuverability in fishes, but there are no appropriate experimental studies with which to test this possibility. As the vertebrae develop in the shark embryo, they constrict the primitive notochord into a series of chambers, rather like a string of fluid-filled sausages instead of one continuous tube. The vertebrae provide strong anchorage for trunk muscles, and are separated from each other by fluid-filled shock absorbers, all conspiring to strengthen the backbone.

The first neoselachian sharks were usually less than 1 meter long, with an elongate, streamlined body. One of the earliest neoselachians known from fairly complete fossils is *Palaeospinax*, from the Lower Jurassic of England and Germany, which had a full series of calcified vertebrae. [See plate 38] *Hopleacanthus*, from the Triassic of Germany, was similar but had fewer calcified vertebrae. These sharks retained teeth similar in shape to the "cladodont" pattern of the Devonian, but the cusps were armored by a thicker layer of dense, enamel-like tissue. This layer is well developed in teeth of living sharks, giving their cusps a shiny appearance and imparting greater strength to the tooth. [See plate 27] Although a similar surface was present in ancient shark teeth, it was not so thick or so complex as in neoselachians.

Curiously, sharks were not the only fishes to evolve solid vertebrae and a constricted notochord so late in the game,

Scyliorhinus elongatus, a dogfish shark from
the Middle Cretaceous of Lebanon (about
90 million years old). Length 23cm. Note
the presence of solid calcified vertebrae;
these are absent in more primitive sharks.

for these features also appeared in several
groups of advanced ray–finned fishes at
about the same time. Was replacement of
a primitive cartilaginous backbone in such
widely different groups merely a coinci-
dence? It is tempting to correlate the
widespread appearance of solid vertebrae
in sharks and ray–finned fishes with the
evolution of large marine reptiles such as
ichthyosaurs and plesiosaurs. Although
tetrapods had made several previous
attempts to return to the water, ichthyosaurs and plesiosaurs were by far the
most highly specialized. Ichthyosaurs were
virtually reptilian dolphins, and both they
and their plesiosaur competitors were
capable of giving most fishes a run for
their money. On the other hand, solid vertebrae also appeared in freshwater fishes,
whose lives were not threatened by such
reptilian leviathans. Moreover, hybodonts,
which were the largest sea–going sharks
around at that time, did not have solid
vertebrae or a constricted notochord, and
yet managed to survive alongside these
reptiles well into the Cretaceous period.

Modern Diversity Unfolds

Primitive neoselachians related to
Palaeospinax survived until the Eocene
period (about 55 million years ago) but
were then eclipsed by more advanced
forms. Today, neoselachians are represented by about 250 species of sharks and 350
species of rays and skates. Much of this
diversity seems to have arisen over the
last 50 million years, although several
modern families have geological histories
going back 150 million years or more. The
earliest fossils, mainly isolated teeth, that
can be reliably classified within modern
families date from the Early and Middle
Jurassic and include cow sharks (hexan-
choids), Port Jackson sharks (heterodon-
tids), and relatives of wobbegongs and
nurse sharks (orectoloboids). Many more
modern families were present by the Late
Jurassic. The beginnings of modern shark
diversity are not as ancient as might be
expected, therefore, but date instead to the
latter part of the Age of Dinosaurs.

Large open-ocean sharks like the bull, great white, and mako were notably absent from Late Jurassic shark faunas, but their ancestors may have resembled generalized forms such as *Palaeocarcharias*, a large shark from the Late Jurassic of Germany. Relatives of sand and mackerel sharks became abundant and very wide-spread in the Early Cretaceous, and by the Late Cretaceous there were very large mako-like sharks, such as *Cretoxyrhina*, which lived in the shallow seas that covered parts of North America and Europe. To judge from the bite marks on fossil mosasaur bones, sharks sometimes made life uncomfortable even for those large marine reptiles. Many complete skeletons of Late Jurassic neoselachian sharks are known from the Solnhofen Limestone of Germany, the same strata in which the famous fossil bird *Archaeopteryx* was found. Equally complete shark skeletons have been found in younger Eocene deposits of Monte Bolca, in Italy, and include primitive relatives of tiger and bull sharks. The diversity of large pelagic sharks has increased continuously since the Late Cretaceous, with no major decline or extinction. [see Plate 26]

Skates and Rays: Sharks That Fly

Rays are close relatives of sharks. They apparently evolved from sharklike ancestors in the Jurassic and therefore are only a little older than the first birds. The principal feature uniting rays is expansion of the front paired fins around the sides of the head, to form a pectoral disk (in the most advanced rays, the disk extends far in front of the snout). The gill slits, originally on the side of the body, ended up beneath the disk, although a large spiracular opening remained on top, just behind the eyes. This enlarged spiracle allows the fish to breathe while resting; water is pumped in and out of the spiracle when the ray is on the bottom and the gills are obstructed by sediment. Most rays are benthic, spending most of their lives near the bottom or even buried in soft

sands. A few, such as mantas, actually swim in the open sea, and all are capable of graceful underwater flight using wave-like undulations of their pectoral disk.

At first, rays probably were marine, as most still are, although some primitive living rays can tolerate brackish or fresh water, and some stingrays have adjusted physiologically to spending all their lives in fresh water. The earliest ray fossils are from the Early Jurassic of Europe. *Belemnobatis* was a Late Jurassic ray that resembled modern guitarfishes (rhinobatoids). Living alongside it were odd-looking flattened sharks including *Pseudorhina*, an extinct angel shark (squatinoid), and *Protospinax*, an extinct relative of squatinoids, saw sharks, and rays. [Plates 40 and 41]

After the Jurassic, many new groups of skates and rays appeared during the Cretaceous and Eocene. There has been no major extinction among rays since their appearance, and their entire history to date has been one of increasing diversity. Skates, characterized by curious "legs" on the pelvic fins, used for "walking" on the seafloor, appeared in the Late Cretaceous, along with sawfishes and the first electric rays.

Stingrays are characterized by special spines in the tail, covered by glandular tissue that is capable of producing dangerous venom. They probably originated in the Late Cretaceous, and their early fossil record strongly suggests they evolved in the sea. Eagle stingrays became common by the Eocene, about 57 million years ago, and their curious lozenge-shaped teeth are commonly found by amateur fossil collectors. By then other stingrays were also fully adapted to life in fresh waters; today, stingrays are the only living chondrichthyans with species obliged to spend their entire life span in fresh water.

One particular fossil from the Eocene Green River Formation of Wyoming depicts a tragic yet revealing event, for it shows a mother *Heliobatis* stingray surrounded by three small pups. [Plates 42 and 43] Evidently the environment

PLATE 40
〜

This scene of a Late Jurassic lagoon in
southern Germany (about 150 million years
ago) depicts three extinct relatives of modern rays. Swimming at left is *Protospinax*
(about 1.5m long), which still retained many
sharklike features. Below it (center) is
Pseudorhina (1m long), an early relative of
modern angel sharks. In the distance are
some primitive rays named *Belemnobatis*
(about 2m long), similar to modern guitarfishes.

PLATE 42

An Early Eocene fresh water stingray,
Heliobatis, gives live birth to her young
before dying, some 57 million years ago.
The mother is about 30cm long, and the
babies are less than 4cm. Stingrays appar–
ently evolved rapidly during the Eocene,
and are today the most diverse chon–
drichthyans.

PLATE 43

Heliobatis, female freshwater stingray with
aborted young, from the Eocene of
Wyoming, USA (about 57 million years old).
Length 30cm.

became stressful, perhaps from heat, or desiccation, or some oxygen-robbing algal bloom, causing the mother to release the pups from her uterus before dying; the lives of the unfortunate babies were all too short, for they swam barely a few centimeters before succumbing to their mother's fate. Sad though it is, this fossil nevertheless reveals that some Eocene stingrays were able to reproduce in fresh waters, a feat matched by only a few modern forms such as the freshwater stingrays (potamotrygonids) of South America. These dangerous rays represent a distinct group that probably evolved from freshwater ancestors that were anatomically similar to *Heliobatis*. How many early horses and primates came to grief after unwittingly stepping on the tail of an Eocene stingray?

Steno's "Tongue Stones"

Some fossil shark teeth have played a critical role in the advancement of science. In the mid-17th century Nicholas Steno, who served as physician to the Duke of Florence, was interested in the anatomy of vertebrate animals. While dissecting the head of a large shark, he noted similarities between its teeth and the curious "tongue stones" that for centuries had been dug out of soft rocks in cliffs from the island of Malta. In hindsight, we recognize these "tongue stones" as fossilized teeth of the extinct great white shark, *Carcharodon megalodon*. Steno had no prior understanding of fossils or of the processes that created them, but in 1667 he published a little book (*The head of a shark dissected*), in which he argued that tongue stones were indeed the teeth of long dead sharks. To illustrate

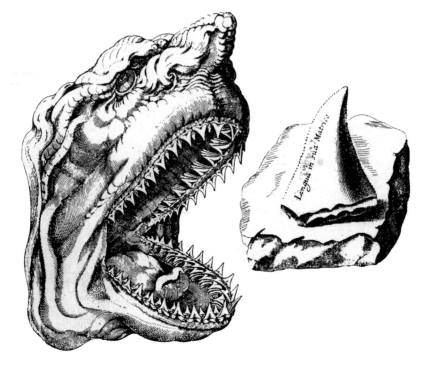

FIGURE 18

Reproduction of Nicholas Steno's original illustration of a modern shark head and a fossil tooth, from a 1667 woodcut.

his point, Steno published a now famous woodcut of a shark head, some shark teeth, and a tongue stone—the *first* published illustration of a fossil, ever. [Figure 18]

To Steno, tongue stones were structurally identical with modern shark teeth because they shared features with them (such as a triangular shape, a serrated edge, and laminated internal structure) that are lacking in mere stones on the beach. How can a stone have the features of a tooth unless it *was* once a tooth? Steno argued that because his tongue stones looked like shark teeth, they *were* shark teeth that had somehow become embedded in the strata (he postulated that this occurred during the Biblical flood).

Steno's simple argument is important, because it recognizes that features of living creatures can be discovered in some non-living objects (what we now recognize as fossils), and suggests that these non-living objects represent parts of long-dead creatures similar to those surrounding us today. Paleontologists today accept fossils (including Steno's tongue stones) as the petrified remains of once-living creatures, because of their structural similarity with living organisms. Homologous structures in living *and* fossil species can be compared, and hypotheses of evolutionary relationship can be developed and improved.

At a stroke, Steno the physician became the world's first paleontologist, but he probably had no idea where his flash of insight would lead. Paleontology accepts that these patterns have a history and that similar patterns existed in the past. Creationism accepts the patterns, but denies the history.

≈⫸ **Simple, or Just Subtle?**

PLATE 44
∽

Semionotus gathering to spawn in a Late Triassic lake in eastern North America, about 210 million years ago. We have no direct fossil evidence that these fishes behaved this way, but it is a common behavior pattern among ray-finned fishes. *Semionotus* was rarely longer than 20cm. (see Plate 63)

*T*he illustrations in this book, particularly in the following chapters, show how little fishes have changed over millions of years. When we compare portraits of Paleozoic, Mesozoic, or even Cenozoic fishes, we don't see a tremendous amount of difference. Aside from some armored placoderm fishes, there are few Dimetrodons, Tyrannosauruses, or pterosaurs in the fish world. The extinct great white shark of the Miocene is a monster, but it is still just a big shark. Stingrays and rabbitfishes are bizarre offshoots from more primitive sharks, but their chondrichthyan ancestry is still evident in their skeletal anatomy. Some very peculiar true bony fishes, or osteichthyans, certainly can be found today, such as those that live in the depths of the oceans, or the snakelike eels or eccentric seahorses, but in their fundamental design most fishes have retained their craniate and gnathostome features almost unchanged. Tetrapods have also retained many of these features, but in tetrapods the early features often are often concealed or modified by an overlay of additional features that reflect tetrapods' secondary terrestrial lifestyle.

Why, among terrestrial craniates, is there such fantastic morphological radiation, while among aquatic craniates there is so much morphological stability? Several evolutionary reasons could be offered as an explanation, but the most important reason probably is environmental stability. The aquatic environment is the primitive one in which craniates first evolved, and the subsequent evolutionary history of aquatic craniates has taken place entirely in this *unchanged* environment. When the first craniates emerged, 450 million years ago, the physical conditions of Earth's oceans, such as temperature and salinity, were much as they are today. Living on land, by contrast, presented new physical and physiological challenges that have been successfully met in several ways by the tetrapods. Such challenges simply never arose in the 450 million years of unbroken aquatic evolution of fishes.

Most biologists regard fishes as primitive craniates because they have retained much of the basic craniate architecture, without the overlays of tetrapod specialization. Modern geneticists who study the humble zebrafish, found in many tropical fish tanks, point out the highly conserved aspects of its regulatory homeotic genes. But we must ask, highly conserved relative to what? Opinions about primitive and advanced conditions only have any meaning within an evolutionary hypothesis substantiated by empirical data. Are the almost identical homeotic genes of a frog or a chick or a mouse any less highly conserved than those of the zebrafish? No, because the zebrafish, too, has a pedigree, separate from that of tetrapods, with its own overlay of higher features. These aren't tetrapod features, but they do reflect the 400-million-year evolutionary history of ray-finned fishes, including 200 million years of teleostean evolution and a relatively short 25 million years of cypriniform evolution (the group of teleosts to which the zebrafish belongs). It is important to remember that fishes didn't stop evolving millennia ago but have continued to refine their adaptations to life in the water. Bony fishes have become the most abundant animals with a backbone and have colonized almost all the waters of the world. Their past history was similarly rich, judging from the abundance and diversity of their fossils.

The intrinsic anatomical stability of most fishes often means that evolutionary changes important to an ichthyologist may seem trivial in scope to a specialist working on dinosaurs or some other dramatic group of tetrapods. With osteichthyans, the problem is magnified by the sheer number of species and even families involved. The number of features available for study in fossil skeletons is woefully insufficient to account for all this diversity, a point that is underlined by the hundreds of closely related species, with practically identical skeletons, that may be found together in some restricted environments such as lakes.

Ichthyologists are thus faced with the formidable task of identifying evolutionary relationships among a forest of modern bony fishes (mostly teleosts), many of which have little or no fossil record. Paleontologists, on the other hand, have been able to glean a lot of information about primitive extinct bony fishes, but are limited in what they can learn from the few surviving primitive examples. When we attempt to piece together the evolutionary history of bony fishes, by putting together what is known about living and extinct species, we are confronted by phenomenal diversity, but little evolutionary change on a scale comparable to that found in tetrapods. Historically, the challenge has been to discover a key to unlock this mystery.

⇒‖⊳ Louis Agassiz and Fishes through Time

Bony fish diversity is as great as tetrapod diversity, but the evolutionary complexities of bony fishes are far more subtle and have remained shrouded in mystery for the better part of two centuries. Although various schemes for classifying extinct and extant fishes had appeared earlier, modern systematic investigation began in the 1830s and 1840s. In those decades the German ichthyologist J. Müller was working on a classification of all living fishes, and at about the same time the Swiss paleontologist Louis Agassiz was completing a multivolume treatise on fossil fishes, *Recherches sur les poissons fossiles*, which was published in parts between 1833 and 1844. At the time these classifications were being developed, *The Origin of Species* with its revolutionary ideas about evolution was still some years in the future, for Darwin was at sea on the HMS *Beagle*. Neither Agassiz nor Müller intended their schemes to reflect any evolutionary pattern. They were simply constructing a system of convenient categories by which to classify fishes. Agassiz nevertheless made a startling contribution to evolutionary studies in his *Poissons fossiles* by publishing, in 1844, a chart of fishes through geological time. This remarkable diagram clustered groups of fishes together and depicted them diverging from each other in treelike fashion through time, although it stopped short of linking the various branches together or identifying any common ancestor.

Agassiz was not looking for ancestors, but he was interested in the changes shown by fossil fishes through time, and his diagram was the first ever published to trace the history of a major group of animals by combining a classification with the geological record. Geology was still a young science. The first geological map that identified and sequenced strata according to the fossils (particularly shells of various invertebrates) they contained had been published only in 1815 by William Smith, the famous English geologist. One of Agassiz's major contributions to science was in showing that fossil fishes showed similar patterns of stratigraphic distribution as invertebrates, and that older fishes were very different than modern ones. Between them, Müller and Agassiz were to lay a foundation for the classification of fishes that would endure almost unchanged into the mid–20th century, until a clearly defined empirical procedure for recognizing evolutionary relationships, known as phylogenetic (or **cladistic**) analysis made its appearance.

Fishes and the "New Systematics"

Fishes became one of the first groups of organisms to be subjected to the new analysis. The methodology was introduced by European entomologists Willi Hennig and Lars Brundin in the 1950s, and was greatly elaborated in the 1960s and 1970s by ichthyologists such as Gareth Nelson and Donn Rosen, at the American Museum of Natural History, in New York, and Colin Patterson, at the British Museum, in London, although many others were also quick to recognize its potential. It is probably significant that the first scientists to appreciate the importance of this "new systematics" specialized in some of the largest and most diverse groups of organisms, the insects and ray–finned fishes. Systematic biology underwent a revolution that rapidly gained momentum in many fields, but its first impact was felt in entomology and ichthyology. Since the 1960s, the patterns of relationship among fishes have become clearer than ever before, and their evolutionary history can now be traced in greater detail.

How does phylogenetic analysis work? We can classify objects in a variety of ways, but scientists who are interested in evolution attempt to classify living and extinct species according to how **primitive** or **advanced** they seem in comparison with each other. This approach relies on the belief that anatomical features have evolved in a recognizable pattern. By discerning the pattern, scientists hope to resolve the evolutionary history of different species.

Phylogenetic analysis focuses on evolutionarily advanced features, not primitive ones. This is an important distinction from classifications based simply on likeness. For example, the presence of paired limbs with digits helps define tetrapods, while paired fins characterize fishes. But paired fins are primitive relative to limbs, because they evolved in the common ancestor of both tetrapods and fishes, the gnathostomes (jawed craniates).

Limbs evolved in the common ancestor of tetrapods, and nowhere else in craniates.

Now let's try and classify these animals. In classifications based on likeness, fishes are defined as craniates with fins, and tetrapods as craniates with limbs, and the two groups would be given equal rank. But a classification based on phylogenetic analysis would recognize a larger group (gnathostomes), defined in part by the presence of paired fins (and jaws, of course!), and a smaller group of tetrapods contained within it, and defined by the presence of limbs. No group comparable to "fishes" in the likeness classification therefore exists.

The results of the phylogenetic analysis reflect the advanced evolutionary nature of tetrapod limbs; they are not merely the equivalent of fins, they are *derived* from fins. So tetrapods are evolutionarily advanced *relative to all other craniates* in possessing limbs, whereas the presence of paired fins in a fish tells us only that it is a gnathostome. "Primitive" and "advanced" status is always *relative* in these kinds of analyses. For example, ray-finned fishes are evolutionarily advanced *relative to all other craniates* (including tetrapods) in the structure of their paired fins. Just as ray-finned fishes lack the advanced features of tetrapods, so do tetrapods lack the advanced features of ray-finned fishes.

Phylogenetic analysis is thus a tool used by modern biologists and systematists, to map the pattern of distribution displayed by these advanced features. These patterns usually are depicted in a branching diagram linking creatures in a sequence that reflects the acquisition of new features in the most plausible (usually shortest) way. [see Figure 1] From such diagrams we can extrapolate plausible evolutionary trees and construct evolutionary charts that explain the relationships of living and extinct organisms.

The technique can be applied at any evolutionary level, whether between different species of guppies or between larger groups such as sharks, placoderms, and bony fishes. In fact, several of the evolutionary scenarios presented earlier in this book are based on such analytical procedures, and the branching diagrams that accompany most chapters are simplified representations of phylogenetic analyses made by scientists.

The addition of new data can change the results of a phylogenetic analysis and scientists' subsequent interpretation of evolutionary history. For example, some advanced features in skull anatomy, thought in the 1980s to unite lungfishes and tetrapods, were shown by subsequent fossil discoveries to be absent in primitive members of both groups. This new information affected the interpretation of the old because it no longer provided the most plausible (shortest) explanation of the observed facts. The similar skull features in lungfishes and tetrapods are still considered to be evolutionarily advanced, but are thought to be an example of **convergence** and are no longer regarded as being shared by a common ancestor of tetrapods and lungfishes.

Throughout this book, groups of fishes are characterized by features that are regarded as evolutionarily advanced, relative to all other groups. This holds true whatever the size of the group, whether it is all bony fishes, or teleosts, or herrings. These features uniquely characterize each group, even though each may also share various primitive features with other groups. The evolutionary heirarchies presented in this book are thus based upon the distribution of advanced anatomical features within each group. With this in mind, let us turn our attention to the greatest of all craniate groups, the bony fishes or osteichthyans.

⇒⫸ What Is an Osteichthyan?
Except for the jawless fishes and sharks and their relatives, all modern craniates (including all tetrapods) are osteichthyans (*bony-fishes*). [Figure 19] Among the many compelling differences separating osteichthyans from other craniates such as sharks and lampreys are a lung or **swim**

Osteichthyans (bony fishes)

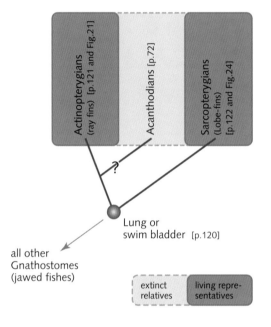

all other Gnathostomes (jawed fishes)

Lung or swim bladder [p.120]

extinct relatives | living representatives

FIGURE 19

Evolutionary relationships of the "true" bony fishes (osteichthyans), including acanthodians.

bladder, an outgrowth of the esophagus that forms a hollow chamber used in respiration, buoyancy control, and sometimes hearing; a pericardial cavity for the heart, that is completely separate from the rest of the body cavity; a brain that does not extend forward between the eyes; solid crystalline ear stones (otoliths or otoconia) inside the labyrinth organ; and a short gill septum that does not completely separate the pink respiratory surfaces of the gills, so that the gills are located inside a common gill chamber (rather than being separated by partitions, as in sharks and chimaeras). This separation is better developed in ray-finned fishes than in coelacanths and lampreys.

Unfortunately, few of these features are observable in fossils, and paleontologists have naturally favored skeletal features to establish evolutionary relationships and schemes of classification among bony fishes. Widely cited skeletal features include a braincase composed of two parts, one behind the other, either connected by cartilage or sometimes hinged together; a large bony plate (operculum) supported by the hyoid arch; two paired jaw bones (a maxillary and premaxillary) with teeth fused to them that form the upper biting margin of the mouth; and large overlapping body scales, usually arranged in diagonal rows and (in primitive osteichthyans) articulating together internally (unlike the placoid scales of sharks). These features clearly represent ancient conserved traits in bony fishes, and were probably present in their common ancestor.

You Are an Osteichthyan

In a cladistic analysis, humans are osteichthyans, because tetrapods—craniates with arms and legs—evolved from a group of lobe-finned fishes that in turn evolved from the true bony fishes, the osteichthyans. Humans have been happy to classify themselves as primates, mammals, amniotes, tetrapods, gnathostomes, craniates (or vertebrates!), and chordates, but they intuitively shy away from regarding

themselves as bony fishes. Why omit this intermediate category from our pedigree? We may not look very fishlike, and in traditional schemes of classification tetrapods are sharply distinguished from fishes, but this distinction takes no account of anatomical features reflecting our piscine pedigree. In fairness, the concept that we evolved from fishes came along after most of the organic world had been categorized and classified, and we should not fault the early systematists for blurring a distinction that was beyond their comprehension. Nevertheless, we should come to terms with the idea that we belong to a highly specialized group of bony fishes.

Osteichthyans are usually divided up into two groups, based largely on skeletal features, including fin structure, although some fossils (and one or two living fishes as well) do not fit well within such a dichotomous classification. The first division contains the **ray-finned** osteichthyans or **actinopterygians** (the vast majority of bony fishes), characterized by fins consisting of little more than flexible fin rays supported at their base by a series of small bones. The fins are thin and delicate, and the fin muscles are largely confined to the base of the fin. Another identifying feature is found in the jaws: the upper jaw lacks the direct attachment to the braincase that is found in other gnathostomes and instead is supported entirely by the hyomandibular bone; it has only ligamentous attachments to the skull. Other features, seen also in the extinct acanthodians, include three (instead of two) pairs of crystalline ear stones inside the labyrinth organ, and extensive separation of gill lamellae on each side of the gill septum (see page 75). Living actinopterygians include the **reedfishes** of Africa, **paddlefishes** and **sturgeons** of the northern hemisphere, **gars** and **bowfins** of North America, and the **teleosts** (by far the most diverse and abundant group, living in salt and fresh waters worldwide). The distinguishing features and evolutionary histories of all these fishes will be examined in Chapter 9.

The second division of osteichthyans includes three modern groups of **lobe-finned** osteichthyans or **sarcopterygians**—the **coelacanths**, **lungfishes**, and **tetrapods**. All are united by the presence of fleshy fins or limbs, well supplied with muscles and containing a series of internal bones, one of which is attached to the shoulder girdle. Our limbs are elaborate structures, yet they agree primitively with the paired fins of a coelacanth or lungfish, not with the fins of other craniates. Lobe-finned fishes, including extinct relatives of tetrapods, are treated in Chapter 10.

⟫⟫ The Antiquity of Bony Fishes

Living osteichthyans or bony fishes thus include all ray-finned fishes plus the lobe-finned coelacanth, lungfishes, and tetrapods, but not sharks and rays, chimaeras, lampreys, or hagfishes. If we total up all the tetrapod species living today (mammals, birds, reptiles, and amphibians) and throw in the half-dozen living lobe-finned fishes (lungfishes and the coelacanth), we see that the two groups, the sarcopterygians (all tetrapods and lobe-fined fishes) and the actinopterygians (all ray-finned fishes), are about equal in size.

Within sarcopterygians and actinopterygians most of this diversity lies with the tetrapods and teleosts respectively. In the Late Devonian, however, tetrapods accounted for a much smaller part of sarcopterygian diversity than they do now, whereas lungfishes and coelacanths were much more abundant and diverse, and were accompanied by other kinds of sarcopterygians that are now extinct. With time, the balance has shifted dramatically among lobe-fins so that the tetrapods now dominate, with their remarkable anatomical peculiarities so different from their fishy cousins'.

By contrast, teleosts did not exist at all in the Devonian, or for that matter at any time during the Paleozoic era. Their incredible diversity has arisen since the Jurrasic in one-third of the time available to tetrapods. Since the Devonian, only the tetrapods and ray-finned fishes have seen a dramatic increase in their diversity, with sharks and rays running in a poor third place.

Although ray-finned fishes certainly existed as long ago as the Devonian, none of those belonged to any modern family of ray-fins. Most were members of now extinct lineages, sharing only general features with living forms. No extant ray-fin family, not even the reedfishes, currently has a fossil record that extends back to the Paleozoic. In fact, no contemporary group of ray-fins has a fossil record extending farther back in time than the Jurassic or Triassic (about 200 million years ago), so their evolution can be fitted into the same time frame as that of mammals or birds. As we saw earlier, the same is also true of all modern sharks and rays.

⟫⟫ Primitive versus Old

When scientists talk about primitive and advanced conditions, our intuition suggests that "primitive" also should mean "older," but the fossil record is hardly so obliging. The supposed antiquity of reedfishes predicted by their primitive position in cladistic analysis is not supported by fossil evidence, for the oldest reedfishes so far discovered are only about 90 million years old (see Chapter 9). The fossil occurrences of paddlefishes and sturgeons suggest they probably diverged from a common ancestor in the Early Jurassic (about 200 million years ago), at about the same time that teleosts and extinct relatives of the modern bowfin diverged from their common ancestor. The earlier heritage of these lineages must extend much farther back in time, but this fundamental diversity among modern ray-finned fishes seems to have originated at about the same time that mammals first evolved and dinosaurs ruled the land, not in the world of placoderms and ostracoderms. Reedfishes, paddlefishes, sturgeons, gars, and bowfins may be primitive (relative to teleosts), but they aren't primeval!

Evolutionary changes in ray-finned fishes may be more subtle than those seen in tetrapods, but several important trends are evident, mainly toward improved biting mechanisms, more powerful swimming, and greater agility. Important trends are manifested in greater freedom and protrusibility of jaw bones, a reduction of heavy bone in the scales and dermal bones, more solid vertebral columns, more symmetrical tails with strengthened internal skeletal support, and experiments with neutral buoyancy that include novel body shapes.

All the Better to Bite You With

The evolution of jaws in early craniates widened their menu of food sources and opened up many possibilities for feeding on the move. Subsequent elaboration of the jaws occurred in every major gnathostome group, but nowhere is there such a range of structural adaptation as in ray-finned fishes. In most modern ray-fins the jaws are highly mobile, but fossils reveal that this mobility is the result of gradual evolutionary changes that began in the Paleozoic. [Figure 20] In primitive ray-finned fishes, the jaw joint is a simple hinge between the lower mandible and the upper **quadrate** bone. The jaws are primitively propped against the side of the braincase by a large endoskeletal bone called the hyomandibular. In the most primitive living and fossil ray-finned fishes, the dermal bones of the cheek region overlying the jaw bones are attached to the braincase, limiting the range of movement of the jaws, particularly their ability to expand and seize large prey. This ancient condition is retained today by reedfishes, and sturgeons, although paddlefishes have secondarily modified their mouthparts into a gaping chasm used to filter small food particles from the water.

Among higher ray-finned fishes there has been a tendency for some of these bones to become mobile, allowing the mouth to expand laterally as it opens. This creates a drop in pressure, so that water and food are sucked into the mouth. Many adaptations of teleosts, the most advanced ray-fins, involved further elaboration of this suction-feeding

mechanism. Paired **premaxillae**, toothed bones in the front of the upper jaw, were primitively fixed to other dermal bones of the cheek. In some early ray-fins the premaxillae became free, allowing the front of the mouth to expand and providing the superficial jaw bones with a greater range of movement. This feature evolved in more than one group of ray-finned fishes, so although it represents an advanced condition, it is an example of convergence and therefore not a reliable indication of common ancestry among those fishes that possess it.

The bite was further improved by separating the **maxillae**, the principal outer tooth-bearing paired bones of the upper jaw, from the other cheekbones. In addition, the maxilla, acquired a bony process that articulates with the side of the braincase. This kind of maxilla, seen in modern teleosts and the bowfin *Amia*, can be rotated outward and downward, stretching the skin and enlarging the depth of the mouth. By quickly opening the mouth and swinging the maxilla down, the bowfin can create a strong suction to draw prey into its mouth. In modern gars the maxillae are fixed to the sides of the skull roof, and until a few years ago this was regarded as a primitive condition. The discovery of *Obaichthys* [see Plate 64], a primitive extinct gar in which the maxilla was movable against the side of the braincase, suggests that modern gars have returned secondarily to the primitive condition, perhaps as the snout became longer.

In gars, bowfins, and teleosts there is also a small **symplectic** bone below the hyomandibular, reinforcing the jaw joint. In gars and teleosts this bone lies behind the jaw joint, but in the bowfin an articulation is developed between the symplectic and lower jaw, and the mandibular hinge is therefore doubled up, with both a quadrate and a symplectic articulation. This feature is not noticeable in living bowfins because the two joints are positioned close together, but the tandem arrangement offers a mechanical advan-

FIGURE 20

Improved mobility of bones surrounding the mouth in ray-finned fishes. Primitively, the maxilla and premaxilla are fixed, as in *Moythomasia* (A). In many neopterygians and some extinct primitive ray-fins, the maxilla is attached to the skull only at its front end, and can rotate downward to expand the cheek and suck water and prey into the mouth, as in the living bowfin, *Amia* (B). In advanced teleosts such as cich-lids (C), the premaxilla can slide forward as the maxilla rotates down, creating a tube-like extension of the mouth. When deployed rapidly, this tube creates powerful suction, drawing water and prey into the mouth.

A PRIMITIVE RAY-FIN *Moythomasia*

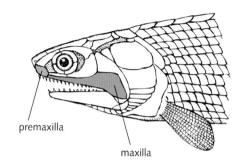
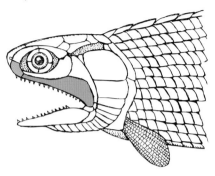

B PRIMITIVE NEOPTERYGIAN *Amia*

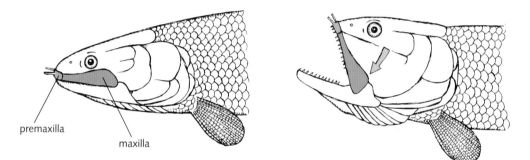

C ADVANCED TELEOST (Cichlid)

tage to the jaw joint and probably increases its strength.

In teleosts the upper jaw usually is capable of a wide range of movements because the premaxillae are also movable. If the maxillae are rotated downward and the premaxillae are protruded, an even more effective suction is produced. Most teleosts use suction feeding, closing the gills and opening the mouth rapidly to suck water and prey into the mouth. Deep-sea anglerfishes can dislocate their jaw bones in order to swallow prey larger than themselves. Higher teleosts such as pikes, codfishes, and spiny-rayed fishes have evolved unique muscles associated with their gill arches, used to manipulate prey once it is inside the pharynx.

Clearly there has been a general trend in the evolution of ray-finned fishes toward greater mobility of the jaw bones, a trend involving elaboration of the toothed bones around the mouth and various adaptations of the jaw hinge. But separation of the maxilla from the cheek-bones may have occurred several times in different groups, for it is seen in some Paleozoic actinopterygians that (according to phylogenetic analysis of their features) are only distantly related to modern forms.

⟫ Toward a Stiffer Fish

A bony vertebral column is less compressible than cartilage and more solid than a fluid-filled notochord. Bony outgrowths of vertebrae provide greater surface areas for anchoring the body muscles used in swimming, although they also add weight, which can affect buoyancy. Tetrapods and some extinct lungfishes have bony vertebrae, but bony vertebrae have not been found in fossil coelacanths, and *Latimeria*, the only living coelacanth, has a continuous fluid-filled notochord. In paddlefishes and sturgeons the vertebrae are cartilaginous. Gars, bowfins, and teleosts all have bony vertebrae but probably evolved them independently in the Jurassic or Cretaceous – another example of convergent evolution – because many extinct

relatives of bowfins and teleosts lack them. The distribution of bony vertebrae among extinct teleosts suggests that vertebrae also evolved several times in this group during the Jurassic and Cretaceous periods. The primitive reedfishes of Africa also have bony vertebrae, and they occur in a few primitive Carboniferous and Permian ray-finned fishes, but because these fishes are classified as remote from other living ray-fins, these occurrences of vertebrae likely represent additional examples of convergent evolution. Although the distribution of bony vertebrae among actinopterygians cuts across patterns of evolutionary relationship determined by other anatomical features, their occasional appearance in primitive ray-finned fishes suggests that the regulatory genetic pathway to form these structures was present but not always expressed, in the ancestors of all modern ray-fins.

Vertebrae are formed by the deposition of bone both around and within the membranous sheath that surrounds the primitive notochord. Primitively this remained a continuous fluid-filled tube, as in the coelacanth, and even where bony vertebrae began to constrict it (as in some extinct teleosts, for example) the notochord remained continuous. In the bowfin and most teleosts the notochord became completely restricted and even obliterated, as vertebrae invaded more and more of the notochordal sheath. We see a similar tendency in lungfish and shark vertebrae, and in tetrapods the notochord is almost completely obliterated by solid bone.

The vertebral column of sharks, lobe-finned fishes, and primitive ray-finned fishes usually consists of a high number of vertebrae that tend to be of the same size and shape, no matter whether they are abdominal (associated with ribs) or caudal (found in the trunk region). Only the ural (tail) vertebrae differ in size, gradually tapering toward the tip of the tail. In comparison, tetrapods are exceptional in having different kinds of vertebrae (for example, cervical, thoracic, lumbar, sacral) that are restricted to distinct regions of the vertebral column. Most fish vertebrae are concave both in front and in back (a condition known as amphicoelous), and in the spaces between them are pads made from the remains of the notochord. Similar vertebrae occur in ichthyosaurs and whales, where they represent an advanced or evolved rather than primitive condition because the primitive terrestrial relatives of these marine tetrapods had more complex vertebrae. The simple vertebrae of most fishes are really an efficient adaptation to aquatic life, allowing the vertebral column to resist compression but retain flexibility. Gars have vertebrae that are concave in back, convex in front (a condition known as opisthocoelous), with almost no intervertebral space between them, so that the vertebral column is stiffer than usual.

The vertebral column in teleosts is specialized in several ways. First, the column is differentiated into regions of greater and lesser flexibility. Second, there is a trend in several groups toward fewer vertebrae. Third, in many advanced teleosts the backbone is stiffened—especially in the trunk, where the propulsive muscle mass is concentrated—by lengthening of individual vertebrae and reducing the number of vertebrae (and hence the number of compressible intervertebral pads) to decrease flexibility and increase compression resistance. Fourth, in the most advanced teleosts, the spiny-finned acanthopterygians, the proportions of the spinal column have shifted: the caudal (trunk) region is relatively longer than in the more primitive ray-finned fishes.

As with trends toward greater jaw mobility in actinopterygians, the presence of bony vertebrae in osteichthyans does not represent a single evolutionary progression. Lobe-finned fishes evolved a bony vertebral column far earlier than any group of ray-finned fishes, and their vertebrae are constructed differently. Fossils reveal that bony vertebrae were primitively absent in both the bowfin

and teleost lineages, and they evolved independently in each of these groups. In general, the presence of bony vertebrae doesn't say much about evolutionary relationships, but differences in their structure (for example, between sarcopterygians and actinopterygians or between bowfins and teleosts) support the view that bony vertebrae evolved independently in different groups of fishes.

Fish Tails

A stiffer fish is a faster fish, especially when the vertebral column is truncated at its rear end to form a vertical hinge with the tail. A primitive, asymmetrical shark-like tail was conserved by most Paleozoic ray-finned fishes and is seen even in modern reedfishes, paddlefishes, and sturgeons. Fossils suggest that shortening and modification of the tail skeleton, with the associated development of external symmetry of the tail, apparently occurred independently in teleosts and in the ancestors of bowfins.

The evolution of the teleost tail has been mapped in considerable detail. Although each modification may seem slight, involving only a fiddly little bit of anatomy, the net result was the evolution of a highly efficient propulsive mechanism that was far more effective than the primitive tail of other fishes. One of the first modifications affected the neural arches—the bones over the spinal nerve—belonging to the last few tail vertebrae. Several arches moved forward to overlie the vertebrae at the base of the tail, becoming splints of bone called **uroneurals**. Later in teleost evolution these uroneurals secondarily took on a more horizontal position and became fewer in number.

Primitive ray-finned fishes (including the most primitive teleosts) had heavy scales that stiffened the upper and lower leading edges of the tail. Early in teleost evolution the lower series was lost. Most (but not all) modern teleosts also lack the upper series. The number of principal fin rays also lessened in the tail (principal rays are those running all the way to the trailing edge of the fin). Early in teleost evolution the upper fin rays became reduced to nine; in later teleosts the lower fin rays were reduced to just eight. These numbers are remarkably constant in modern teleosts and can be easily counted because the fin rays are clearly visible in the tail. (Check it out the next time you cook a whole fish, but remember to count only those extending right across the fin, not the short accessory fin rays at the base of the tail.)

Inside the teleost tail, the number of ural (tail) vertebrae became reduced to only two or three. The first of these is specialized to support two triangular bony plates (hypurals) instead of only one, helping support the lower fin rays. As the number of ural vertebrae was reduced, so too was the number of hypurals; there were about nine in many extinct teleosts, but there are usually far fewer in modern forms. The tail vertebrae also became upturned sharply where they joined the last trunk vertebrae, and the upper fin rays became rearranged, so that in modern teleosts only one ray overlies each hypural bone.

Collectively, these specializations have resulted in a more compact tail skeleton with a narrow attachment to the trunk (the peduncle). The chief hydrodynamic advantage offered is the ability to "feather" the tail constantly, to adjust its angle relative to the water current as it swings from side to side. An asymmetrical shark tail generates enormous thrust, but as it swings laterally its surface is more broadside to the water current, increasing its drag. The teleost tail, with its shorter hinge and symmetrical form, can be angled to the left as it sweeps right, and vice versa. Even at maximum swing, the tail's angle generates thrust but minimizes drag, improving its mechanical efficiency enormously. A variety of swimming patterns have evolved in consequence of these changes. Some teleosts, such as barracudas, tunas, and marlins, are fast-swimming predators. Large groupers can use their fins to maintain position in

shifting currents. Boxfishes and pufferfishes are highly maneuverable and can swim sideways and backward, using their tail, which has evolved a vertical hinge with the body. Eels, which are highly modified teleost fishes, are exceptional: they have lost their "fishy" tail and instead use snakelike muscular contractions to push themselves through the water.

Sinkers and Floaters

Not all fishes are streamlined bullets or torpedoes. Many are flattened from top to bottom, as in modern rays and many teleosts (flatfishes such as sole). A similar flattening has been observed in ancient extinct ostracoderms and placoderms, and among aquatic tetrapod such as turtles and plesiosaurs. A flattened body frequently is associated with a bottom-dwelling mode of life, although rays, flatfishes, and turtles can venture into the open ocean. Being flat does not necessarily involve anatomical modification (although rays and flatfishes are certainly specialized in comparison with their closest relatives). It is a physically stable shape, with a low center of gravity, and helps with concealment on the bottom.

By contrast, a deep-bodied shape flattened from side to side is intrinsically unstable, and it has not found favor among most aquatic craniates. We do not find deep-bodied sharks, placoderms, lobe-fins, or ostracoderms (with the possible exception of some thelodonts), and we do not find deep-bodied aquatic tetrapods either. A body shape that is flattened from side to side and deepened from top to bottom is an actinopterygian trait without equal. Among modern teleosts this body shape is so common that we hardly give it a thought, but the physiological and physical constraints of a deep-bodied fish apparently are stringent, and only the ray-finned fishes have consistently been able to meet these constraints.

It is all the more remarkable, then, that some ray-finned fishes called **platysomoids** (*broad belly form*) first accomplished this more than 350 million

PLATE 45
~

Bobasatrania (1m or more in length) is a primitive deep-bodied ray-finned fish from the Triassic (about 225 million years ago). Its fossils are distributed worldwide in marine strata, suggesting that it lived in open seas.

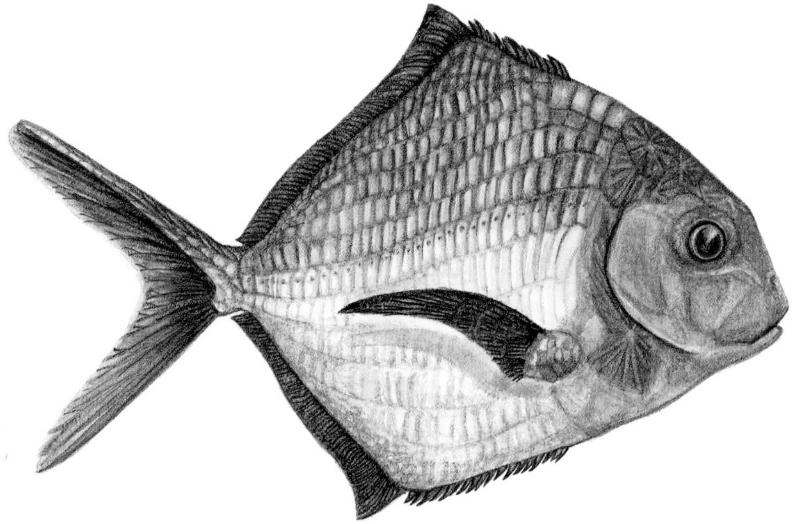

PLATE 46
~

Bobasatrania canadensis, a deep-bodied ray-finned fish from the Triassic of British Columbia, Canada (about 225 million years old). Length of preserved part 67cm. Restoration in metal by Richard Weber, American Museum of Natural History.

years ago. *Bobasatrania* from the Triassic (about 225 million years ago), possibly a later representative of this lineage, shows how far even these primitive ray-finned fishes could take this extreme body shape. [Plates 45 and 46] Another extinct group of fishes called **pycnodontids** (*crowded tooth*) which lived from the from the Triassic to the Eocene, 55 million years ago, were also deep-bodied.

What significant feature of actinopterygians has made it repeatedly possible for them to evolve such an elegant yet unlikely anatomy? The answer is almost certainly the swim bladder, although we cannot be absolutely certain because traces of this structure are rarely preserved in fossils. A swim bladder or lung is present in lobe-fins and reedfishes. Even if Devonian ray-finned fishes had a swim bladder, their heavy, enameled scales and armored head added weight that almost certainly gave them negative buoyancy. Any object (and a fish is no exception) that has a specific gravity greater than that of water will tend to sink. In many primitive fishes a sharklike heterocercal tail was (and is) necessary to provide lift as well as thrust at the rear end, while the pectoral fins acted as hydrofoils to provide lift at the front end.

In the majority of ray-finned fishes the gas-filled swim bladder functions as a hydrostatic organ to provide buoyancy. By regulating its own buoyancy internally, a fish can rise, sink, or remain level in the water without the need for tail thrust or paired hydrofoils. Once it was relieved of these duties, the fish body no longer was limited to the hydrodynamic teardrop shape seen in the earliest ostracoderms such as *Sacabambaspis*. The advantages of a swim bladder are clear: fishes in hydrostatic equilibrium with water were free to evolve into new shapes, and they did not have to keep swimming in order to maintain their position in the water column. Streamlining remained important for faster swimmers, for neutral buoyancy did not alter the laws of physics relating to drag. For other fishes, however, evolution-

ary progress meant being able to swim more slowly, which permitted them to nibble at sponges or corals and graze the algae. Fast-swimming fishes are poorly suited to using these stationary food resources; high maneuverability at low speed is more advantageous when navigating the nooks and crannies of the seafloor.

A fish is balanced when its center of buoyancy lies directly above its center of gravity, and the farther apart these points are, the greater is the vertical stability. A deep body allows the center of gravity to lie farther below the center of buoyancy, improving up-and-down (pitch) control. The primitive hydrofoil function of the pectoral fins becomes unnecessary, and instead they can be relocated higher on the body immediately behind the head, where they are more effective in braking and turning maneuvers and in controlling rotation about the body axis (roll). [see Figure 14]

Studies of modern fishes reveal that elevated pectoral fins have one drawback: they impart an upward motion to the body when they are extended. The extra lift can be canceled by moving the pelvic fins forward, so that they lie in front of the center of gravity, which produces an opposite, downward motion. The pelvic fins are located far forward in many living spiny-rayed teleosts (acanthomorphs). Many platysomoids and pycnodontids retained their pelvic fins in the primitive position, behind the pectoral fins, but *Bobasatrania* lost its pelvic fins altogether. Pelvic fins sometimes are absent in modern deep-bodied teleosts, such as the freshwater moonfish *Monodactylus* and the carangid *Parastromateus*, and they are absent in the extinct deep-bodied teleost *Araripichthys* from the Early Cretaceous of South America.

Deep-bodied Paleozoic fishes and *Bobasatrania* had externally symmetrical tails in which the lower lobe was as large as the upper one, although the body still primitively extended far into the upper tail lobe, making it stiff and internally asymmetrical. This primitive tail anatomy may actually have increased drag, because the stiff upper lobe would not have permitted adjustment of tail angle as the tail swept from side to side. This became possible only in more advanced ray-fins such as pycnodontids and teleosts, whose internal skeleton no longer extended into the upper lobe of the tail, allowing the tail angle to be constantly adjusted.

Many deep-bodied fishes have continuous dorsal and anal fins along the back and belly that converge on the base of the tail at a high angle. This arrangement improves control of side-to-side yaw and facilitates faster turns. Some modern fishes are able to create waves of movement up or down these fins, providing supplemental forward or even backward thrust. Elongate dorsal and anal fins were present in most extinct deep-bodied ray-fins, suggesting that they possessed swimming agility comparable to that of their modern analogues.

No single evolutionary trend in body shape can be discerned among bony fishes. Instead, various shapes have arisen repeatedly among different evolutionary lineages. The recurrent deep-bodied shape among living and extinct actinopterygians is a good example, for its disjunct distribution cuts sharply across established evolutionary relationships. Examples of convergence in body shape are well known among modern teleosts, so that the discovery of similar cases in fossils should come as no great surprise, but these examples nevertheless illustrate that ancient ray-finned fishes were no less adaptable than those of today, and that the range of body form displayed by modern bony fishes is nothing new.

⩘ Flocking Together

The anatomical adaptations of ray-finned fishes (particularly teleosts) provide many functional advantages for aquatic life, and teleosts have clearly made significant evolutionary progress over their primitive craniate ancestors. The structure of their mobile jaws has made them effective predators, their redesigned tails generate thrust more efficiently, and their neutral buoyancy has freed them from the morphological constraints that still bind other gnathostomes. But better teeth, tails, and buoyancy do not account for the phenomenal richness and diversity of species. In fact, the secret of teleost success probably is not to be found in the skeleton but in the behavior patterns of these fishes.

Among living teleosts, we find many cases of high taxonomic diversity among closely knit fish communities. For example, before its fauna was obliterated in the 1960s and 1970s by human introduction of the Nile perch and *Tilapia*, Lake Victoria in Africa supported over 300 endemic species of cichlids. These fishes, with hundreds of species living in close harmony, have been cited as a prime example of a **species flock**. Other lakes along the East African rift valley are home to comparable flocks. In such communities, each species may occupy a narrowly defined ecological niche and may have distinctive coloration and behavior patterns, but skeletal anatomy in closely related species may differ only in minute details. It is thought that speciation rates—the rates at which new species evolved and branched off from a common ancestor—were extremely rapid when the new lake habitats became available for colonization. These teleosts have partitioned their aquatic environment in ways that are still poorly understood, and that ability has become translated into taxonomic diversity that is often minimally reflected by anatomical variation. For the teleosts, success involved maintaining this delicate complex of ecological niches; for the introduced Nile perch and *Tilapia*, success required the obliteration of that same complex.

Semionotids (*flag back*; see Page 150) were very successful fishes from the Triassic to the end of the Cretaceous, especially in lakes, rivers, and shallow seas. [see Plate 44] Among semionotids, the genus *Semionotus* is interesting because there are cases of many species apparently living together in the same environment. *Semi-*

onotus lived during the Triassic and Early Jurassic (220 to 200 million years ago), and many species lived in lakes that lay along what is now the eastern seaboard of the United States. These species are distinguished only by subtle differences in scale ornamentation patterns and slight variation in body shape, with almost no other differences in their skeletal anatomy. Were it not for these variations, especially in scale ornament, we would be unable to discern differences among these fossils and might conclude they all belonged to a single species.

A comparison with the African cichlid fishes suggests that collectively, the Triassic semionotids of the eastern United States represent ancient species flocks that were established as the lakes were formed. Up to 250 separate lake cycles, each with an estimated life span of around 21,000 years, are represented in four formations of strata, found in an area stretching from eastern Pennsylvania to New Brunswick. In the lowest formation only two *Semionotus* species occur, but in the overlying formation there are at least six. Twenty-one species of *Semionotus* have been identified in the third formation, but only nine in the fourth.

By studying ornamentation patterns of the scales in these fossils, supposed colonist species were recognized from which the others could have been descended. Unfortunately, the genetic evidence needed to prove actual ancestor-descendant relationships is not available from fossils, at least for the moment, but the fossils lend compelling support to the idea that ray-finned fishes long ago had behavior patterns similar to the ones they exhibit today, and that they were able to partition the environment in ways that optimized the number of resident species.

Examples of past biodiversity such as this are rare, and their empirical study is difficult, first because original faunas and populations undoubtedly have been biased (not every fish became a fossil), and second because paleontologists must rely on hit-or-miss collecting methods.

But such samples nevertheless possess a unique attribute, unrivaled by any modern population study—the element of *time*. Paleontologists can observe the evolution of successive lake communities from birth to death, something a modern ecologist cannot do, and we can collect samples of colonist species instead of merely supposing that they once existed. This line of investigation added support to the theory, held by most ecologists, that lake environments initially are colonized by a few hardy species which could survive in conditions that are generally unsuitable for most other fishes, perhaps because of limited food resources or fluctuating physical conditions. Fish diversity may increase as the lake environment becomes more settled and increasingly compartmentalized. Although many nuances and subtleties of environmental partitioning may be lost in the fossils (we don't know whether particular species were nocturnal or whether they swam upside-down, for example), we can map the temporal and geographic range of species in considerable detail, so providing a novel perspective for ecologists interested in the evolution of modern fish communities.

What Is Success?

We could measure the evolutionary success of ray-finned fishes in ways other than taxonomic abundance. There is success in numbers: actinopterygians include some of the most abundant species in the world, many of which (such as herrings) form the basis of important fishing industries. The small Eocene herring *Knightia* may well be the world's most abundant fossil fish. With fossils, we can measure the longevity of groups over geological time, and in this way we can talk about their long-term success. Other measures of success, such as physiological adaptations to changes in salinity, oxygen availability, and temperature, cannot be obtained from fossils (although isotopes in fossil bones have revealed some physiological clues). Some living ray-finned fishes can tolerate steaming hydrothermal waters at 1100 F, others can survive in subzero Antarctic waters; some live at depths greater than 11,000 meters below the ocean surface, others live in high mountain meltwaters 4,500 meters above sea level. Finally (and reiterating a point made in Chapter 1), almost half of the world's fish species live in 0.01% of its surface waters, a remarkable success in terms of sharing a precious resource!

Although we have no way to estimate the total biomass of fishes represented by teleosts, in absolute terms it is far greater than any other living vertebrate group, and may well be greater than that of any group in the past. Their biomass is decidedly biased in favor of the sea: millions of metric tons of sea fishes are caught each year, but total catches and harvests of freshwater fishes are measured only in thousands of tons.

Evolutionary success is thus an elusive concept. It is something we judge with hindsight, and humans have tended in the past to seek tangible reasons for the success of one group or another. Paleontologists have sometimes sought to explain evolutionary success by discovering anatomical structures that may have conferred some advantage on (usually unknown) ancestors. Yet it is hard to explain the enormous success of teleost fishes by the few evolutionary novelties we see in their skeletons, or to explain the enormous prior success of ray-finned fishes that lacked these structures. The actinopterygian fossil record sends us a powerful message: success is ephemeral, and the real reasons why a group becomes abundant, or species-rich, or has Methuselah-like persistence may not be related to anatomical features we can see in fossils. Of course, some anatomical features have played an important role in determining the subsequent success of certain groups; birds would not have mastered the skies without wings, for example, nor would tetrapods have succeeded on land without legs. But wings do not explain the diversity of birds or legs the diversity of tetrapods.

Success evidently comes in many different guises, even among living organisms, and the fossil record adds yet another dimension, for we can look back through time and compare the longevity of lineages, examine the past and present geographic distribution of groups, and see patterns of design that are no longer around (ostracoderms or placoderms, for example). But our view is restricted to a few particularly rich fossil deposits. Usually these strata were deposited over a short interval of geological time, with huge intervening gaps from which mere scraps of fossils are known, so our windows on time are really small. The record is more complete for aquatic than terrestrial organisms, but it is still constrained by the geological processes of deposition and erosion, continental drift, and plate tectonics. A measure of evolutionary success is obtained from fossils if a particular group is recognizable through more than one window, but the views through successive windows may be completely different.

Patterns and Bias Through the Windows of Time

Most of our knowledge concerning past teleost diversity and success has come from just a few famous fossil localities around the world. Early Jurassic marine localities include the Holzmaden fossil beds in Germany and comparably aged strata in England and France. For the Middle Jurassic, the Todilto Formation of the western United States has another marine fauna. The Late Jurassic is represented by marine lithographic limestones of France and Germany (also famous for the fossil bird, *Archaeopteryx*), and by other marine fossil deposits in Chile and Cuba. Freshwater Late Jurassic or Early Cretaceous teleosts are rare, but some are known from China. The Early Cretaceous Santana Formation of Brazil has both marine and freshwater strata with teleosts; freshwater teleosts of this age occur in Australia, and contemporaneous marine teleosts occur at various sites in Europe, Africa, and Central America. Late Cretaceous shallow-water marine strata in various parts of the world have produced many teleost fossils, particularly the chalk beds of Europe and North America and their equivalent in North Africa and Australia. In the Eocene, the best marine sample is from Monte Bolca, in Italy, and the most famous freshwater occurrences are from the Green River Formation of western North America.

These windows on time can be spectacularly informative, but they are few and far between. Fossil fishes from marine strata may have close relatives in nearby freshwater deposits (for example, the teleosts *Tharrhias* and *Dastilbe* from the Santana Formation; see pg 179), but such contemporaneous occurrences are rare. The view through windows in different parts of the world may enable us to make comparisons between continents. For example, in the Early Cretaceous most fishes inhabiting the southern continent of Gondwana were different from those inhabiting the northern land masses, not only in fresh waters but in marine strata as well. This early Cretaceous pattern fades away during the Late Cretaceous, and cosmopolitan faunas occur in both northern and southern marine strata, but it is difficult to determine whether this change in the pattern represents a real event (for example, reflecting global shifts in oceanic circulation associated with opening of the equatorial Atlantic Ocean) or merely that the Early Cretaceous sample from many parts of the world is inadequate.

Similarly, we might question whether there were really upsurges in teleost diversity during the Late Jurassic and Eocene; maybe we simply have better samples from places such as Solnhofen and Monte Bolca. The dramatic first appearance of more than 100 teleost families in the Eocene means either that there is a gaping hole in the teleost fossil record prior to that time or that the Early Tertiary marked a crucial turning point in the success of these fishes. More primitive teleosts certainly were abundant in the Cretaceous, so unless we suppose that all the advanced teleosts were hiding in Cretaceous deep-sea trenches, it seems more plausible to conclude that their rates of evolution suddenly accelerated after the close of the Cretaceous.

It is tempting to correlate this explosion of teleost biodiversity with global events such as the Cretaceous–Tertiary extinction, which marked a great faunal and floral turnover on land, in the air, and in salt and fresh waters. That time marked the disappearance of large dinosaurs and the rise of mammals, the extinction of pterosaurs and the success of birds, the extinction of major marine invertebrate groups such as ammonites and belemnites, and the displacement of coniferous plants by those with flowers. Among fishes, it saw the end of hybodont sharks, shallow salt- and freshwater coelacanths, and some primitive teleosts. On the other hand, some ray–finned families survived the Cretaceous–Tertiary boundary event and hung on locally into the Tertiary, such as pycnodontids in Europe, aspidorhynchids (see page 165) in North America, and perhaps ichthyodectids (see page 171), primitive extinct teleosts that appeared in the Late Jurassic in South America. Others, such as gars and bowfins, managed to survive into the present, in dramatically reduced habitats.

Although the initial successes of acanthomorphs and other advanced teleosts in the Early Tertiary may be linked to a biodiversity crisis at the end of the Cretaceous, it is hard to imagine what that had to do with their subsequent diversity. The replacement of known Cretaceous teleost fauna by thousands of new species and over 100 new families in the Tertiary is poorly described by "faunal turnover." It is more as though fishes had rediscovered water, and were diversifying within it all over again. Acanthomorphs, the largest group of advanced teleosts, today include around 15,000 living species and 300 families, including such diverse groups as flatfishes, blennies, gobies, scombroids, pufferfish, and their allies. There are also several thousand species of generalized perchlike acanthomorphs whose relationships have not yet been resolved.

Just as the anatomical features that characterize teleosts are insufficient to account for all their diversity, so the terminal Cretaceous extinction event is insufficient to account for subsequent teleost success. It is implausible that lakes and shallow sea environments changed dramatically after the Cretaceous, suddenly becoming capable of supporting complex communities of fishes as never before.

Part of the answer may lie in the ability of teleosts to compartmentalize environments that were previously uncompartmentalized, so that many more species could occupy the same piece of watery real estate simultaneously. Specialized feeding habits and behaviors serve to separate many modern teleost species living in close harmony, but such subtleties are lost in the fossil record. The fossil record shows us the anatomy of early teleosts, but rarely what they did with it. Just occasionally, however, we can glean something about the past behavior of extinct teleosts, for example by studying the way they are preserved, their stomach contents, bone structure, and even their fossilized eggs.

The Daily Lives of Extinct Fishes

The numerical success of teleosts such as herrings may lie in their behavior patterns, for vast shoals of individuals belonging to the same age class swim together for most of their lives; indeed, separation from the group can mean death in the jaws of a predator. We sometimes find groups of non–teleost fossil fishes together, but rarely in the same abundance as fossil herrings. When we examine fossilized herring death assemblages from the Green River Formation of Wyoming and Montana, for example, most of the individuals are of the same size and apparently represent a single population. [see Plate 91] Although we cannot be certain these fishes swam together, it is hard to think otherwise.

By finding the bones of different species in the stomachs of fossil teleosts, we can determine that those species really lived together, instead of simply being washed together after death. Given a sufficiently large sample of predator–prey relationships (for example, in Early Cretaceous fishes from the Santana Formation of Brazil), analysis of stomach contents reveals links in the ancient food chain. [Plate 47] Stomach contents of Late Jurassic fishes from Solnhofen, in Germany, suggests that the Solnhofen oceanic environment was more open than in the Santana Formation, because the food chain is less well defined in terms of specific predator–prey relationships. Also, Solnhofen fishes tended to eat only other fishes, whereas the diet of some Santana fishes included benthic and planktonic invertebrates. [Plate 48]

Further research into the paleoecology of Early Cretaceous fishes from Brazil includes studies of their fossilized eggs and measurements of age, seasonal growth rates, and the season of death based on features in the bones and scales of dozens of individuals. These studies, like those of stomach contents, do more than reveal new facts about extinct fishes and community structure, for they also put flesh back on the bones, providing tangible proof (if we needed any) that as living organisms they were subject to the same kinds of environmental pressures as are operating today. Every successful strike by a predator represents unsuccessful avoidance by the prey, but a fossilized predator with stomach contents intact suggests something went suddenly wrong, and a fossil teleost with a belly full of eggs represents a failed reproductive cycle, just like the aborted fossil stingray fetuses seen in Plate 41.

Windows on time are rarely as clean as the Santana Formation, and such opportunities to explore the life habits of extinct creatures are exceptional. Most paleontological studies are limited to skeletal anatomy and are concerned with establishing evolutionary relationships.

PLATE 47

A complete skeleton of *Rhacolepis buccalis*, a primitive teleost, revealed after acid preparation inside the stomach of another teleost, *Notelops brama*, from the Early Cretaceous of NE Brazil (about 110 million years old). Length of *Rhacolepis* 15cm; estimated length of *Notelops* 40cm.

The evolutionary history of the vast ray-finned group of bony fishes is not easy to comprehend, and only a bare outline will be offered in Chapter 9.

⇒⫸ Success on Land, success in water

If we measure evolutionary success simply in terms of taxonomic abundance, two groups of osteichthyans are outstanding; the tetrapods on land and the teleosts in water. Both these groups have obvious anatomical specializations (limbs instead of fins, lungs instead of gills in tetrapods; movable jaw bones, a more rigid backbone, and modified tail skeleton in teleosts). Stages in the evolutionary transformation of these advanced structures from more primitive (ancestral) states can be discovered in fossils. When we add the dimension of geologic time, we discover that both groups were emplaced into their dominant position within the span of about 50 million years (tetrapods during the late Devonian and Early Carboniferous, teleosts between the Late Triassic and Middle Jurassic). Terrestrial habitats probably offered early tetrapods a great many new ecological niches, for the Devonian fossil record reveals little evidence of competition there from other creatures. Teleosts, on the other hand, had to compete with established fish faunas, and in this sense the success of tetrapods and teleosts is different.

Anatomical specializations may have endowed some adaptive advantages on both tetrapods and teleosts, but are insufficient to account for all the subsequent diversity seen in these groups. If this diversity was originally linked to ecological adaptations rather than to anatomical specializations, however, we are never likely to identify the causes from the fossil record. For example, it is unclear whether the few observable differences among Triassic semionotids reflect an ancient species flock, just as it would be difficult to reconstruct a modern species flock of African cichlids simply by looking at their bones. Fossils certainly help us understand the evolution of anatomical features, but are far less revealing about other aspects of evolutionary success. The abundance and diversity of modern teleosts defies explanation in purely anatomical terms, although the fossil record offers a tantalizing glimpse of how and when it evolved.

⫷⊘⫸

PLATE 48
☙

Oblivious to some fish-eating pterosaurs passing overhead, an elopocephalan *Notelops* almost 1m long chases a group of 20cm *Rhacolepis*, a related fish, in an Early Cretaceous interior sea of NE Brazil, 110 million years ago. An meter-long bonefish, *Paraelops*, rests near the shallow sea floor (lower right). Fossilized stomach contents have revealed parts of the food chain in these fishes.

OF RAY-FINNED FISHES

Finding a Tree in a Forest of Fishes

RAY-FINNED FISHES or actinopterygians, one of the two major divisions of the osteichthyans or true bony fishes, are the most abundant and diverse group of backboned fishes on Earth today, for they have achieved a level of diversity matched only by tetrapods. In 1994 the American ichthyologist Joe Nelson estimated that 23,681 species and 42 orders of living ray-finned fishes had been described in the scientific literature. In a book the length of this one, only two or three words could be devoted to each species!

Actinopterygians do not represent our ancestors, nor are they even closely related to our own evolutionary lineage. The ray-fins are the cousins to all the lobe-finned sarcopterygians, which include the coelacanths, lungfishes and all tetrapods. [Figure 21] Actinopterygians represent a different success story than ours, with its own unique attributes and history. In this chapter we will discover some of these features and will sample the history of ray-finned diversity.

Some idea of the tremendous diversity of *extinct* ray-finned fishes can be obtained by looking at the evolutionary relationships among *living* ray-fins. With this as a framework, we can examine unfamiliar fossils in order to see where they fall and how they relate to the more familiar fishes of today.

PLATE 49

Two *Cheirolepis* search for prey in a shallow Middle Devonian lake, 380 million years ago. These primitive ray-finned fishes were up to 20cm long, and were covered in small diamond-shaped scales resembling those of acanthodians.

Our first task, then, is to construct a very simple pattern of evolutionary relationships among the living ray-fins—in other words, to find the tree that defines the forest. Briefly, modern ray-fins are composed of three groups, representing different levels of evolutionary complexity. In the first group are the primitive reedfishes, in the second group are the more advanced **chondrosteans** (*cartilage bone*; paddlefishes and sturgeons), and in the third group are the **neopterygians** (*new fin*) , which in turn are made up of three groups: the gars, the bowfins, and the teleosts.

That is the basic tree of the living ray-fins. But it provides a very biased view of the forest, because the more primitive ray-fins, representing the earlier branches of ray-finned evolution, are poorly represented. The vast majority of living ray-fins belong to a single, evolutionarily advanced group known as **teleosts** (*whole-boned*); in total, fewer than 50 species of reedfishes, paddlefishes, sturgeons, gars and bowfin are alive today.

The fossil record has a completely different bias, with as many non-teleostean as teleostean ray-fins (perhaps even more). There are certainly far more fossil non-teleosts than living ones. Conversely, fewer than 150 out of roughly 425 modern teleost *families* are known from fossil skeletons, plus about 60 more known only from fossil ear stones (otolith**s**), so that only about half of the modern teleosts have a fossil record—and much of this is fragmentary. In addition, almost 70 extinct teleost families are recognized from fossils, but even so, there are far fewer fossil teleost species than there are living ones.

Fossil ray-finned fishes can be categorized within or around these living groups, according to whether or not they share particular advanced features. Despite their diversity, these fossils can be viewed as falling into just two categories. There are fossil ray-fins with no living direct descendants, belonging to lineages now extinct, and there are fossil ray-fins with closer ties to living groups, for example,

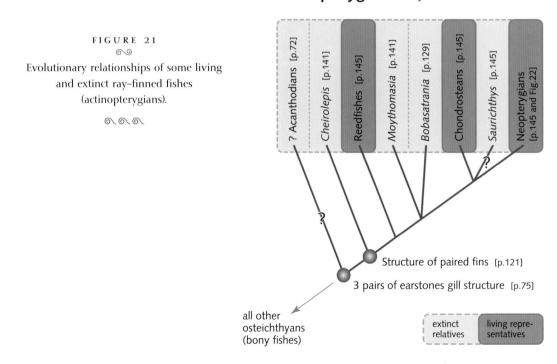

Actinopterygians (ray-fins)

FIGURE 21

Evolutionary relationships of some living and extinct ray-finned fishes (actinopterygians).

? Acanthodians [p.72]

Cheirolepis [p.141]

Reedfishes [p.145]

Moythomasia [p.141]

Bobasatrania [p.129]

Chondrosteans [p.145]

Saurichthys [p.145]

Neopterygians [p.145 and Fig.22]

Structure of paired fins [p.121]

3 pairs of earstones gill structure [p.75]

all other osteichthyans (bony fishes)

extinct relatives

living representatives

fossil gars, bowfins, herrings, catfishes, or surgeonfishes. The first category is represented mostly by older fossils, from the Paleozoic and early Mesozoic. Most extinct relatives of still-living groups, especially teleosts, are geologically younger, and no fossils of any living ray-finned group (even the primitive reedfishes) have yet been discovered from Paleozoic strata.

As one might expect from the paltry survivors, the vast majority of primitive ray-finned fishes are extinct. Fossils of these primitive fishes reveal features uniting them in a very general way with modern groups of ray-finned fishes, but they may not lie on the same evolutionary branch. The position of a fossil on the tree depends on the particular features it has; a fossil with only primitive ray-finned features would be placed lower on the tree than one showing, say, features shared by teleosts, gars and bowfins but not by reedfishes, paddlefishes or sturgeons. Many fossil ray-finned fishes are missing links between the few remote primitive survivors and the plethora of fishes we know as teleosts.

⇒⫶⫶⫶◗ **Ray-fins at the Base of the Tree**
One of the most primitive ray-finned fishes is *Cheirolepis*, from the Middle Devonian. [Plate 49] It closely resembled some acanthodian fishes (which may themselves be primitive ray-fins; see page 75) but lacked fin spines. Like all ray-finned fishes, *Cheirolepis* had a single dorsal fin supported by an internal skeleton. [Plate 50] Its shape and fin configuration suggest that it was capable of high swimming speeds, and its large mouth, armed with pointed teeth, would have made it an efficient predator. [Plate 51] *Cheirolepis* lived alongside acanthodians and placoderms (especially antiarchs) in fresh waters, but apparently did not venture into the oceans. Other Paleozoic ray-fins such as *Mimia* and *Moythomasia* were abundant in shallow seas around the northern and southern continents, where they probably swam in large schools and were hunted by early sharks and placoderms.

Moythomasia was particularly widespread, and its fossils have been found in Europe and Australia, suggesting that this was a pelagic fish that sometimes went inshore. Most of these ancient ray-fins were only a few centimeters long. An exception was *Tegeolepis*, from the Late Devonian of North America, which grew to lengths of about 1 meter and shared the same habitat as the primitive shark *Cladoselache* and giant arthrodires such as *Dunkleosteus*.

Our sample of Devonian ray-fins is small – only five families are currently recognized – and it is difficult to detect any evolutionary trends among them, although in the more advanced forms the mouth tended to be shorter, the scales and the large opercular plate that covers the gills tended to be larger, and the braincase was more bony. None of the recognized Devonian ray-fin families survived into the Early Carboniferous, but diversity nevertheless increased dramatically with the appearance of about 17 new families, including the first distant relatives of neopterygians. About half a dozen families were short-lived and disappeared before the Late Carboniferous, but several others proved more resilient. Three or four of them survived until the Middle Permian, half a dozen others lasted until the Late Permian and Early Triassic, and two survived into the Jurassic. Among these fishes were the deep-bodied platysomoids (see page 129).

A curious group of small freshwater fishes known as **redfieldiids** (named for J.H. Redfield) were common in the fresh waters of Australia, South Africa, Zambia, Morocco, and North America during the Triassic and Jurassic periods. Redfieldiid fishes such as *Cionichthys* and *Redfieldius* [Plate 52] have an interesting distribution. The most primitive ones occur in Australia and South Africa, which suggests that the group may have originated there. More advanced redfieldiids invaded North America and Morocco at the time when these two areas formed a single continent, before the opening of the North Atlantic. Redfieldiids have no representatives in the

PLATE 50
◔

Cheirolepis trailli, a primitive ray-finned fish,
from the Middle Devonian of Nairnshire,
Scotland (about 380 million years old).
Length 25cm.

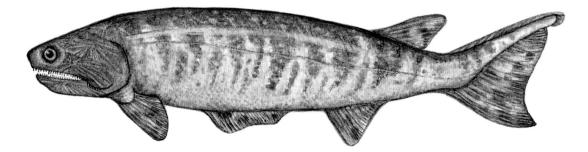

PLATE 51
◔

Cheirolepis (20cm long) is among the most
primitive ray-finned fishes, with no close
relationship to any living forms. This 380-
million-year-old (Middle Devonian) fresh
water inhabitant has elongated pelvic fins
and a small tuft of fin rays at the tip of its
tail, but the function of these features is
unknown.

PLATE 52
❧

Redfieldius gracilis, a redfieldiid from the Late
Triassic of Connecticut, USA (about 210 mil‑
lion years old). Length 19cm.

PLATE 53

Saurichthys (about 75cm long) from the
Triassic (225 million years ago) has an
extremely streamlined shape and pointed,
sharp teeth, suggesting it was a fast-swimming oceanic predator.

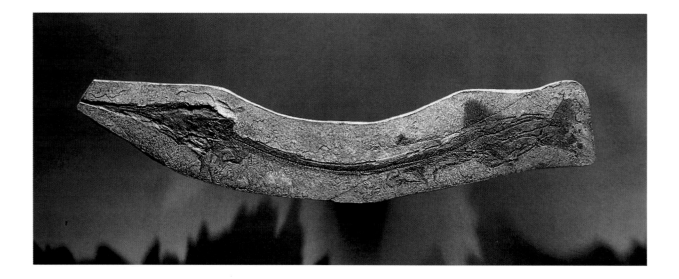

PLATE 54

Saurichthys megacephalus, a streamlined ray-
finned fish from the Middle Triassic of
Como, Italy (cast), about 225 million years
old. Length 57cm.

Late Carboniferous or Permian, so their ancestry is largely unknown, and they apparently died out without leaving any descendants. These ancient freshwater ray-finned fishes were as widespread as many more modern groups, and display potentially meaningful patterns of distribution.

The Fossil Record of Reedfishes

The reedfishes (also known as **bichirs** or polypterids, *Polypterus* and *Calamoichthys*, with just a few species living today in lakes and rivers of Africa) are peculiar fishes with a heavily armored bony skull roof and an elongate body encased by thick, bony scales. They are very different anatomically from all other ray-finned fishes, and are usually regarded as extremely primitive surviving actinopterygians, although some scientists have suggested removing them from this group altogether. Polypterids (*many fins*) have muscular lobed fins, but their internal skeleton is more like that of other ray-finned fishes than that of sarcopterygians.

We might expect that such a basal position within bony fishes would be reflected by a long fossil record stretching back into the Paleozoic era. If that were so, reedfishes would be wonderful examples of "living fossils." In fact, reedfish fossils were for many years known only from the same parts of Africa where they now live, and had no great antiquity (a few million years or so). The discovery of fragmentary polypterid fossils of Late Cretaceous age (about 75 million years old) from strata in Bolivia has extended reedfish history to the Late Mesozoic of western Gondwana, before this southern supercontinent broke up. Beyond these tantalizing clues, we have no further knowledge of reedfish prehistory.

Lizard fishes: extinct relatives of paddlefishes and sturgeons?

The freshwater paddlefishes of North America and China, and the freshwater and anadromous sturgeons of the Northern Hemisphere are rare today and have a low number of species. These fishes, collectively known as chondrosteans, have largely cartilaginous internal skeletons and were once regarded as survivors of an ancient ray-finned lineage that primitively lacked bone. Chondrosteans share some evolutionarily advanced features with remaining ray-finned fishes, especially in the arrangement of bones in the skull roof.

Perhaps the earliest fossils sharing particular advanced features with paddlefishes and sturgeons are the saurichthyids (*lizard fish*), from the Triassic and Jurassic. A relationship is suggested by similarities in the arrangement of the nasal openings and some other features in the braincase. *Saurichthys* [Plates 53 and 54] is considered too specialized to have given rise to paddlefishes or sturgeons, but perhaps shared an unknown common ancestor with them. Saurichthyids had a long snout, an elongate, streamlined body, and a tail in which the upper and lower lobes were of equal shape and size, suggesting that these fishes were fast open-water predators. Lizard fishes survived until the Early Jurassic before going extinct.

Extinct Relatives of Neopterygians

All other living ray-finned fishes are grouped together as neopterygians (*new fins*). Living neopterygians include gars, represented by several species of predominantly freshwater fishes, at least some of which are capable of entering the coastal seas of North and Central America; bowfins, represented by a single North American freshwater species, *Amia calva*; and the **teleosts**, represented by over 23,000 species worldwide. Neopterygians are considered to be evolutionarily higher—to have more derived features—than other ray-finned fishes. Advanced evolutionary trends seen in neopterygians but not in chondrosteans or reedfishes include greater mobility of mouthparts and modifications of the internal skeleton. Some of the advanced features are of considerable adaptive value, improving the swimming and feeding capabilities of creatures endowed with them. [Figure 22]

In the 1980's, some paleontologists suggested that the neopterygian evolutionary lineage, which eventually leads to gars, bowfins, and teleosts, may extend to the Early Carboniferous, around 350 million years ago. No fossil gars, bowfin or teleosts are known from that time, and this is much earlier than previously supposed for the origin of neopterygians, suggesting that their ancestors diverged from those leading to modern chondrosteans (paddlefishes and sturgeons) before that time.

Evidence for the great antiquity of neopterygians comes from small dermal bones (called supraorbitals) above the eye. These are regarded as an advanced feature in neopterygians, and are present in fossils such as *Palaeoniscum*, [Plates 55 and 56] from the Late Permian, and its earlier

relatives such as *Elonichthys*, about 350 million years old, from the Early Carboniferous. *Palaeoniscum* had a central place in 19th- and early 20th-century works on fossil fishes, and the term "palaeoniscoid" was once used to distinguish primitive actinopterygians from more advanced ones, but according to the new interpretation *Palaeoniscum* would be an early neopterygian with many primitive features such as a sharklike tail and non-movable maxillary bones in the upper jaw. That interpretation has proven controversial, however, for other phylogenetic analyses suggest that *Palaeoniscum* and its Paleozoic relatives were not closely related to neopterygians, and supraorbitals evolved independently in neopterygians and the ancestors of *Palaeoniscum*.

Perleidus, [Plates 57 and 58] from the

FIGURE 22
❧

Evolutionary relationships of some living and extinct neopterygian fishes. Modern neopterygians include gars, bowfins and teleosts.

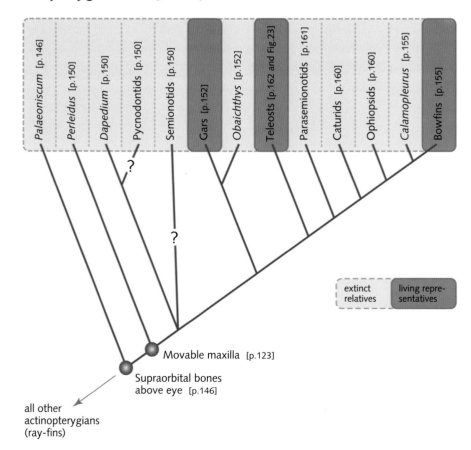

PLATE 55
෧෧

Palaeoniscum (about 20cm long) was a common marine ray-fin of the Permian period
(250–290 million years ago). It retains primitive features such as a fixed maxillary
bone in the jaw, and an upturned, shark–
like tail.

PLATE 56
෧෧

Palaeoniscum freislebeni, a primitive ray–finned
fish from the Late Permian of Saxony,
Germany (about 250 million years old).
Length 19cm.

PLATE 57

Perleidus (about 15cm long) from the Triassic (225 million years ago) lived in seas in many parts of the world. Advanced features include a movable maxillary bone in the jaw, and internal shortening of the tail skeleton, so the body no longer extends to its tip.

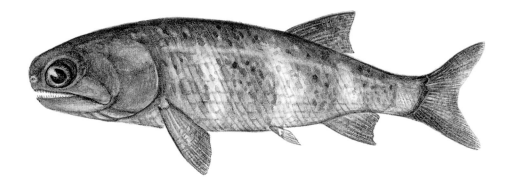

PLATE 58

Perleidus madagascariensis, a primitive extinct relative of neopterygian ray-finned fishes, from the Early Triassic of Madagascar (about 225 million years old). Estimated complete length 12cm. The rock has been split open to reveal the external impression of both sides of the head.

PLATE 59
〜

Dapedium (up to 40cm long) was a primitive
sea-going neopterygian of the Early
Jurassic (about 200 million years ago). It
had a moderately deep body, with pelvic
fins located at its deepest part, and also
had long, low dorsal and anal fins. Its tail
skeleton was short, and it had a movable
maxillary bone in the jaw.

PLATE 60
〜

Dapedium pholidotum, a primitive extinct
neopterygian from the Early Jurassic of
Wurtemberg, Germany (about 200 million
yeas old). Length 26cm.

Triassic, shared several more advanced features with modern neopterygians, and it is commonly regarded as lying close to the origin of modern higher ray-finned fishes. It is certainly a more convincing candidate for **stem** neopterygian than *Palaeoniscum*. The most evident external feature is that the body no longer extended to the tip of the tail, an important first step in developing a hinge joint between the tail and trunk. Internally, the number of fin rays equaled the number of internal bony supports in the dorsal and anal fins, another advanced feature shared with neopterygians. The development of separate premaxillary bones in *Perleidus* and higher ray-fins represented an important step in providing the superficial jaw bones with a greater range of movement.

Dapedium, [Plates 59 and 60] from the Early Jurassic, lived alongside those gigantic marine reptiles, the ichthyosaurs and plesiosaurs. In the past, *Dapedium* was classified as a primitive teleost, but it lacks the advanced features by which teleosts are recognized. It shares advanced features with neopterygians, including those found in *Perleidus*, plus additional features such as movable maxillary bones facilitating protrusion of the upper jaw.

Dapedium also shares a few features with an extinct but highly successful group of deep-bodied neopterygians called pycnodontids (*crowded tooth*). Fossil remains of these succesful fishes are abundant, widely distributed around the world, and have an impressive span of about 170 million years, from the Triassic to the Eocene. Together, *Dapedium* and pycnodontids may represent a now-extinct lineage of primitive neopterygians, characterized by a particular arrangement of their pebble-like teeth and some peculiarities in the skull.

Like *Dapedium*, pycnodontids had movable maxillary bones, but the mouth was smaller. Although they had a similar tooth arrangement, that of pycodonts was more specialized, with "nipping" teeth in front and batteries of rounded, crushing teeth farther back. The stomachs of some fossil pycnodontids contain small pieces of coral, swallowed perhaps while the fish was browsing for algae on the reefs. These fishes probably occupied similar ecological niches as do modern teleosts such as surgeonfishes, angelfishes, and butterflyfishes. In fact, some of the last pycnodontids lived right alongside the first of these reef-dwelling teleosts, whose evolution probably contributed to pycnodontid extinction. Other pycnodontids lived in places where there were no reefs, and their fossils have even been found in river and lake deposits. *Neoproscinetes*, [Plates 61 and 62] from the Early Cretaceous of Brazil, lived in a brackish inland sea devoid of corals, where it probably fed on smaller fishes as well as on the limited bottom community of molluscs and small shrimps.

Temporally and environmentally, Triassic pycnodontids overlapped with the last of the deep-bodied platysomoids from the Paleozoic, just as Eocene ones overlapped with deep-bodied teleosts; no direct evolutionary relationship exists between these three groups, but it is interesting to see how similar extremes of body shape have repeatedly evolved in these fishes. The oceans have contained deep-bodied ray-fins continuously for at least 300 million years.

Semionotids represent another long-lived group with the same neopterygian features seen in *Dapedium* and pycnodontids. [see page 131] They range from the Triassic until the Late Cretaceous, and an older Permian genus *Acentrophorus* is sometimes classified as a semionotid, although its sharklike tail skeleton suggests that it is really more primitive. Semionotids had thick, enameled scales and usually had jaws full of peglike teeth. [Plate 63; and see Plate 44]

Many species of *Semionotus* lived in fresh water lakes during the Triassic and Early Jurassic, but their skeletal anatomy was always conservative, and species are distinguished by subtle variations of scale shape and ornamentation. (see page 131) Some specimens of *Lepidotes*, a semionotid from marine Late Jurassic strata of Ger-

PLATE 61

❧

Neoproscinetes (about 35cm long) was an Early Cretaceous pycnodontid found in brackish interior seas of Brazil about 110 million years ago. Its shape and fin config–uration are evocative of many modern teleosts, and it may also have been colored as brilliantly, although the pattern depicted is conjectural.

PLATE 62

❧

Neoproscinetes penalvai, a pycnodont fish from the Early Cretaceous of NE Brazil (about 110 milion years old). Length 30cm. Acid preparation by Walter Elvers and Ivy Rutzky, American Museum of Natural History.

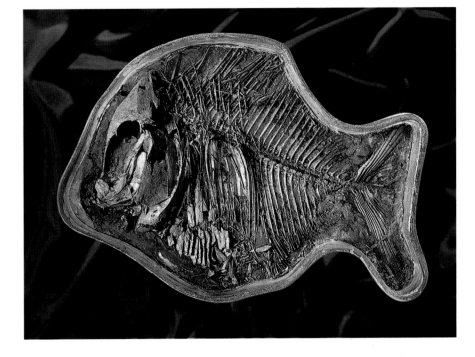

many and freshwater Early Cretaceous strata of Brazil, attained lengths of over 2 meters. *Araripelepidotes*, another Early Cretaceous semionotid from Brazil, resembled *Lepidotes* except for its jaws, which were little more than narrow splints of bone without any teeth. Unable to crush shellfish as its larger cousins could, *Araripelepidotes* may have grazed on algae or sifted the soft bottom muds for particles of food in lagoons and shallow seas.

Palaeoniscum, *Perleidus*, *Dapedium*, pycnodontids and semionotids thus share anatomical features with modern neopterygians, and reveal some of the subtleties of this group's evolution over the past 250 million years. Neopterygians make a controversial Paleozoic beginning, with supraorbital bones in *Palaeoniscum* and its relatives. Otherwise, early neopterygian history is largely confined to the Mesozoic, with Triassic forms such as *Perleidus* having a shortened internal tail skeleton, equal number of fin rays and supports, and separate premaxillary bones. More advanced neopterygians, with movable maxillary bones, are represented by *Dapedium*, pycnodontids and semionotids, from the Triassic and Jurassic. Although the Paleozoic beginnings of neopterygian evolution are clouded with controversy, there is no doubt that neopterygians were well established by the Triassic and, as we will see shortly, had even begun to diverge into their principal modern groups.

Modern neopterygians are classified into three groups; gars, bowfins and teleosts. There is some disagreement among scientists as to how these are related, but the most widely accepted view is that gars are primitive, while teleosts and bowfins share some advanced features not found in gars, and are more closely related to each other. Nevertheless gars are highly specialized fishes in their own right, and have many anatomical peculiarities not found in bowfins or teleosts. Furthermore, the fossil record of gars at present extends only to the Early Cretaceous (about 110 million years), whereas primitive relatives of both teleosts and bowfins have been discovered in strata of Late Triassic age (almost 250 million years old). Thus there is a considerable discrepancy between the apparent geological antiquity of gars and their presumed evolutionary position relative to other modern neopterygians. It has been suggested that gars are related to semionotids, which would certainly provide a lengthier geologic record, but no convincing evidence (in the form of shared, evolutionarily advanced features) has been presented in support of that claim. Nevertheless, neopterygians are treated here in the most commonly accepted way, with gars representing the most primitive surviving neopterygians.

The Evolution of Gars
The most primitive, and oldest fossil gar is *Obaichthys*, [Plates 65 and 66] from the Early Cretaceous of Brazil. Fragmentary gar fossils of almost the same age are known from Niger, in Africa. The maxillary bones of *Obaichthys* are not fused to the skull roof (as in modern and Eocene gars) but were still movable (as in teleosts and bowfins), suggesting that modern gars have reincorporated this bone into the skull roof, perhaps in relation to developing a long snout. *Obaichthys* differs from modern and Eocene gars in having only two large bones behind the eye (a primitive condition), instead of a mosaic of numerous small bones (an advanced condition). In most other respects, *Obaichthys* is just like other gars, right down to its peculiar opisthocoelous (concave in back, convex in front) vertebrae (see page 126).

The past distribution of gars is more closely linked to the land than to the sea. Most fossil gars are from freshwater deposits, but *Obaichthys* occurs in strata deposited in a brackish inland sea. Modern gars can enter seawater, although they are by no means sea-going fishes like herrings or tarpon. Fossil gars and bowfins occur together in non-marine strata, for example in the Eocene of North America

PLATE 63
〜
Semionotus agassizii, a Late Triassic semionotid from New Jersey, USA (about 210
million years old). Length 29cm.
(see Plate 44)

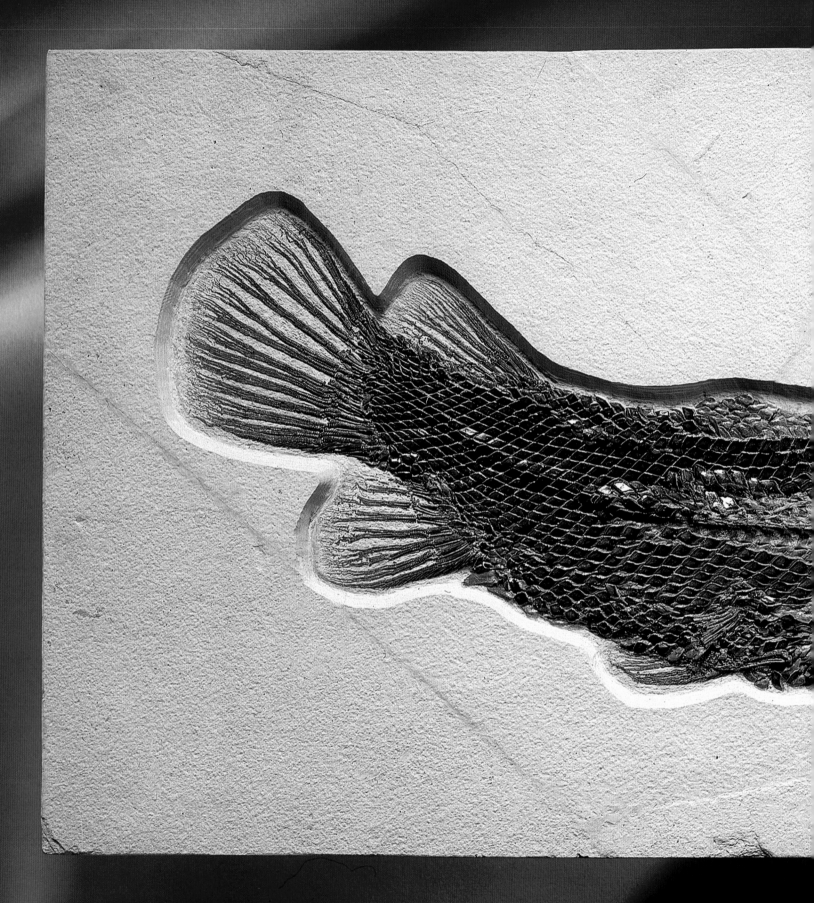

PLATE 64

Lepisosteus simplex, a fossil gar from the
Eocene of Wyoming, USA (between 110
million year old). Length 73cm.

PLATE 65

Obaichthys (about 65cm long) is a primitive
gar from the Early Cretaceous of Brazil. It
had many characteristic features of gars
including an unusual type of vertebrae, but
unlike modern gars it still had a movable
maxillary bone like other neopterygians.

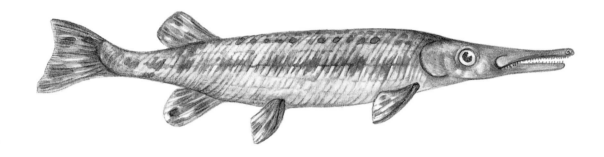

PLATE 66

Obaichthys, a primitive gar from the Early
Cretaceous of NE Brazil (110 million years
old). Length 65cm.

RAY-FINNED FISHES

and the Oligocene of Europe. It is unusual to find fossils of both in marine strata, but the gar *Obaichthys* occurs together with the primitive bowfin *Calamopleurus* in the Early Cretaceous of Brazil. No gars are known from the Late Jurassic marine Solnhofen limestone of Germany, although these strata contain amiids.

Gars seem to have originated in the southern continent of Gondwana, shortly before Africa finally separated from South America. They spread to the Northern Hemisphere by the Late Cretaceous, existing simultaneously in present-day South America, Africa, India, southern Europe, and North America. After that time they apparently became extinct in South America and Africa, but survived across much of Europe, Asia, and North America in the Eocene. Large specimens of *Lepisosteus* (a living genus) are known from beautiful skeletons of Eocene age, from the Green River Formation of Wyoming. [Plate 64] The last Old World gars (from western Europe) date from the Oligocene, about 23 to 35 million years ago. By the Miocene (5 to 23 million years ago) their geographic range had become restricted to its present limits in the Western Hemisphere (from Costa Rica to eastern North America, including Cuba).

⚞ Bowfins: Shadows of Former Glory

Bowfins and teleosts are regarded as each other's closest living relatives. Bowfin evolution is dealt with first here, not because they are intrinsically more primitive than teleosts, but for convenience (teleosts are such a big complex group that they are best left until last).

There is only a single surviving species of bowfin, known to science as *Amia calva*. Today *Amia* is found only in lakes and rivers of the eastern and mid-eastern parts of the United States and Canada, but its present distribution is only a fraction of what it was. Magnificent fossils of *Amia* have been discovered in lake deposits from the Oligocene of Germany and the Eocene of North Ameri-

ca. Less complete fossils dating back from the Late Cretaceous are known from North America, Europe, and Asia. These fossils differ from living *Amia* only in small details, showing that it evolved slowly over the past 65 million years, in the same kinds of freshwater environments that it inhabits today. Appropriate environments for bowfins and gars apparently still exist in the regions they formerly occupied, but these fishes may have lost territory in competition with freshwater teleosts.

Many fossils have been classified along with *Amia*, into a group called **amiids**. Many primitive amiids were marine fishes, especially the oldest ones from the Late Jurassic of Germany. Why freshwater amiids survived but marine amiids became extinct is a mystery, because both had to compete with teleosts. Possibly the demise of marine amiids was linked to competition with teleosts in specific habitats, but the fossil record does not reveal any clues.

Calamopleurus [Plate 67; see Plate 1] was an Early Cretaceous amiid from Brazil. It resembled *Amia*, the living bowfin, in many features, including its curious double jaw joint (see page 123), but its skull was more bony, and it had a shorter dorsal fin. It was a top predator in its environment, and its fossils are sometimes preserved with large fishes in their mouths (commonly a harmless filter-feeding teleost called *Vinctifer*), attesting to a voracious appetite. *Calamopleurus* is unusual in coming from the Southern Hemisphere; most fossil amiids are known from the northern continents, and there are only a few records from Brazil and Africa. Unlike gars, which may have arisen in Gondwana, amiids seem to have arrived there secondarily, and it is possible that amiids from Africa and South America belonged to a distinct lineage, separate from that of *Amia*, that died out in the Tertiary.

Amiids are themselves only one branch of an even larger, more inclusive group called halecomorphs (*shad form*).

PLATE 67

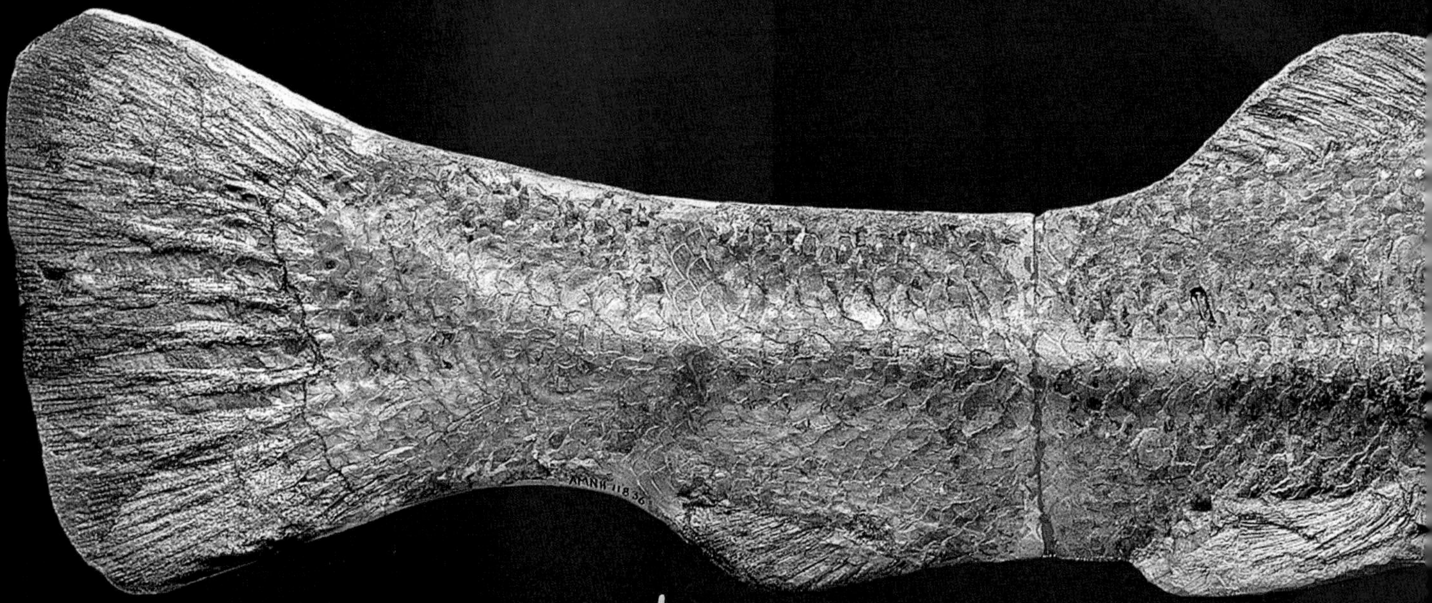

Calamopleurus cylindricus, an extinct amiid
from the Early Cretaceous of NE Brazil
(about 110 million years old). Length 91cm.

All these fishes have a double jaw joint like that of *Amia*, but apart from that have few features in common. Halecomorphs reached a peak of diversity and abundance during the Late Jurassic and Early Cretaceous, then suffered a dramatic decline, leaving only the solitary freshwater bowfin lineage, which has managed to survive until now.

Extinct halecomorphs include caturids (*downward tail*), which first appeared in the Early Jurassic and became extinct at the end of that period. *Caturus* was a top predator among Jurassic marine fishes, and fossils have been recovered with complete skeletons of prey in the stomach. [Plate 68] It resembled amiid fishes in its double jaw joint and in lacking two important paired bones (the opisthotic and pterotic) of the ear region. Other extinct halecomorphs include ophiopsids (*snake look*), which first appeared in the Triassic and became extinct in the Late Cretaceous. *Teoichthys*, from the Early Cretaceous of Mexico, was typical of most ophiopsids. [Plate 69] Rela-

tives of ophiopsids included less specialized fishes such as *Ionoscopus*, from the Jurassic and Cretaceous of Europe, and *Oshunia*, from the Early Cretaceous of Brazil. These fishes had primitive sharklike tails with an unusually high number of ural (tail) vertebrae, up to 16.

The most primitive halecomorphs, from the Late Triassic, belong to a family called parasemionotids (*near flag back*). The name comes from their resemblance to semionotids, which lacked a tandem jaw joint, but the similarities between the two groups are primitive and do not support any direct evolutionary relationship. Parasemionotids are very generalized and may include the ancestors of more advanced halecomorphs.

The living bowfin is thus a relic of a group that was formerly much more succesful than now in terms of anatomical and environmental diversity and abundance. Extinct relatives of *Amia* lived in fresh waters and oceans all over the world, and other related fishes such as caturids were among the top fishy preda-

tors of the Jurassic and Cretaceous. Two separate evolutionary lineages of these halecomorph fishes have been identified, one including amiids and caturids, the other including ophiopsids and ionoscopids. Primitive members of both lineages lacked bony vertebrae, and these structures apparently evolved independently in their more advanced members. The amiid/caturid and ophiopsid/ionoscopid lineages are in turn distantly related to Triassic parasemionotids, by the presence of the peculiar double jaw joint involving the symplectic bone. This former glory, revealed only through fossils, means that *Amia* is no longer a bizarre isolated relic, but can be placed among its extinct relatives and viewed as part of a succesful evolutionary history that lasted the better part of 100 million years, during much of the Jurassic and Cretaceous periods.

⇒‖‖▹ Teleosts Take Over

The three major groups of living neopterygians, gars, bowfins and teleosts, have rather different evolutionary histo-

ries. Gars evolved a single specialized body plan which they have retained and refined for at least 110 million years. The bowfin represents the lone survivor of a formerly much more diverse group, the halecomorphs, which reached a zenith in the Jurassic and Cretaceous, then all but disappeared. Teleosts evolved into a myriad different kinds of fishes, and have become adapted to virtually every aquatic habitat imaginable. Among *living* fishes, more than 99% of ray–finned diversity occurs within a single group, the **teleosts** (*whole-boned*). [Figure 23]

The earliest fossil teleosts had no direct relationship with any living subgroup, but belonged instead to lineages that are now extinct. For approximately the first 90 million years of teleost evolution, none of the modern diversity is recognizable.

How do scientists recognize a teleost? With so many living and fossil taxa, it is difficult to agree on features shared by all teleosts. We can recognize a tarpon, or a herring, or a perch, but we would be

PLATE 69
꩜
Teoichthys kallistos, an ophiopsid fish from the Early Cretaceous of Tepexi, Mexico (cast), about 110 milion years old.
Length 25cm.

hard-pressed to find advanced features shared by all of them. The most consistent features are found in the tail skeleton. Arguably the most important from a systematist's viewpoint is the presence of small paired uroneural bones in the tail (see page 142). These bony splints lie above the other tail bones and help stiffen and support the tail fin.

⋙ Extinct Teleosts

The earliest fossil teleosts (from the Middle Triassic, about 235 million years ago) are poorly classified into two families. Many are grouped together as pholidophorids (*scale bearer*) and ichthyokentemids.

Pholidophorus, [Plates 71 and 72] from the Jurassic, is the best known. It probably evolved from more primitive ancestors during the Triassic. The classification is poor because pholidophorid fishes do not have any unique derived features, and thus they are stem teleosts that may include the ancestors of other teleost groups.

Pholidophorids are arbitrarily distinguished from modern teleosts by the retention of several primitive features, including thick, enameled skull bones and ganoid scales that articulate with each other by means of an internal peg-and-socket articulation. The upper jaw of *Pholidophorus* was movable because the maxilla and premaxilla bones were no longer attached firmly to the skull roof, so the mouthparts were almost as protrusible as in modern teleosts. *Pholidophorus* also had bony vertebrae, although they did not constrict the notochord and mostly consisted of a hollow bony cylinder to which the spines and ribs were attached.

Leptolepides, [Plates 72 and 73] another primitive extinct teleost, was more advanced than *Pholidophorus* in having thin, flexible bony scales lacking enamel, and in important features in the tail, such

Teleosts

FIGURE 23
෨

Evolutionary relationships of some living and extinct teleosts. Living teleosts include osteoglossomorphs, elopomorphs, clupeomorphs, ostariophysans and many different kinds of "higher teleosts".

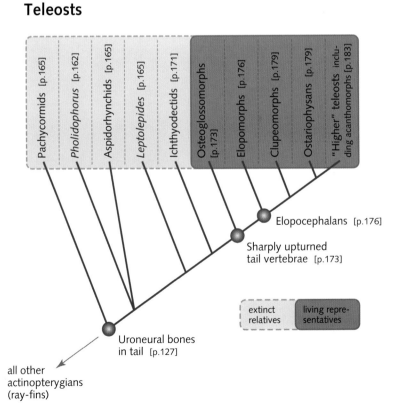

Pachycormids [p.165]
Pholidophorus [p.162]
Aspidorhynchids [p.165]
Leptolepides [p.165]
Ichthyodectids [p.171]
Osteoglossomorphs [p.173]
Elopomorphs [p.176]
Clupeomorphs [p.179]
Ostariophysans [p.179]
"Higher" teleosts including acanthomorphs [p.183]

Elopocephalans [p.176]

Sharply upturned
tail vertebrae [p.173]

extinct
relatives

living repre-
sentatives

Uroneural bones
in tail [p.127]

all other
actinopterygians
(ray-fins)

PLATE 70

Pholidophorus (up to 18cm long) is a primitive marine teleost from the Late Triassic and Early Jurassic (220–175 million years ago). It was abundant and widespread in many parts of the world

PLATE 71

☙

Pholidophorus bechei, a primitive teleost from the Early Jurassic of Dorset, England (about 200 million years old). Length 16cm.

PLATE 72
ᔥᔥ

Leptolepides (up to 15cm long, often smaller),
from the Late Jurassic (about 150 million
years ago), is more advanced than
Pholidophorus in its skull and tail structure
and delicate, thin scales. Many marine and
fresh water teleosts from the Triassic to the
Cretaceous superficially resembled
Leptolepdes.

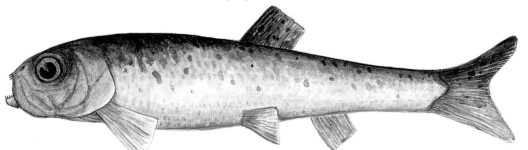

PLATE 73
ᔥᔥ
Leptolepides sprattiformis, a primitive teleost
from the Late Jurassic of Solnhofen,
Germany. Length 10cm.

as a fixed number of fin rays and a single first tail vertebra supporting two platelike hypurals (see page 127). Many fossil teleosts ranging from the Triassic to the Cretaceous were once lumped together as leptolepids, but are now scattered at various points throughout the stem of the teleost tree.

Pachycormids (thick trunk) such as *Pachycormus* [Plates 74 and 75] were streamlined marine fishes of the Jurassic and Cretaceous that were characterized by a pointed rostral bone in the snout, scythe-like, stiff pectoral fins, and a narrow peduncle at the base of the tail, which was strongly forked, as in modern tuna and marlin. Some Late Jurassic pachycormids had triangular finlike projections on each side of the body in front of the tail, probably to smooth the flow of water over the rapidly beating tail. Pachycormids are regarded as a specialized group of primitive extinct teleosts that evolved from a single ancestor, unlike pholidophorids or leptolepids. The tail skeleton in pachycormids was highly specialized and unlike that of other teleosts, although uroneural-like bones were present. Solid vertebrae were absent, a primitive feature in comparison with many other extinct teleosts. Some pachycormids reached enormous size, such as *Leedsichthys*, from the Middle Jurassic of England. Its tail was about 5 meters from tip to tip, and the fish probably was at least 12 meters long, making it the largest teleost ever to have lived. *Protosphyraena*, from the Late Cretaceous of North America and Europe, was another large pachycormid, with a pectoral wing span of up to 2 meters.

Aspidorhynchids (shield snout) such as *Aspidorhynchus* [Plates 76 and 77] and *Belonostomus* form another group of specialized Jurassic and Cretaceous teleosts that evolved from a single ancestor. They had many distinctive features, including an elongate snout and elongate flank scales on the body (usually with enameled ornament). Jurassic aspidorhynchids were sea-going, but in the Late Cretaceous some became tolerant of fresh water. The

last marine aspidorhynchids lived in the Early Cretaceous, but freshwater forms survived until the Early Eocene in North America. Most aspidorhynchids had sharp teeth, and specimens have been found with other fishes in the stomach region, suggesting that they were effective predators. The upper jaw bones were elongate and slender but not particularly mobile, as the maxilla was fixed to the skull beneath the eye. This arrangement would have made suction feeding virtually impossible, and aspidorhynchids probably had to outswim their prey. The pharynx was filled with a delicate array of long gill rakers, suggesting that aspidorhynchids did not rely solely on hunting but were also capable of filter feeding. The Early Cretaceous aspidorhynchid *Vinctifer* [Plate 78; and see Plate 1] had a large mouth with vestigial teeth, but its gill rakers were better developed than in other aspidorhynchids, suggesting it was more dependent on filter feeding. Its fossils have also been found in Brazil, Venezuela, and Queensland, and it may also have lived in Africa; apparently it was restricted to these southern continents and did not venture farther north than the Caribbean region. *Vinctifer* was marine but may have ventured into the brackish or fresh waters of South America, where it sometimes fell prey to the large amiid *Calamopleurus*.

Ichthyodectids are primitive extinct teleosts that appeared in the Late Jurassic and became a successful group of sea-going predators during the Cretaceous. Some grew to an impressive size, and the Late Cretaceous oceans were filled with monstrous 6-meter ichthyodectids such as *Xiphactinus*. [Plate 79] Their elongate body, powerful tail, and bulldoglike jaws combined to make all ichthyodectids efficient predators, and these specializations show they form another natural group that evolved from a single ancestor. Like modern teleosts, they had highly sculptured vertebrae with expanded areas for muscle attachment, and the notochord was constricted or even obliterated by solid bone. Some had small teeth, but the largest

PLATE 74
⟐

Pachycornus (length over 1m) is a pachycormid teleost from the Early Jurassic (205–
175 million years ago). Pachycormids were
succesful streamlined marine predators
during the Jurassic and Cretaceous, but
then became extinct.

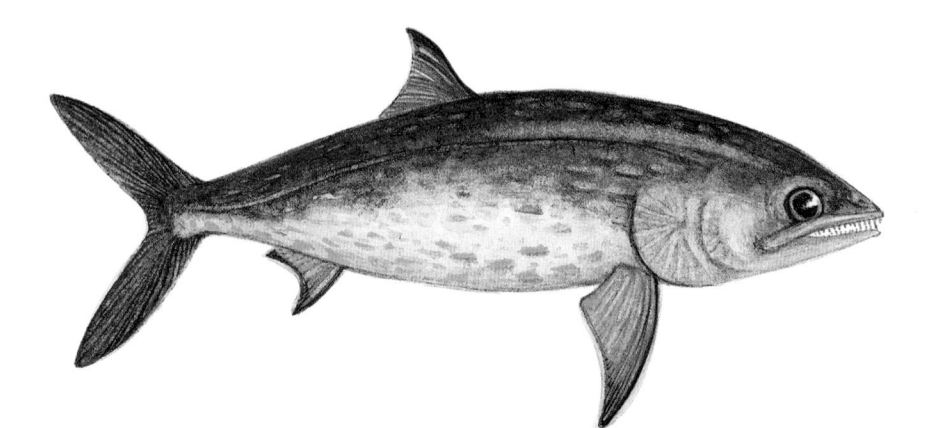

PLATE 75
⟐

Pachycornus esocinus, a pachycormid teleost
from the Early Jurassic of Holzmaden,
Germany (about 200 million years old).
Length 94cm

PLATE 76
ꙮ

Aspidorhynchus (length up to 80cm), from the
Jurassic (205-135 million years ago) belongs
to the extinct group of teleosts called aspidorhynchids, characterized by a long body
and snout, and vertically elongated scales
along the flank. Aspidorhynchids were predominantly marine, and lived from the
Early Jurassic to the Eocene, but the last
survivors were inhabitants of fresh waters.

PLATE 77
ꙮ

Aspidorhynchus acutirostris, an aspidorhynchid
teleost from the Late Jurassic of Solnhofen,
Germany (about 150 million years old).
Length 57cm.

PLATE 78

Vinctifer comptoni, an aspidorhynchid teleost
from the Early Cretaceous of NE Brazil
(about 100 million years old). Length 75cm.

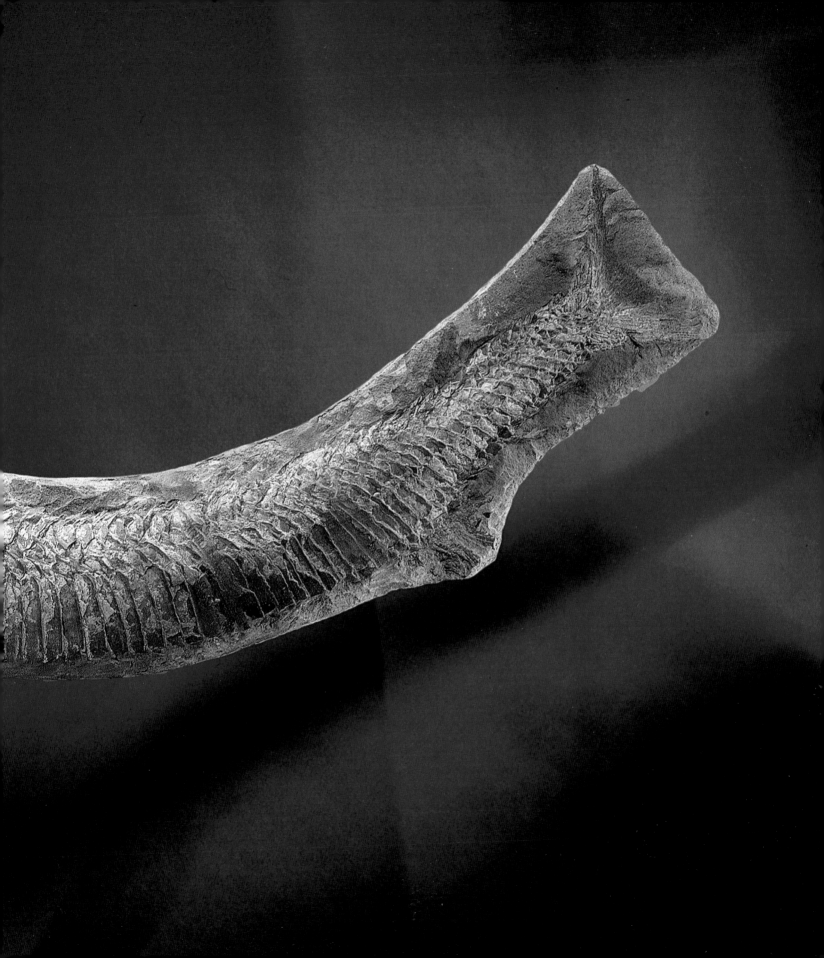

PLATE 79

PLATE 79
A six-meter-long *Xiphactinus*, an ichthyo-dectid teleost, leaps from a vast inland sea that covered much of interior North America during the Late Cretaceous (95–65 million years ago). Ichthyodectids appeared in the Jurassic and reached a peak of diversity, size and abundance during the Cretaceous, then suffered a decline at their end, although a few survived into the Eocene.

ichthyodectids had big fangs at the front of the mouth, usually inserted into small premaxillary bones that were movable. Probably these front teeth were used to strike or impale the prey, perhaps wounding it during an initial strike. *Cladocyclus* was a comparatively small ichthyodectid (1 meter or less) from the Southern Hemisphere. [Plate 80] In Brazil its fossils occur in both marine and freshwater strata, and it was capable of entering lakes, where it may have fed on an abundance of small fishes and aquatic insect larvae. No other ichthyodectid fossils are known from freshwater deposits. Ichthyodectids suffered a major decline at the end of the Cretaceous, but they may have survived until the Eocene in South America. At their peak in the Late Cretaceous, ichthyodectids lived alongside large mako sharks and gigantic marine lizards known as mosasaurs. The extinction of mosasaurs and the decline of ichthyodectids may have allowed modern sharks to become the top sea-going predators after the Cretaceous; they clearly did not occupy that position before that time.

The First Modern Teleosts

In modern teleosts the tail vertebrae are sharply upturned relative to the rest of the backbone, an advanced feature not seen in most extinct teleosts, where the tail vertebrae are more gradually upturned. The common ancestor of modern teleosts probably evolved this feature in the Jurassic, because we can trace the appearance of several modern teleost subgroups to the Late Jurassic and Early Cretaceous, some 90 million years after teleosts first appeared.

Osteoglossomorphs (*bony tongue form*), the most primitive living teleosts, include the bonytongues (Osteoglossidae) of the southern continents, the featherbacks (Notopteridae) of Africa and Southeast Asia, the elephantfishes (Mormyridae) of Africa, and the mooneyes (Hiodontidae) of North America. Osteoglossomorphs are unusual among teleosts in that more fossil than living genera (the category of classification above species) are known; in most other groups the number of living genera far exceeds the number of fossils.

PLATE 80

Cladocyclus gardneri, an ichthyodectid teleost from the Early Cretaceous of NE Brazil (about 110 million years old). Length 111cm.

PLATE 81

~

Lycoptera (up to 10cm long), from the Early
Cretaceous of China and Mongolia (145–120
million years old), is the earliest osteoglossomorph, and may be the earliest skeletal
fossil that can be classified within a living
group of teleosts.

PLATE 82

~

Lycoptera davidi, a primitive osteoglossomorph teleost from the Early Cretaceous of
Manchuria, China (between 145–120 million
years old). Length 7cm.

All modern osteoglossomorphs (about 200 species) live in fresh water, and these fishes occur on all continents except Europe and Antarctica. As far as we can tell from the fossil record, all osteoglossomorphs lived in fresh water in the past. As with terrestrial animals, therefore, the distribution of osteoglossomorphs may be informative about the past history of the continents. Fossil osteoglossids, notopterids, and hiodontids are known from North America.

The world's oldest osteoglossomorph fossils are small fishes from the Upper Jurassic or Lower Cretaceous of China. *Lycoptera*, the best known, is anatomically similar to modern mooneyes (Hiodontidae) in many features. [Plates 81 and 82] Hiodontids occur in north-central and eastern parts of North America. Fossil hiodontids of Eocene age also occur here. Until recently it was thought that *Lycoptera* was a hiodontid, but the similarities between them may be primitive, and it has been suggested that *Lycoptera* is a primitive osteoglossomorph with no particular relationship to any living group.

Phareodus is a North American Eocene relative of modern bonytongues (osteoglossids), which occur today only in the southern hemisphere. [Plate 83] Older ones from the Upper Cretaceous of North America closely resemble *Phareodus*. The oldest osteoglossid fossil discovered so far is *Laelichthys*, from the Early Cretaceous of Brazil. It is clear from the geographic occurrence of these fishes that their present distribution represents only a fraction of their original range. Modern osteoglossid distribution may reflect the former continuity of all the southern continents in a single land mass known as Gondwana.

Stem Elopocephalans

Few non-specialists have ever heard of **elopocephalans** (*sea-fish head*), an enormous subgroup of living teleosts. This subgroup is itself divided into several smaller categories, among which are the **elopomorphs** (tarpons and tenpounders, bonefish, and eels), **clupeomorphs** (herrings), **ostariophysans** (carp, characins, and catfishes), and "higher" teleosts (sever-

PLATE 83

Phareodus testis, an extinct bonytongue from the Early Eocene of Wyoming, USA (about 57 million years old). Length 34cm.

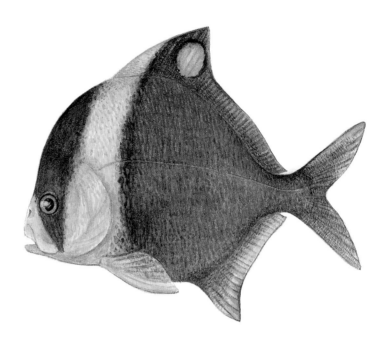

Araripichthys (about 30cm long), from the
Early Cretaceous (110 million years ago) of
South America, is a deep-bodied
elopocephalan with highly advanced
mouthparts reminiscent of those in acanthomorphs.

Araripichthys castilhoi, from the Early
Cretaceous of NE Brazil (about 110 years
ago). Length 33cm. The body and fins are
entirely covered by delicate scales.

PLATE 86
~∽~

Eomyrophis (20–25cm long) is an Early
Eocene eel that lived in seas that covered
parts of northern Italy.

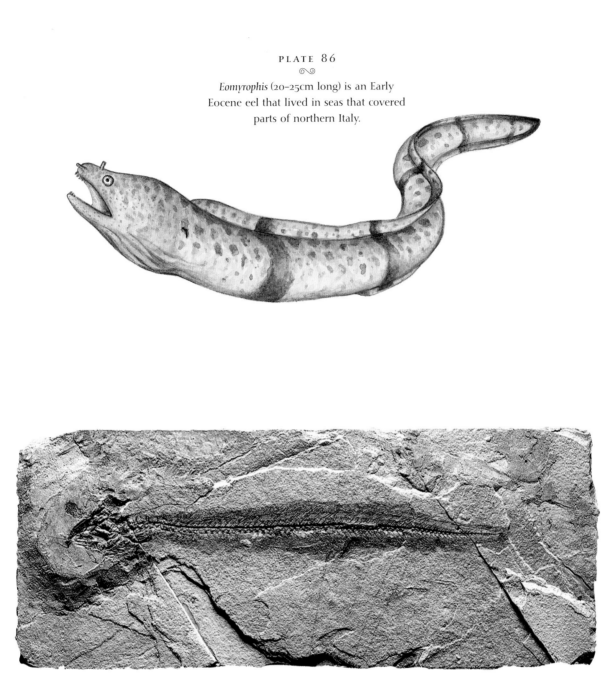

PLATE 87
~∽~

Eomyrophis latispinus, a primitive eel from
the Early Eocene of Monte Bolca, Italy
(about 57 million years ago). Length 24cm.

al categories, including the **acantho-morphs**).

The elopocephalans are useful to know about because many fossil teleosts, mostly from marine deposits of Late Jurassic and Cretaceous periods, fit generally at this level rather than within any particular group of modern teleosts. These fossils are regarded as stem elopocephalans, but like the pholidophorids and leptolepids we reviewed earlier, these do not seem to form a natural group. *Notelops* was a streamlined elopocephalan that lived during the Early Cretaceous in the shallow seas and estuaries of present-day northeastern Brazil. [see Plate 48] Its tail had a deep central notch, as in the fast-swimming mackerels, tuna, or marlin, but *Notelops* was not related to those fishes and must have evolved this feature independently. The stomach contents of *Notelops* reveal that it was a predator of other fishes, including a smaller relative called *Rhacolepis*, [see Plate 47] which is also known from the Early Cretaceous of Venezuela, Colombia, and Mexico.

Araripichthys [Plates 84 and 85] was a deep-bodied marine elopocephalan from Brazil and Venezuela that had some specialized features found otherwise only in very advanced teleosts, such as premaxillary bones that were highly mobile and protrusible, as in the spiny-rayed teleosts (acanthomorphs; see page 185). It also had no pelvic fins and is remarkably similar to modern lanternfishes, but their shared features may reflect similar behavioral patterns rather than any evolutionary relationship.

Elopomorphs

Tarpons and tenpounders, bonefish, and eels are classified together as elopomorphs (*sea-fish form*). Although to some people eels may not even seem like real fishes, in fact, eels are distant relatives of the bonefish and tarpons, with which they share a specialized larval stage (called a leptocephalus). Otherwise, their anatomy has become so highly modified that it is difficult to find any resemblances to other fishes. *Eomyrophis* [Plates 86 and 87] from the Eocene of Italy, was one of the earliest and most primitive eels, but it is not closely related to any particular living ones.

Relatives of tarpons are known from the Eocene of Europe. The oldest fishes related to the modern bonefish (*Albula*) include *Brannerion* [Plates 88 and 89] and *Paraelops* [see Plate 48] both from the Early Cretaceous of Brazil. Variation in tooth

PLATE 88

Brannerion sp., an extinct bonefish from the Early Cretaceous of NE Brazil (about 110 million years old). Length 51cm.

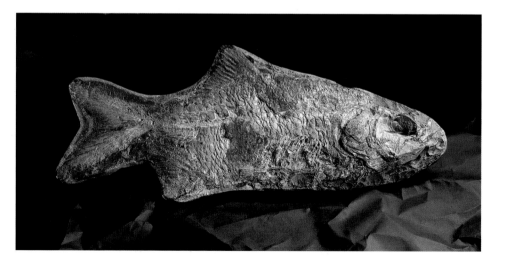

PLATE 89

Nocturnal behavior by the albuloid *Brannerion* (up to 45cm long) from the Early Cretaceous of Brazil is suggested by the size of its eye orbits, a feature also seen in unrelated squirrelfishes (see page XX). Many species of *Brannerion* apparently lived in close harmony with each other, suggesting they had mastered the art of compartmentalizing their environment.

PLATE 90
ை

Knightia (usually 10–15cm long, sometimes larger), from the Early Eocene is a double–armored fresh water herring, with large scutes along its back and belly. Its fossils have been found in North America and China.

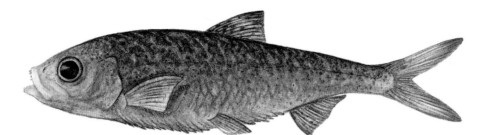

PLATE 91
ை

Knightia eocaena, numerous small herrings representing a mass mortality, from the Early Eocene of Wyoming, USA (about 57 million years old). Length of each individ–ual shown 9cm.

arrangement and vertebral number among specimens of *Brannerion* suggests that many species lived together, and its large orbits suggest that it may have been active at night, like modern squirrelfishes. Both *Brannerion* and *Paraelops* had dentitions consisting of thousands of small pebblelike teeth, and the stomach contents reveal that they liked to eat fishes far smaller than themselves.

Clupeomorphs

Herrings and their relatives (clupeomorphs: *herring form*) are among the most abundant fishes, accounting for about one third of the world's total commercial fishing catch. Most living species are marine, but some spend all or part of their lives in freshwater or brackish environments. About 150 fossil herring species have been described, and they are known as far back as the Early Cretaceous. Clupeomorphs have a distinctive row of enlarged scales (scutes) along the belly, a feature seen even in the earliest examples. Some primitive herrings from the Cretaceous and Eocene also had a second row of scutes along the back. Another feature of living clupeomorphs is an extension of the swim bladder that enters the back of the skull via a pair of small openings and is thought to provide some hearing ability. Skull openings for this system were not developed in some extinct herrings.

Knightia [Plates 90 and 91] was a small Eocene freshwater herring from North America and China that is related to modern herrings from parts of Africa and the Indo-Pacific. *Knightia* was very abundant; records from quarries in Wyoming indicate that in 1978 about 20,000 complete specimens were collected by commercial and amateur fossil hunters, making it one of the most common vertebrate fossils in the world. Hundreds of similarly sized individuals were fossilized together, which suggests that shoals of them were overcome by some catastrophic event and were washed together by winds or tides.

Ostariophysans

Fishes cannot easily detect sound waves, because the density of their soft tissues is very close to the density of water. By far the most elaborate hearing apparatus is developed in fishes known as ostariophysans (*small bone form*). The swim bladder is connected to the ear region by a series of three or four small bones known as **weberian ossicles**. These bones are derived from processes growing out of the first few vertebrae. Ostariophysans include the majority of freshwater fishes (about 6,000 species), such as characins (including piranhas), carps, and catfishes.

Tharrhias [Plates 92 and 93] is a primitive marine ostariophysan from the Early Cretaceous of Brazil. Its first few ribs are thicker, suggesting a primitive stage in the evolution of weberian ossicles. The mouthparts of *Tharrhias* are small and the jaws are toothless, but stomach contents that include planktonic crab larvae suggest that it preferred to feed near the surface rather than in mid-water or close to the bottom. It was closely related to *Dastilbe*, [Plate 94] which thrived in lakes within rift valleys along what would become the margins of Brazil and Africa. *Dastilbe* populations were large, but only one or two species lived in a single lake, and we do not see evidence of species flocks. Possibly *Dastilbe* was a hardy colonist, capable of survival in newly formed lake environments within the Afro-Brazilian rift system.

Notogoneus was a more advanced ostariophysan that belonged to the sandfish family (Gonorynchidae); it lived in the lakes of North America during the Eocene. Other sandfish fossils occur as far back as the Cretaceous in North America, Europe, Africa, and Asia, and they are also known from the Oligocene of Australia. Their present-day distribution (with about 30 species, mostly restricted to African rivers) is thus a relic of a formerly more widespread group.

Catfishes are also ostariophysans, with very distinctive spines in front of

PLATE 92
∾

Tharrhias (20–50cm long) is a primitive
plankton–feeding marine ostariophysan
from the Early Cretaceous of Brazil.

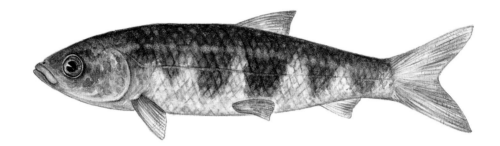

PLATE 93
∾

Tharrhias araripis, an extinct relative of milk–
fish, from the Early Cretaceous of NE Brazil
(about 110 million years old). Length 27cm.

PLATE 94

Dastilbe crandalli, a freshwater teleost from
the Early Cretaceous of NE Brazil (about
110 million years ago). This individual is
about 17cm long, but most others are
much smaller.

PLATE 95

Hypsidoris (about 16cm long) is a fresh water
catfish from the Early Eocene of North
America. The antenna-like barbels and adi-
pose (fat-filled) second dorsal fin are reconstructed; they have no solid skeleton to
become fossilized.

PLATE 96

Hypsidoris farsonensis, a primitive catfish from
the Eocene of Wyoming, USA (about 57
million years old).. Length 16cm.

RAY-FINNED FISHES

their pectoral fins. These spines fossilize well and are usually all that we find. Complete catfish fossils are unusual, because the rest of their skeleton is often delicate, but many examples have been found in the Green River Formation of Wyoming, such as *Hypsidoris*, [Plates 95 and 96] a very primitive catfish that still has teeth on its maxillary bones of the upper jaw (in all but one living catfish, maxillary teeth have been lost). The oldest catfish fossils known at present are pectoral spines from the Late Cretaceous (about 70 million years ago) of South America. All the modern catfish families were in existence in the Eocene. Some modern South American catfishes have thick scales and bony plates covering the head, and are among the most heavily armored fishes still living. Fossils of similar armored catfishes from the Miocene of South America superficially resemble bony placoderms from the Devonian.

Tinca, the tench, [Plate 97] belongs to another branch of ostariophysans, the carp and minnow family (Cypriniformes), a group that also includes the geneticists' favorite, the zebrafish. Cypriniform fishes occur today in fresh waters of Europe and Asia. Fossils from Europe show that modern cypriniform diversity was well established there in lakes in the Oligocene. Cypriniforms occur today in all kinds of habitats throughout the temperate and tropical regions of the world except South America, Madagascar, and Australia, but their fossils are uncommon and usually not very old, suggesting that their evolutionary history is fairly modern.

"Higher" Teleosts

Several other subgroups of teleosts are collectively more advanced than those just surveyed. These include pikes and mudminnows, classified together as esociforms (*pike form*), with fossils from the Late Cretaceous of Alberta. Another group is represented by salmon, trout, and smelts, classified as salmoniforms (*salmon form*), which include fossils from the Early

PLATE 97

Tinca tarsiger, a tench from the Late Oligocene of Rott, Germany (about 24 million years old).

PLATE 98
⚮

Eurypholis (10–15cm long), from the Late
Cretaceous of Lebanon is a voracious-look-
ing distant relative of deep-sea teleosts and
advanced acanthomorphs.

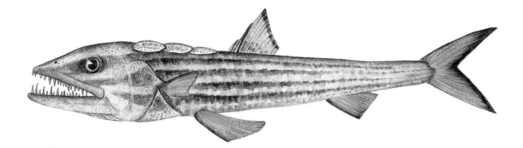

PLATE 99
⚮

Eurypholis boisseri, an extinct teleost from the
Late Cretaceous of Lebanon (about 90 million years old). Length 11cm.

Cretaceous. By the Eocene there were separate lineages of salmonids and smelts, and modern-looking fossil capelins and salmon a few million years old have been found in parts of Canada and Greenland. Specialized deep-sea teleosts known as stomiiforms (*big-mouth form*; with about 300 species) are more advanced than salmonlike fishes and are thought to have appeared in the Cretaceous, although no stomiiform fossils older than the Eocene are known. Two other groups (aulopiforms {*unkown fish-form*}, with about 200 species of mostly deep-sea fishes, and myctophiforms {*snout-snake form*}, with some 250 deep-sea species) are known from rare Middle and Late Cretaceous fossils found in strata deposited in shallow seas on the once submerged continental margin of Lebanon. Groups that include deep-sea fishes may have appeared first in shallower waters, but much of their bizarre anatomical diversity surely arose after they entered deeper environments, from which we have been unable to recover their fossils.

Some Late Cretaceous teleost families, possibly lying close to the ancestry of acanthomorphs, include eurypholids (*wide scale*) and enchodontids (*spear tooth*). These were fast-swimming marine predators with needle-like teeth. *Eurypholis* [Plates 98 and 99] was about 20 centimeters long. It had large scutes arranged in a row along the back and an enormous mouth with sharp teeth, reminiscent of some modern deep-sea fishes. Enchodontids were considerably larger, sometimes over 1 meter. They had saber-toothed fangs at the front of the mouth and were common in many parts of the world.

The greatest subgroup of advanced teleosts is the **acanthomorphs** (*spine form*), represented by about 15,000 living species and 300 families. They were so named because their fins bear sharp, bony spines instead of soft fin rays. Defensive structures, these spines are strong and firm, but they are also retractable (to reduce drag). When erected, they expand the dimensions of the fish so that it

becomes more difficult to be swallowed by a predator. Among acanthomorphs we frequently find that the size and position of the fin spines are linked closely to body shape, with an emphasis on protecting the abdomen. These defensive spines also need a firm base; they would be useless if they flopped about, and each spine has a well-developed bony support at its base. A well-defended spiny fish is less dependent on speed as a means of escape, and many slow-swimming or sedentary acanthomorphs, especially in the huge perch family, are reminiscent of the heavily armored fishes of the Devonian.

The oldest acanthomorph skeletons date back only about 100 million years, to Late Cretaceous. The earliest record of the group consists of ear stones (otoliths), from the Middle Jurassic of England, but no skeletal remains of that age are known. Three modern families of primitive acanthomorphs are known from Late Cretaceous otoliths, but no skeletal fossils of these or other modern families are known until the Eocene. These examples show the value of otoliths in extending the geological record of ray-fin families beyond what is revealed by their bones.

The Eocene Explosion

By the time we get a good look at the acanthomorph fossil record in the Eocene, the action is virtually over. Charts showing the range of fishes through geological time suddenly sprout hundreds of new families. Many of the fossils come from the famous marine strata of Monte Bolca, in northern Italy. These and other fossils from around the world leave no doubt that modern family-level acanthomorph diversity is rooted in the Early Eocene (about 55 million years ago), and that this teleost explosion was the most dramatic evolutionary radiation ever seen in vertebrate history, eclipsing the evolution of mammals and birds in numbers of families and species.

Many acanthomorph fossils are known from Eocene and younger strata. Their study is best left to specialists of the living forms, because their evolutionary relationships can only be understood by reference to extant species. The few fossil acanthomorphs shown here are but a small and inadequate sample of their richness and diversity. There would be little point in illustrating one example after another of essentially modern-looking fossil acanthomorphs, for they would teach us little about the past history and diversity of fishes. The interest of fossils really lies elsewhere, in suggesting how this modern diversity arose and, by revealing the former existence of intermediate stem ray-finned fishes, linking all the modern groups together.

Eoholocentrum, [Plates 100 and 101] from the Eocene of Italy, was related to modern squirrelfishes, a primitive acanthomorph group. It had several acanthomorph features, including spiny fin rays, thin scales with comblike margins, and fusion of the pelvic and pectoral girdles so that the pelvic fins lay just behind the head. This feature, commonly observed in acanthomorphs, is possible only because the swim bladder provides neutral buoyancy and frees the paired fins from their primitive function of generating lift and stability; they were now able to function together as an advanced braking system. Modern squirrelfishes are nocturnal and are characterized by large eyes. We cannot be sure that fossil squirrelfishes were nocturnal, but their large orbits offer a provocative clue, like those of the Cretaceous albuloid *Brannerion* (see page 176).

Priscacara [Plates 102 and 103] was a common perchlike fish that lived in lakes of central North America during the Eocene. More than 9,000 living and several hundred fossil species of perchlike fishes are recognized—about the same number as there are species of songbirds. Perches may contain primitive members of many other acanthomorph families, and almost certainly do not form a natural group. This "group" is widely regarded as the last great unsolved problem in ichthyology. Currently it contains about 150 nominal families.

Surgeonfishes are common reef-dwelling acanthomorphs. Their fossil record extends back to the Eocene. A unique single specimen of a fossil surgeonfish, *Eonaso*, [Plates 104 and 105] was found on the Caribbean island of Antigua and was deposited in the collections of the American Museum of Natural History at the beginning of the 20th century. No other specimens have ever been found, and the original collecting site is now thought to lie under a luxury hotel complex! *Eonaso* is anatomically similar to the modern genus *Naso*, a Pacific form that does not occur today in the tropical waters around Antigua or other Caribbean islands. The precise age of this unique fossil is in doubt, but probably it is no more than a few million years old. More primitive surgeonfishes have been discovered in Eocene strata of Monte Bolca, in Italy, but their relationships to modern species are not well documented. Another spectacular Eocene fossil from Monte Bolca is called *Mene*. [Plate 106] This beautiful fish may have been related to modern carangids (jacks and pompanos), and it has a deep pompano-like body. Carangid fossils first occur in the Eocene, along with many other modern groups of reef fishes. The shape of the body and fins in such fossils can evoke in our imagination the grace and dignity of many modern reef fishes.

The path through the forest

The fossil record of ray-finned fishes suggests that their modern diversity largely evolved over the past 200 million years, not longer, and that the range of forms seen today among acanthomorphs and some other advanced teleosts is, in geological time, a relatively modern phenomenon. In particular, rates of diversification among these fishes accelerated dramatically during the Eocene. Diversity among more generalized living teleosts began earlier, as we might expect, but is mainly concentrated in the Cretaceous. Modern neopterygian diversity can be traced to the Jurassic and Late Triassic, although

PLATE 100
◠

Eoholocentrum (about 12–20cm long), from
the Eocene of Italy, is a relative of modern
squirrelfishes (holocentrids). Its large eyes
suggest it was nocturnal, like many living
holocentrids.

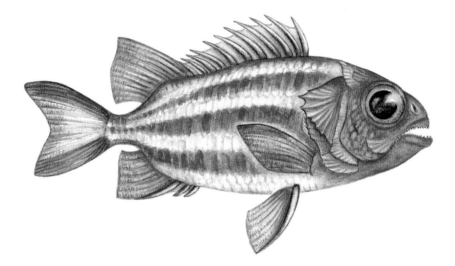

PLATE 101
◠

Eoholocentrum macrocephalum, an extinct
squirrelfish, from the Eocene of Monte
Bolca, Italy (about 57 million years old).
Length 13cm.

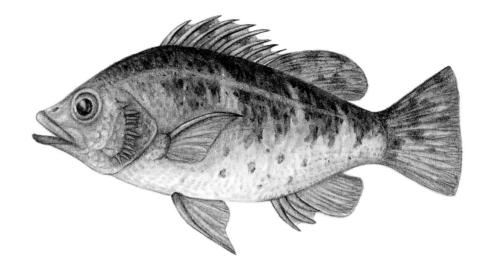

PLATE 102
⟋⟍

Priscacara (20–30cm long) is a fresh water perch–like acanthomorph from the Early Eocene of North America. More than 9000 living species of perches have been discovered, but their evolution is poorly understood and the significance of fossils such as *Priscacara* is still a mystery.

PLATE 103
⟋⟍

Priscacara oxyprion, from the Early Eocene of Wyoming, USA (about 57 million years old). Length 24cm.

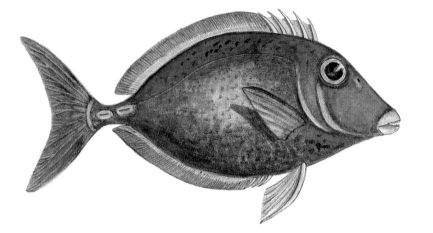

PLATE 104
◦◦

Eonaso (about 30cm long) is an extinct Caribbean relative of modern surgeonfishes, but its exact age is unknown. It is more advanced than Eocene surgeonfishes from Italy, and seems closest to *Naso*, which today lives only in the Pacific.

PLATE 105
◦◦

Eonaso deani, a surgeonfish from the island of Antigua. Length 29cm.

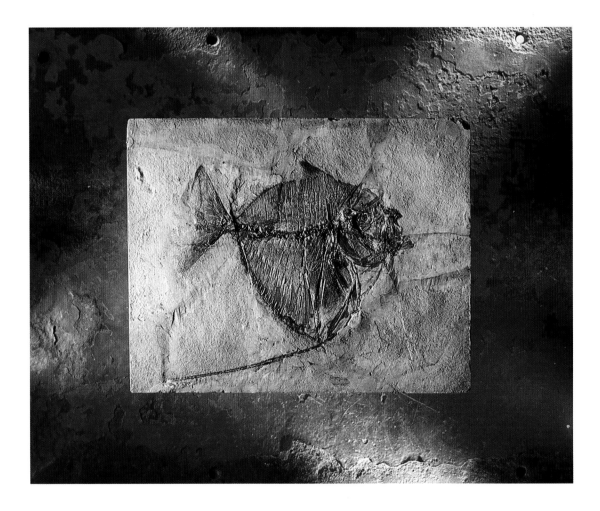

PLATE 106
෨

Mene rhombeus, a carangid–like acantho–
morph from the Early Eocene of Monte
Bolca, Italy (about 57 million years old).
Length 20cm.

gars, supposedly more primitive than teleosts and bowfins, currently are known only from the Early Cretaceous to the Present. Neither the first neopterygians nor the first teleosts witnessed such an explosive radiation as that experienced by acanthomorphs, but their early diversity nevertheless included several specialized groups that subsequently became extinct, as well as lineages that survive to the present day. The pedigrees of chondrosteans and reedfishes are less clear, but no Paleozoic fossils have yet been recognized as direct relatives of these fishes.

Compared to today's rich faunas of ray-finned fishes, those of the Devonian, Carboniferous and Permian seem taxonomically impoverished, despite the fact that some species were abundant and widespread. Moreover, little of that early diversity is apparent today; even though modern phylogenetic analyses have predicted that the ancestors of modern reedfishes and chondrosteans evolved in the Paleozoic, we have so far failed to discover or recognize them among the fossils at our disposal. The oldest fossil skeletons belonging to an extant group of ray-finned fishes are teleosts and chondrosteans about 200 million years old, and the oldest fossil bowfins are about 150 million years old. We still have a great deal to discover about the early evolution of primitive living ray-finned fishes.

The subsequent history of teleosts is somewhat clearer. There are over 400 extant families, and almost 100 more extinct families have been recognized. Fossils reveal that modern teleost diversity was not gradual, but arose rapidly between 75 and 50 million years ago, during the Early Tertiary (Paleocene and Eocene periods). Less than half a dozen modern teleost families are known from the Early Cretaceous, and only about 20 more are known from the Late Cretaceous, but over 180 additional modern families are represented by fossils from the Paleocene and Eocene. That time of maximum diversification was also a time of higher extinction; about half a dozen teleost families disappeared in the Jurassic, and about a dozen more in the Early Cretaceous, but around 30 families became extinct during the Late Cretaceous and over 30 more during the Paleocene and Eocene. Many of the Late Cretaceous extinctions were of older families extending from the Jurassic, but most of the extinctions in the Early Tertiary involved geologically short-lived families, many of which were allied closely to surviving groups. Extinction of teleost families outran new appearances in the Late Cretaceous, but new appearances swamped extinctions in the Early Tertiary.

Of more than 23,000 living species of teleosts, 21,000 belong to just two groups, the ostariophysans (with over 6,000 species) and the acanthomorphs (with about 15,000 species). It is thus no exaggeration to say that teleost success is really acanthomorph and (to a lesser extent) ostariophysan success; no other teleost group even comes close! There are about 180 acanthomorph families with a fossil record; of these, more than 160 are extant. As might be expected, the vast majority of these families first appeared in the Early Tertiary, so the "rise of teleosts" is more appropriately the rise of acanthomorphs. That event is geologically contemporaneous with the rise of mammals and birds, and seems to have involved a moderate failure rate (represented by extinctions) similar to that discovered among these "higher" vertebrates. More specifically, however, the evolutionary history of acanthomorph teleosts parallels that of placentals among mammals, or songbirds among our feathered friends. All three groups represent remarkable independent vertebrate success stories, yet the acanthomorph story has remained largely hidden from popular view. ✌

OUT OF WATER

*T*ODAY THERE ARE about 23,500 species of lobe–finned sarcopterygians
(*flesh fin*) of which 23,494 or so are air–breathing tetrapods, mostly with
four legs and living on land. Five are lungfishes, with strangely modified
bodies and fins (so strange, in fact, that when the South American lung–
fish *Lepidosiren* was discovered in 1836 it was originally identified as a
reptile), and one is the **coelacanth** (*hollow spine*), *Latimeria*. For a century
lungfishes were the only known surviving fishy relatives of the
tetrapods, until the discovery of a living coelacanth in 1938 revealed
more about our more generalized Paleozoic ancestors. [Figure 24] Only
these six living species still have fins, for although flippers are present in
ichthyosaurs, plesiosaurs, turtles, whales, and dolphins, all these creatures
evolved from ancestors with limbs adapted for terrestrial life. The sup–
posedly primitive fin is really the optimal design for swimming, and it
has been copied and recopied by tetrapods that returned to water.

An important advanced feature of all sarcopterygians is that the
internal skeleton of the paired appendages, whether they are fins or
limbs, is attached to the shoulder or pelvis by a single bone, the
humerus or **femur**. The flexible shoulder and hip joints between these
bones and the body allow great freedom of movement by the paired
appendages, which contain strong muscles. The fleshy appearance of the
fins in lungfishes and coelacanths gave rise to the name "**lobe fins**." In

PLATE 107
〰

Eusthenopteron (up to 1m long) lived in fresh
to brackish waters covering parts of Canada
during the Late Devonian (365–355 million
years ago). This lobe–finned relative of
tetrapods retained many primitive (i.e.
"fish–like") features, and was much better
adapted to life in water than its limbed
relatives.

Sarcopterygians
(lobe-fins)

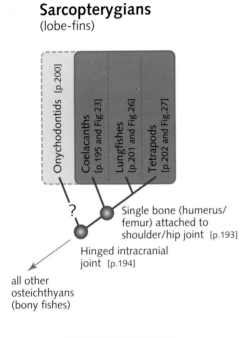

FIGURE 24

Evolutionary relationships of lobe-finned fishes (sarcopterygians).

the coelacanth, the anal and second dorsal fins also form fleshy lobes, but the first dorsal fin consists of stiff fin rays similar to those of actinopterygians.

Some lobe-fins such as the coelacanth have a two-part braincase, with a movable intracranial joint in the middle. The front and back part of the skull are hinged transversely, allowing limited movement (but not too much, because the cranial cavity for the brain passes beneath this joint). The upper jaw is separate from the skull but is attached by ligaments to the front part of the braincase. The advantage of the intracranial joint is not clear, because live coelacanths have not been studied sufficiently, but it may serve to cushion the shock of biting stresses in the braincase and body. Although no living lungfishes or tetrapods have this joint, fossils reveal that it was primitively present in the ancestors of both of these groups and was lost independently in their evolution when the upper jaw became fused to the underside of the skull to form a palate.

Lungfishes and coelacanths are truly living fossils, for they are the *only* finned relatives of tetrapods to have survived a major extinction in the Permian (290 to 245 million years ago). Unlike sharks and ray-finned fishes, which flourished and diversified after that extinction, coelacanths and lungfishes barely survived. Before that time, diversity among lobe-finned fishes was far greater than it is today, not only among the lungfishes and coelacanths, but in other related groups now long extinct. Lobe-fin diversity was greatest in the Paleozoic, with about 19 families occuring in the Devonian, and with peak diversity (about a dozen families) in the Late Devonian, when it was about equal to that of all chondrichthyans, acanthodians, and ray-finned fishes *combined*. At that time there were as many families of lungfishes as there were of chondrichthyans. Up to ten lungfish and three coelacanth families lived at some time in the Devonian.

Lobe-finned fishes were also the earliest vertebrates to evolve a backbone that included solid vertebrae, although these never evolved in coelacanths and probably arose independently in lungfishes and tetrapods.

Fish Lungs

A great many fishes can breathe or gulp air at least some of the time. Besides lungfishes, the list includes the African reedfishes (*Polypterus*), the tarpon, the Amazonian pirarucú (*Arapaima*), loaches, knifefishes, many catfishes, some eels, climbing perches, paradisefishes, fighting fishes and mudskippers. It was also once suggested that the placoderm *Bothriolepis* had lungs (see pg. 81). A lung or swim bladder is present in most osteichthyans, and although the living coelacanth *Latimeria* does not have a lung, it does have a large swim bladder completely filled with fatty tissue. The swim bladder in *Latimeria* does not function as an air-filled hydrostatic organ in the same way that it does in ray-finned fishes, but it may still provide some buoyancy. Curiously, the swim bladder in many extinct coelacanths was encased in thin bony plates, helping to preserve its shape. In fossils it is sometimes preserved in three dimensions, perhaps because it was also filled by fatty tissue and resisted compaction after burial in sediment.

Lungfishes, as their name implies, have a lung whose internal wall is folded to increase its surface area, much like our own. The technical name for lungfishes is dipnoan, or *two-lunged*, not because of the number (some have only one lung), but because they have two modes of respiration (using either gills or lungs). Despite this, the gills of modern lungfishes are small and generally cannot meet the respiratory demands of the fish. Modern lungfishes, many of which live in environments subject to periodic desiccation, may be more reliant on lung respiration than were the Paleozoic forms that lived in open waters.

We are so used to thinking of lungfishes as semiterrestrial freshwater fishes that the idea of them swimming in the ancient oceans seems almost absurd. Throughout most of the Mesozoic era, lungfishes were largely confined to freshwater habitats, much as they are today, but things were not always this way. Many early lungfishes of the Devonian and Carboniferous eras were marine, and some may have lived in seas at depths greater than 300 meters, perhaps feeding on algal debris and bottom-dwelling invertebrates. Probably they were unable to swim repeatedly to the surface in order to breathe air, and it is far more likely that they were obligate gill-breathers. Most Devonian lungfishes had large gill chambers covered by a big round opercular bone. The back of the braincase was raised, increasing the space available for gills to several times that in modern lungfishes, and the gill arches were well developed and carried large blood vessels to the gill surfaces.

Could these early lungfishes have gulped air? Modern lungfishes all have an orobranchial pump that enables them to expel old air from the lung, gulp fresh air into the mouth, and then pump it quickly into the lung, using the tongue to seal the mouth. By gulping air this way a few times, *Lepidosiren* (the sole South American lungfish) can remain submerged for up to 20 minutes. Anatomical features linked to this ability include the shape of the upper jaw bones (especially the quadrate), the way the palate fits against the tongue, and an increased size of the shoulder girdle (which provides anchorage for powerful muscles needed to work the pump). Many primitive extinct lungfishes lacked the skeletal prerequisites necessary to gulp air in this way, and probably none of the marine forms were air breathers. The orobranchial pump may have arisen only in freshwater forms.

When did lungfishes develop the ability to breathe air? Indirect evidence comes from supposed lungfish burrows in strata from the Late Devonian onward. These could only have been made by lungfishes that could estivate (burrow into mud and undergo a form of deep sleep,

with a reduced metabolism), and in order to do that they must have breathed air. The most compelling evidence of estivation behavior comes from the Early Permian of the south-western United States, where burrows have been found still containing skeletons of the lungfish *Gnathorhiza*. These lungfishes lived in freshwater streams that were subject to periodic drought. The large size of their opercular apparatus and gill chamber suggests that these lungfishes used gills as well as lungs in respiration. Facultative air breathing probably arose during the Late Devonian (about 375 million years ago), but many early lungfishes probably still used their gills much of the time.

Last Dance of the Coelacanths

Anyone who has watched Hans Fricke's amazing footage of coelacanths swimming cannot fail to be impressed. They don't swim, they *perform*! Sculling with paired pectoral and pelvic fins and flicking its tail as it does headstands, *Latimeria* shows no sign of walking on all fours, as scientists in the 1930s had predicted it would. "Old Fourlegs," it was dubbed, but what a misnomer! The paired fins certainly function in unison, turning and orienting the body, but there is no trace of a side-to-side "walking" gait, and the fish doesn't appear to stand on its fins at all. Curiously, it uses its anal fin and second dorsal fin in unison too, like a third pair of fins in the vertical plane. All the fins are coordinated in an elegant ballet of underwater motion, the last dance of the coelacanths.

Latimeria is on the way out. Estimates of its numbers vary, but there may well be more coelacanths pickled in jars than there are left in the wild. It is protected, but since its discovery in 1938 human ignorance, greed, and scientific curiosity have continued to take their toll. Almost 400 million years of evolutionary history are about to end. Paradoxically, the coelacanth's longevity is part of its downfall, for there are people who actually believe that *Latimeria* contains an elixir of life, as if this fish had itself survived for so many millions of years. In fact, *Latimeria* has no fossil record and is merely the last survivor of a remarkably conservative lineage. Part of the coelacanth myth is attributable to its lost heritage, for there are no known fossil coelacanths from strata younger than the Cretaceous 65 million years ago (it was for this reason that scientists were surprised and delighted when *Latimeria* showed up in 1938).

The coelacanth body plan is remarkably conservative, yet coelacanths have managed to enter a wide range of fresh- and saltwater habitats without appreciable modification to their basic design. [Figure 25] Some of the most primitive coelacanths had a sharklike, asymmetrical tail, but most have an externally symmetrical tail that includes a small central tuft (epicaudal lobe) with its own special muscles that enable it to twitch, like a kitten's tail. *Rhabdoderma*, typical of most early coelacanths, was common during the Early Carboniferous in North America and Europe, where it lived in the lower reaches of rivers and swamps, but it could also tolerate brackish and even salt waters (Triassic relatives of *Rhabdoderma* were fully marine). From the Triassic onward, two principal coelacanth lineages are distinguishable. One of these gave rise to giant coelacanths that mostly lived in fresh water, and the other included forms closer to *Latimeria*.

The first of these lineages included *Diplurus*, a small (15 to 25 centimeters long) coelacanth that lived with semionotids in lakes along the eastern margin of North America during the Late Triassic and Early Jurassic. [Plate 108] *Chinlea*, also from the Triassic, was larger (50 to 75 centimeters long) and lived in interior lakes of North America. Related coelacanths of the Early Cretaceous, such as the gigantic *Mawsonia* (up to 3 meters long) and *Axelrodichthys* (about 1.5 meters), lived in brackish waters of Brazil and Africa. [Plates 109 and 110] These giants of Gondwana were the last and the largest coelacanths ever to inhabit the continents of Earth.

Coelacanths

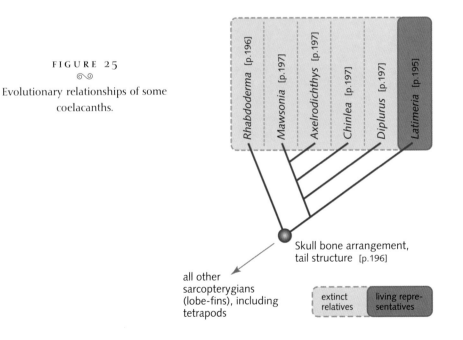

FIGURE 25

Evolutionary relationships of some coelacanths.

PLATE 108

Diplurus newarki, a coelacanth from the Late
Triassic of Princeton, New Jersey, USA
(about 220 million years ago). Length 15cm.

PLATE 110

PLATE 110
⁓

Axelrodichthys araripensis, a coelacanth from
the Early Cretaceous of NE Brazil (about
110 million years old). Length 70cm.

PLATE 109
(*left*)
⁓

The coelacanth *Axelrodichthys* (about 1m
long) performs a headstand as it investi-
gates some bottom-living shrimps while
Mawsonia, an even larger coelacanth (about
3m long) looms from the depths of a
brackish Early Cretaceous inland sea of
north-eastern Brazil, about 110 million
years ago. Despite their size, these coelacanths were toothless, unlike their living
relative *Latimeria* and most extinct coelacanths, but what they ate is still a mystery.

By the Late Cretaceous only saltwater coelacanths were left (including extinct relatives of *Latimeria*), mostly living in shallow, warm seas extending across the continents of Europe, North America, and North Africa. Some were small, but those living in a central seaway across North America during the Late Cretaceous were the largest coelacanths that ever lived, probably reaching lengths close to 4 meters. And all that time, presumably deep in the Indian Ocean, the ancestors of *Latimeria* survived, past the extinction of their freshwater relatives, past the demise of their shallow-sea cousins, until their chance discovery in the mid-20th century. Now *that's* a gap in the fossil record, extending anywhere from 65 to 200 million years!

⇒⫴⫸ Onychodontids: Fishes in Search of Their Relatives
When scientists don't understand the evolutionary relationships of a fossil, they sometimes place in it a class by itself.

Strunius, from the Devonian of Germany, is such a fossil. [Plate 111] *Strunius* was a small fish with two dorsal fins and a coelacanth-like tail, but its fins completely lacked fleshy lobes. The pattern of bones in its skull was remarkably similar to that of primitive ray-finned fishes, although it seems to have had a functional joint in its braincase. *Onychodus*, from the Devonian and Carboniferous of many parts of the world, was a much larger fish that resembled *Strunius* in many primitive features, but its fins have been reconstructed with fleshy lobes. These two fishes have been classified together as **onychodontids** (*claw tooth*), though for no very good reason. *Strunius* looks like a link between ray-fins and lobe-fins, and it could be a primitive "hinge-head." *Onychodus* could be viewed as a more advanced "lobe-finned hinge-head," more closely related to all other lobe-fins. Despite the availability of informative fossils, surprisingly little has been published on these enigmatic fishes.

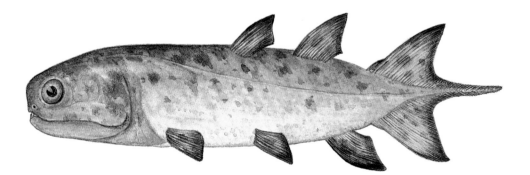

PLATE 111

⟳

Strunius (about 7cm long), from the Middle Devonian of Germany (380 million years old) had no lobed fins, but its skull was divided into front and rear sections as in other sarcopterygians. Its evolutionary relationships to other fishes are still poorly known.

Lungfishes

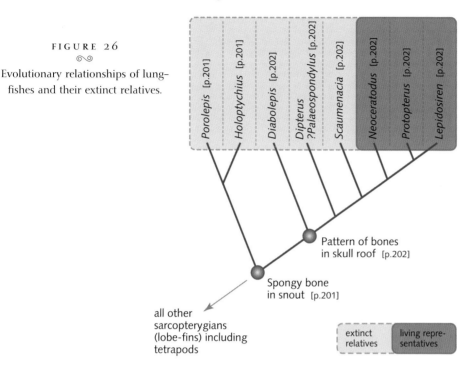

FIGURE 26

Evolutionary relationships of lung-fishes and their extinct relatives.

Pattern of bones
in skull roof [p.202]

Spongy bone
in snout [p.201]

all other
sarcopterygians
(lobe-fins) including
tetrapods

extinct
relatives | living repre-
sentatives

PLATE 112

Holoptychius quebecensis, an extinct porolepiform, distantly related to lungfishes, from the Late Devonian of Escuminac Bay, Quebec, Canada (about 375 million years old). Length 43cm.

Unlikely Success: The Lungfishes

Excluding tetrapods, fully *half* of the families of Sarcoptergians (*lobe-fins*) are lung-fishes. That estimate admittedly includes some fossils that some scientists would exclude from lungfishes, but even if these forms are excluded, 14 of the 33 lobe-finned families that ever existed are lung-fishes. These were the most diverse group of aquatic sarcopterygians during the Devonian and were second only to placo-derms in Devonian family-level diversity. Among lobe-fins, only the tetrapods have achieved greater diversity than lungfishes. [Figure 26]

Extinct lobe-fins primitively related to lungfishes probably include Devonian forms such as *Porolepis* and *Holoptychius*. [Plate 112] These fishes were too late to be directly ancestral to lungfishes, but they probably resembled their ancestors. They were stocky, rotund fishes with heavy, bony scales and a sharklike tail. One specialized feature uniting them with primitive lungfishes was the presence of bony tubules inside the snout and at the front of the lower jaw. These tubules connected with sensory canals of the head and may have formed part of a pressure-sensitive or electrosensory organ. Unfortunately, this bony tissue is absent in modern lung-fishes, and we cannot determine its function directly. Another specialization of lungfishes is their large upper and lower tooth plates. [Plate 113] These evolved early in lungfish history, and lungfish tooth plates are common fossils. *Diabolepis*, from the Early Devonian of China, is one of the oldest and most primitive lungfish-es. Its upper jaw was not fused to the floor of the braincase, and the biting surfaces of its jaws were covered by small teeth that were periodically shed and replaced, instead of forming large tooth plates. The bones of its skull roof show distinctive features shared by more advanced lungfishes.

Lungfishes became widespread very early in their evolution and their fossils are found on every continent, including Antarctica. Modern lungfishes live in harsh, arid environments unsuitable for most other fishes, but many Devonian lungfishes lived in waters teeming with other kinds of fishes. For example, *Scaumenacia* lived in fresh to brackish waters that also supported a diverse and abundant fauna of ostracoderms, antiarchs, and many ray-finned and other lobe-finned fishes, [Plate 114; and see Plate 120] while *Dipterus* lived in fresh water along with arthrodires and acanthodians. [Plate 115] Other Devonian lungfishes have been found in marginal coral reef environments, and their early success may have been due to their ability to adapt to a wide range of environments. These primitive lungfishes looked more fishlike than modern ones, with heavy scales, many dermal bones, and large fins.

Palaeospondylus from the Devonian of Scotland is known from many enigmatic little fossils that have been the subject of controversy for over a century. For years it was thought to be a fossil hagfish, but the fossils have paired fins, bony vertebrae, and derived features in the braincase that place them within the jawed vertebrates, not with hagfishes. *Palaeospondylus* fossils resemble larval lungfishes in many features, and they could be the larvae of *Dipterus*, which occurs in the same strata. It is even possible that they are the larvae of primitive tetrapods, which may make them the world's oldest pollywogs.

Living lungfishes are classified into two families, the Neoceratodontidae, which includes the Australian lungfish *Neoceratodus*, and the Lepidosirenidae (with both the African and South American lungfishes, *Protopterus* and *Lepidosiren*). The earliest neoceratodontids are from the Early Triassic, and later ones have been found as far afield as the Urals and South America, so the family was formerly much more widespread than it is today. Neoceratodontids are anatomically primitive in having large scales and dermal bones, and big, fleshy lobe fins. Fossil lepidosirenids have been found only in Africa and South America, the oldest coming from the Late Cretaceous. These fossils fall within the current continental range of the family, and they postdate the separation of Africa and South America, which suggests that modern lepidosirenid diversity (one species in South America and at least three in Africa) has arisen only in the past 70 million years.

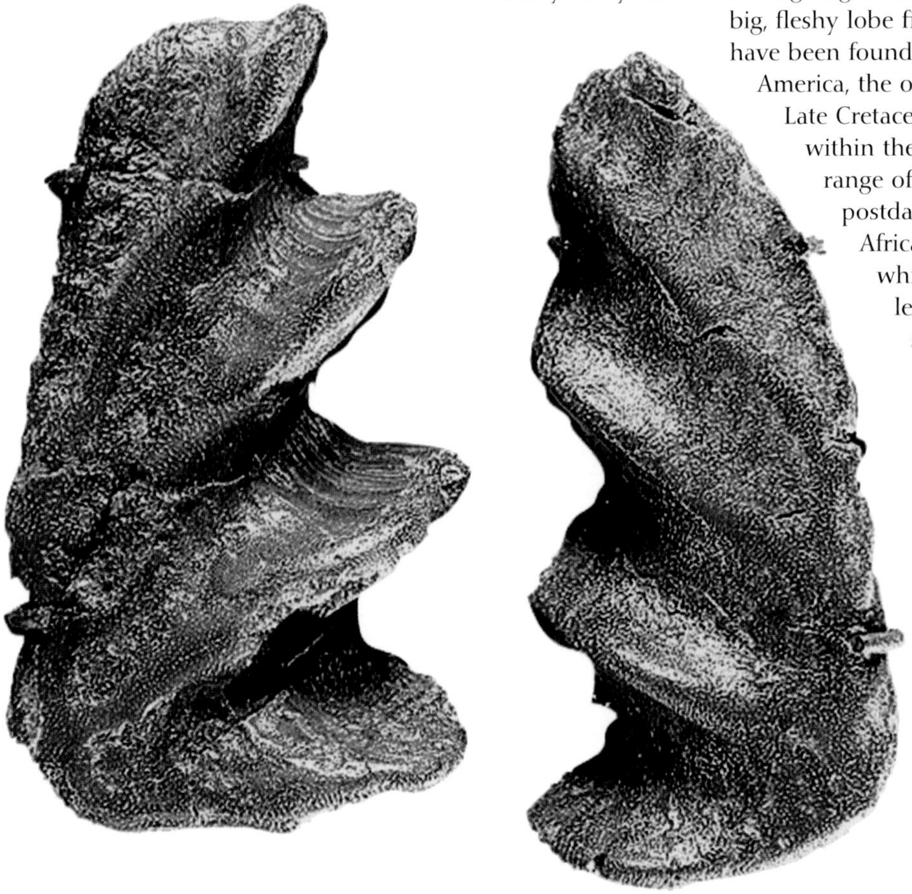

Toes and Lungs

The principal anatomical feature by which scientists have characterized terrestrial craniates is the presence of digits (toes and fingers), as if these digits, the frayed ends to the lobed fins, were the most significant

PLATE 113

Ceratodus rumcinatus, two lungfish tooth-plates, each about 4cm long, from the Late Triassic of Würtemberg, Germany (about 210 million years old). Very similar tooth-plates occur in modern lungfishes.

PLATE 114
ↂ

Scaumenacia sp., an extinct lungfish from the
Late Devonian of Escuminac Bay, Quebec,
Canada (about 375 million years old).
Length 27cm.

PLATE 115
ↂ

Dipterus valenciennesi, an extinct lungfish
from the Middle Devonian of Achanarras,
Scotland (about 380 million years old).
Length 17cm.

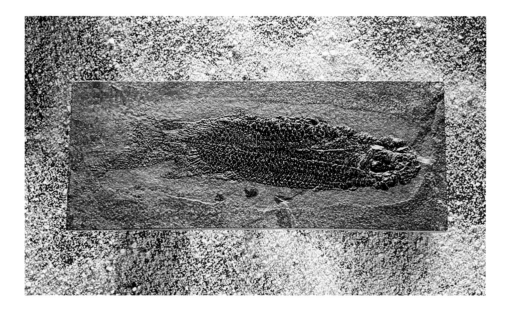

anatomical feature separating tetrapods from fishes. [Figure 27] We have probably focused too much attention on the evolution of our digits, however, because a far more fundamental anatomical and physiological feature separating us from our fishy cousins is our reliance on air-breathing. Humans will drown after a few minutes underwater if unaided, and large whales will drown after two hours. The transition from gill to lung respiration effectively prohibited tetrapods from remaining submerged. We speak of something inappropriate as "a fish out of water", but could just as easily speak of "a tetrapod in water".

In fact, the internal skeleton of the tetrapod limb is generally similar to that of a coelacanth or lungfish, and is even more similar in many details to the paired fin skeletons of fossils such as *Eusthenopteron*. [Plate 116; and see Plate 107] Embryologists and geneticists have studied the development of tetrapod limbs, and have determined that the formation of separate digits is controlled by special genes that regulate whether particular cells will live or die in the limb extremity. Cells that live will grow into digits; cells that die create gaps between them.

This developmental peculiarity is apparently all that distinguishes limb development in tetrapods, and hardly seems sufficient to account for their rise to dominance on land. Nor does it seem to endow them with any apparent advantage in water, for separate digits are one of the first features to be lost in the evolution of aquatic tetrapods (for instance whales, ichthyosaurs, and plesiosaurs). As a device for swimming, a limb with separate digits is pretty inefficient. And yet we find the earliest and most primitive tetrapods with toes in strata that were deposited in shallow water, and some of these fossils show clearly the presence of gills. Limbs with digits apparently evolved first in aquatic animals, not on land.

It was suggested in the early years of the 20th century that the driving force behind the evolution of tetrapods was climatic. Devonian strata in many parts of the world consisted of "red beds," sands and muds laid down in hot, arid

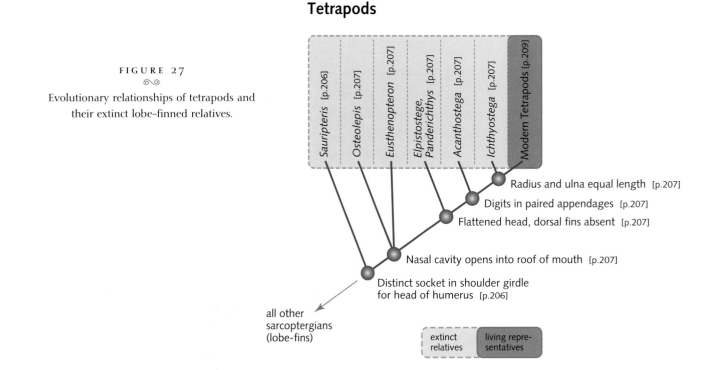

FIGURE 27
⊙〜⊙

Evolutionary relationships of tetrapods and their extinct lobe-finned relatives.

Tetrapods

Sauripteris [p.206]
Osteolepis [p.207]
Eusthenopteron [p.207]
Elpistostege, Panderichthys [p.207]
Acanthostega [p.207]
Ichthyostega [p.207]
Modern Tetrapods [p.209]

Radius and ulna equal length [p.207]
Digits in paired appendages [p.207]
Flattened head, dorsal fins absent [p.207]
Nasal cavity opens into roof of mouth [p.207]
Distinct socket in shoulder girdle for head of humerus [p.206]

all other sarcoptergians (lobe-fins)

extinct relatives | living representatives

environments and cemented together by ochers of red and brown iron oxides. Through the mid-20th century this view of tetrapod origins prevailed, and after the discovery of primitive tetrapod fossils from the Late Devonian of Greenland and elsewhere it was thought that the first limbed vertebrates must have lived in hostile, dry environments unsuitable for "typical" fishes. Devonian lobe-finned fishes thought to be related closely to the ancestors of tetrapods were popularly depicted crawling out of dwindling pools of fetid water to make temporary excursions on land, brave explorers of a hostile world.

Significant discoveries made in the closing years of the 20th century have forced us to discard such images. Late Devonian fossils such as *Elpistostege* [see Plate 120] from Canada and *Acanthostega* from Greenland suggest instead that limbs first evolved in fully aquatic, gill-breathing fishes.

Nor can we cling to the notion that the terrestrial world at the time was a hostile desert, for deep red ocher also forms abundantly in tropical countries today,

under conditions of very high humidity. Usually, soils in such areas are constantly in demand by verdant tropical vegetation, but when this is stripped away, the shallow red soils are quickly lost.

Here is an important clue for the new model of tetrapod origins, for these creatures were entering a newly evolved landscape of green. Inland waters and coastal margins now supported stable wetland communities of aquatic and semi-terrestrial plants. Marshes and swamps, among the deltas, lagoons and bayous of river systems provided new ecological opportunities that had never previously existed. The greening of the swampy margins of the continents was a welcome mat for tetrapods.

It has long been recognized that a great blooming of tropical forests occurred in many parts of the world during the Carboniferous (after all, the plants gave rise to coal, and the coal gave rise to the name "Carboniferous"). It is less well appreciated that the invasion of land by plants began much earlier, in the Silurian period, and that by the Devonian period the first

PLATE 116

Eusthenopteron foordi, a primitive extinct lobe-finned relative of tetrapods, from the Late Devonian of Escuminac Bay, Quebec, Canada (about 375 million years old). Length 25cm.

vascular plants and terrestrial arachnids and simple insects had evolved. The Devonian landscape certainly offered potential sources of food for early tetrapods, but if they were all in the water, they were hardly in a position to utilize this terrestrial resource.

It was apparently in such swamps and marshes that early limbed tetrapods first evolved, not crawling on land but wriggling in ungainly fashion among half-submerged plant stems, and trying to avoid being eaten by faster swimming fishes. The evolution of feet with (presumably) webbed digits may have been an adaptation to life among aquatic weeds, and the first limbed tetrapods probably used their limbs for wading or crawling, not for supporting the body. Some of these tetrapods were able to supplement their oxygen supply by gulping or breathing air, and it is not hard to imagine how their descendants gradually shifted to an obligate air-breathing existence. Once that step was taken, water no longer offered a safe haven, and became a death-trap unless the creatures could periodically surface in order to breathe. The colonization of land

by limbed, air-breathing tetrapods may have been almost accidental.

In the open water, limbed tetrapods stood little chance of avoiding predation from large placoderms or fast-swimming lobe-fins such as rhizodontids (*root-tooth*). These were among the largest lobe-finned fishes, some reaching estimated lengths of 3 or 4 meters, although such giants are known only from fragmentary fossils and teeth as big as a tyrannosaur's. One such fragment is central to theories of limb evolution in tetrapods.

In 1845, just a few years before Charles Darwin published *The Origin of Species*, the fossil of a large fish fin was discovered in Late Devonian strata of Blossburg, Pennsylvania. Despite its fragmentary nature, the fossil was classified as an early rhizodontid and was given the name *Sauripteris*. Aside from the fin – fortuitously, one of the most informative parts of the skeleton – only some scales and tiny bone scraps have ever been found, but the fin skeleton was quickly recognized as having many similarities with the limb bones of terrestrial vertebrates. [Plate 117] Today it provides compelling evidence that

PLATE 117

Sauripteris taylori, pectoral fin and shoulder girdle of a large extinct rhizodontid fish, primitively related to tetrapods, from the Late Devonian of Blossburg, Pennsylvania, USA (about 375 million years old). Length of fin 28cm; estimated length of fish 2m.

tetrapods evolved from sarcopterygian fishes. The equivalent of our humerus is preserved, still articulated with a simple socket in the shoulder girdle and connected to two more bones, the radius and ulna. Recognition of these bones in the fossil suggests that there would have been a complex muscular system allowing the fin to move, but not necessarily providing a terrestrial capability. One important difference from more advanced tetrapods is the unequal lengths of the radius and ulna in *Sauripteris*, for in most tetrapods these two bones are of equal length, allowing the development of a primitive but flexible wrist joint.

Another feature that unites rhizodontids with tetrapods is the particular pattern of skull bones, including large paired frontal bones. These apparently were newly evolved, and although some skull bones in ray-finned fishes are also called frontals, they probably are not the same pair. Coelacanths and lungfishes also lack these bones, although the pattern of skull bones in most lungfishes is so bizarre that it is impossible to equate any of them with the bones of other fishes.

Other extinct lobe-fin families seem to have been evolutionarily even closer to tetrapods than the rhizodontids. Opinions still differ among scientists as to how these fossils should be classified, and they may belong to one or several groups. *Osteolepis* was a small (15 centimeters long) lobe-fin from the Late Devonian that had heavily enameled scales and skull bones, a primitive feature. It gave its name to a family known as osteolepids, which were rather generalized but long-lasting. The last known osteolepid was *Ectosteorhachis*, from the Early Permian of Texas. *Eusthenopteron* was another Late Devonian lobe-fin known from many well-preserved fossils from Quebec, and it has become one of the most intensively studied fossils because of its supposed evolutionary proximity to primitive tetrapods. One such feature is the presence of an internal nostril (choana) within the roof of the mouth. It may have allowed the fish to gulp air without bringing the mouth entirely out of the water, or it may have offered improved olfactory sense in water; it may even have allowed the fish to detect airborne scents. The backbone of *Eusthenopteron* was poorly adapted to support the body in air, even though it had bony vertebrae like those of primitive tetrapods. The unique combination of fin structure, nostril arrangement, backbone, and perhaps lungs in these lobe-finned fishes endowed them with many advantages in the burgeoning wetland environments.

Elpistostege and *Panderichthys* were Late Devonian fishes from Quebec and Latvia that shared several derived features with tetrapods, including a flattened head with eyes set close together, a non-movable intracranial joint, a flattened body without median fins, and expanded ribs. The skull became a solid triangle of bone, with the eyes bulging from its upper surface. *Acanthostega*, from the Late Devonian of Greenland, had limbs with many digits (more than the five we are used to), but its radius and ulna were still of unequal length, like those of rhizodontids and osteolepids. [Plates 118 and 119] Toes, it seems, evolved before wrists and ankles. *Ichthyostega*, also from the Late Devonian of Greenland, is a more advanced aquatic tetrapod in which the radius and ulna are of equal length. Its tail was long and flattened from side to side, but it still retained a fishy feature, the presence of fin rays.

Tetrapods as Fishes

To a great extent, tetrapods closed the door on water when they gave up using gills for respiration. The transition to breathing air created the most potent barrier to tetrapods returning to the aquatic world. The demands of oxygen consumption and the removal of waste gases place the greatest physiological limitations on aquatic tetrapods. Other features of tetrapod anatomy are more readily adapted toward life in the water; for example the limbs have repeatedly been modified "back" to swimming paddles, flippers, and

PLATE 118
᳇

Acanthostega sp., a primitive aquatic tetrapod
with limbs and a well developed internal
gill skeleton from the Late Devonian of
Greenland (about 375 million years old).
Length 63cm. Model by Elliot Goldfinger.

PLATE 119
᳇
Restoration of how *Acanthostega* may have
appeared in life, during the Late Devonian.
Model by Elliot Goldfinger.

fins. Ichthyosaurs and dolphins are unquestionably specialized toward fishlike locomotion, but they have no trace of gills. The Devonian tetrapod *Acanthostega* was among the last tetrapods to have internal gills with sufficient capacity to meet its respiratory needs. Although a lot of tetrapods live in the water, every species is a *visitor* to the water world; none can live permanently beneath the waves.

Extinction has created an enormous anatomical gap between tetrapods and their closest living relatives, the lungfishes and coelacanths. Only ancient Devonian fossils are able to bridge that gap, showing the emergence of tetrapods – and therefore of humans – from the world of fishes about 400 million years ago. The fossils also reveal that, as these creatures began along the path that would lead ultimately to fully terrestrial existence, they gave up many of their primitive fishy attributes *before* escaping from the water. It is therefore legitimate to compare them with fishes generally, and to place their anatomical specializations within a broader context of fishes as a whole.

Extinct finned tetrapods such as rhizodontids and *Eusthenopteron* retained a generalized fishlike form with a full complement of fins. Their swimming abilities were undoubtedly excellent, and probably far better than the swimming abilities of contemporaneous lungfishes and coelacanths. These extinct finned tetrapods were apparently still fully dependent on their gills for respiration, and they may have held honors as top predators. By contrast, *Panderichthys* and *Elpistostege* were probably far less efficient swimmers. *Panderichthys* was not streamlined; its enormous flattened head made up almost a quarter of its body length, and it had no dorsal or anal fins, which would have compromised its ability to control yaw (turning about the vertical axis) and roll in the water. It may instead have rested on the bottom and moved by undulating its body and using the paired lobes as paddles. *Acanthostega* had paired appendages that were incapable of supporting it on land, but were also incapable of generating lift or preventing roll. It was surely not among the great swimmers of its time, for although its tail would have generated thrust, the shape of its body probably created high inertial drag.

With the extinction of the last osteolepid in the Early Permian, 290 million years ago, all that was left were the acrobatic coelacanths, the bizarre lungfishes, and the crawlers on land. Despite a promising start, lobe-fins ultimately were not a successful group of fishes. Their promise lay elsewhere, out of the water. Today, tetrapods constitute slightly less than half of the world's vertebrate species. They have conquered the land and the air, and many of them have secondarily returned to the water. They even gave rise to humans! How, then, could tetrapods be considered unsuccessful?

This book is about fishes, and tetrapods first evolved as aquatic organisms, so it is fair to compare them in that light. Although tetrapods secondarily returned to aquatic habitats many times during the course of their evolution (the water was, after all, teeming with sources of food), rarely have they approximated the graceful combination of streamlined form and function seen in fishes. Attempts to recolonize aquatic habitats by limbed vertebrates (for example, turtles, ichthyosaurs, plesiosaurs, whales, and penguins) are short-lived in comparison, and none of these groups has succeeded in displacing fishes from their dominance of the water.

The point is simple: having left the waters, tetrapods took about 150 million years to return as fishlike ichthyosaurs, and almost 300 million years to return as whales and dolphins. Tetrapods have repeatedly failed in their challenge to fishes for mastery of the oceans. No tetrapods have colonized fresh waters as successfully as fishes, and no tetrapod group has ever attained comparable. ❧

OF FISHES

⫸ Two Great Discoveries

*T*HE SEAS ARE FULL of fishes, and the land is dominated by tetrapods—or is it? For the land is also full of fishes, half the known species in fact, hidden from our gaze in the thousands of freshwater islands scattered across the continents. Largely hidden from view, fishes represent another universe from our own, a universe whose unique identity and evolutionary history are waiting to be explored. We share part of that history with fishes, for our primordial vertebrate ancestry lies in the water. Ancient bony ostracoderms not only were the ancestors of fishes, they were the ancestors of humans, too. And even after the earliest tetrapods crawled and gasped their way out of the water, fishes continued evolving endless ways to live in it. By exploring the evolutionary history of fishes, therefore, we make two great discoveries, one having to do with our own aquatic origins and the other having to do with the tandem evolution of fishes and tetrapods.

Earth is unique in supporting extensive watery environments from which the richness of life could evolve. The oceans are ancient, perhaps more than 4 billion years old. They are vastly older than the volcanic rocks and oozes that lie beneath them, and they could even be older than the continents. The oceans were already well established, and their physical conditions were essentially like those of today's oceans, when the first chordate creatures, such as *Yunnanozoon* and *Pikaea*, wriggled

PLATE 120
∾

A variety of fishes lived in Canada during the Late Devonian (365-355 million years ago), including *Alaspis*, one of the last armored ostracoderms (lower right), placoderms such as *Bothriolepis* (upper right), lungfishes such as *Scaumenacia* (lower left), and primitive aquatic tetrapods such as *Elpistostege* (upper left).

through them half a billion years ago. This enduring stability of oceanic environments is one of their most important features and helps to explain the conservative anatomy of fishes in contrast to terrestrial vertebrate anatomy. The shape of *Sacabambaspis* from the Ordovician reflects accommodation to hydrodynamic demands that still apply to modern anchovies, and 200 million years of progressive fine-tuning of teleost tail anatomy can be interpreted in simple terms, as improvements for greater thrust and diminished drag.

Hox Genes and Fossils

We have discovered that the anatomical features that separate craniates from other organisms are profound, not only because of their great complexity (especially in the head region), but also because they involve significant new developmental strategies and embryonic tissues. These new strategies and tissues in turn are correlated with modifications of fundamental regulatory genes such as Hox. We have discovered that the wide anatomical gap between primitive craniates and their closest living relatives, such as amphioxus, is reflected in differences in embryonic and genetic features. The extinct conodonts form a controversial "missing link" in craniate evolution, and a modern interpretation of conodont structure suggests that some Hox mutations and corresponding gene expressions in the embryo had already occurred in these enigmatic creatures. When we look carefully at the distribution of advanced features among early chordate and craniate fossils and compare what we know about the development and genetic regulation of these same features in living species, a fascinating story of the evolution of embryonic development, or ontogeny, begins to emerge.

The earliest reliable occurrences of the bone-clad craniates we call ostracoderms are about 450 million years old, although controversial bonelike fragments from the Cambrian may push their age back. Furthermore, these primitive marine craniates have been discovered in many parts of the Ordovician world, and their diversity suggests they had already enjoyed a lengthy history, if one hidden from us. These ostracoderms were able to synthesize bone tissue in the skin, and they were well endowed with bony plates and scales, but we can discover no trace of any internal bone formed around or within cartilage. By the Silurian and Devonian, ostracoderms were freely roaming into fresh waters, and several distinct groups were established, some with strongly localized (endemic) distributions that may be the result of isolation following the break-up of prehistoric land masses. Ostracoderm species diversity was high, particularly in Devonian freshwater habitats of the northern continent, and some species became very abundant. The decline and eventual demise of ostracoderms is still a source of mystery, but widespread habitat reduction toward the end of the Devonian, coupled with the rise of new predators, the gnathostomes, probably hastened their end.

One ostracoderm group, the anaspids, may have survived into the present, disguised today as lampreys, and it has been suggested that the scaly thelodonts are relatives of sharks, but the supporting evidence is weak. Although some ostracoderms—the cephalaspids, for example—may be distantly related to gnathostomes, no fossils that would provide an unambiguous link between them have been found. This lack could simply reflect erosion of the appropriate fossil record. Alternatively, the most primitive gnathostomes may not have had bone, and so may not have been preserved as fossils. But there is a distinct third possibility, namely, that the genetic and developmental transformations leading to gnathostomes could have occurred rapidly instead of gradually, in which case the likelihood of finding critical intermediate stages preserved in fossils is minimal.

We have discovered that the gnathostome evolution—the acquisition of jaws—represented almost as profound an evolutionary leap as the craniate evolution, the acquisition of a head. The development of jaws involved a host of new and complex anatomical features, associated with additional mutations of the regulatory Hox genes but apparently without the addition of new kinds of embryonic tissues. Instead, new structures appeared, especially in the head, as the result of altered developmental strategies in the embryo. It may seem inconceivable that the evolution of so many features could have occurred in a very short span of time, geologically speaking, but the Hox genes expressed in their formation may have mutated rapidly, thereby setting the stage for the next scene in the blink of an ostracoderm's eye.

≡⫸ Fishes and Diversity

The basis of modern gnathostome diversity was established more than 400 million years ago, with sharks, ray-finned and lobe-finned fishes. Furthermore, all three modern lobe-finned lineages—coelacanths, lungfishes, and tetrapods—were distinct by the mid-Devonian, 380 million years ago.

Past eras saw as well two groups of jawed craniates with no living representatives, the placoderms and acanthodians. These groups represent divergent and ultimately unsuccessful gnathostomes, but each met with some success before disappearing. Placoderms rapidly underwent a dramatic radiation into marine and freshwater environments, evolving a dazzling array of species and families before they took an equally dramatic dive and went extinct at the close of the Devonian. Acanthodians never achieved the diversity of the placoderms, but they do represent a distinct branch of early gnathostome variety. The fascination of the acanthodians lies elsewhere: they are among the oldest known gnathostomes, sharing some features with the osteichthyans, and they may even be related to ray-finned fishes.

Once this basic division of gnathostomes was established, each lineage followed its own destiny. Placoderms waxed and waned dramatically in the Devonian, while acanthodians stayed reclusively in the background until their disappearance in the Early Permian. Coelacanths followed suit but have resisted extinction, just barely, into the present. Lungfishes were second only to placoderms in diversity during the Devonian, with more families than contemporaneous sharks and ray-finned fishes combined, but then declined to approximately their present level of diversity and abundance almost 200 million years ago.

Somewhat surprisingly, only three of the gnathostome groups present in the Devonian subsequently experienced significant increases in diversity and abundance—the tetrapods, the sharks, and the ray-finned fishes. The tetrapod story is well known, although we are just now discovering how almost accidental those beginnings were. The sharks (and rays) are a poor third in terms of species diversity but are sometimes abundant, especially in marine environments. Without a doubt, the ray-finned fishes, the actinopterygians, take first place today, both in abundance and diversity. Unfortunately, the ray-fins must compete with humans for precious freshwater resources, and their commanding diversity on land will likely be devastated within the next few decades, while human overexploitation of fish stocks in the oceans may similarly damage the ray-fins' abundance.

Although lobe-finned diversity is rooted in the Devonian, the beginnings of neoselachian-like sharks, neopterygian-like ray-finned fishes, and the earliest amniote tetrapods (amniotes include all the higher tetrapods whose embryonic development takes place inside an amniotic egg) apparently lay in the Carboniferous. Most of the diversity we see in these groups today is rooted in the Mesozoic rather than the Paleozoic. Just as there are no Paleozoic mammals or birds, crocodiles, turtles, or frogs, so there are no known Paleozoic reedfishes, paddlefishes, or sturgeons, gars, bowfins, or teleosts, or mako sharks, dogfishes, or rays. All this diversity of form arose in the Mesozoic and was subsequently fine-tuned from the Eocene onward, until by middle of the Miocene, about 15 million years ago, the world teemed with essentially modern-looking backboned animals. In particular, ray-fin diversity apparently exploded in the Late Cretaceous and Eocene, easily eclipsing that of mammals and birds. We sometimes speak of that time as the Age of Mammals, but we could just as easily call it the Age of Teleosts.

It used to be thought that new species replaced older ones in more or less unchanged habitats, but it is more probable that loss of habitat leads to the extinction of species dependent on it. New versions of the habitat, or even entirely new habitats, provide opportunities for new specialists to occupy new niches. For example, the African rift lakes are geologically young environments, and the local fishes have hardly had time to replace earlier occupants; instead, the diversity found in the lakes where the continent is sundering probably evolved in situ, from just one or two original species. We have discovered evidence of analogous colonizations of Triassic lakes in North America. But while the environment may be new, the ecological niches occupied by fishes often seem to be of their own creation. Maybe these examples are microcosms of a grander fishy universe, which would help to explain how teleosts came to dominate the world's seas and lakes, by compartmentalizing aquatic environments in new ways around the beginning of the Cenozoic.

We can detect little difference in the pace of major evolutionary change among tetrapods, sharks, and ray-finned fishes. All are about equally different anatomically from their Jurassic, Carboniferous, and Devonian counterparts. A similar *pace* of evolution does not mean that the *scale* of evolutionary change was comparable in these groups, however, for we have already seen that fishes have conserved many aquatic adaptations of primitive craniates. The anatomical diversity of tetrapods is truly fantastic, encompassing terrestrial, volant (flying), and secondarily aquatic

lifestyles. Apart from mudskippers and flying fishes, few ray-finned fishes ever leave the water, and sharks have never experimented in these directions. The discovery here is that key evolutionary innovations occurred in sharks and ray-finned fishes at about the same rate as they occurred in tetrapods, even though the scale of the transformations involved was different.

Fishes and Extinctions

Over the past half-billion years of Earth's history, five major extinction episodes occurred: at the end of the Cambrian, within the Late Devonian, at the end of the Permian (supposedly the most severe), at the end of the Triassic, and at the end of the Cretaceous. Each was followed by a period of rapid radiation—the evolution and branching of new species—and each event represents a major collapse and re-establishment of Earth's fauna and flora. The evolutionary history of fishes is curious because it sometimes reflects these events and sometimes does not.

We don't know enough about early chordate evolution to determine the impact of the Cambrian mass extinction on the rise of bony ostracoderms. During the Ordovician (a period of glaciation on a global scale), we discover the earliest evidence of diverse craniate faunas in shallow marine environments, including ostracoderms and perhaps the first acanthodians and sharks. With the exception of thelodonts, none of the Ordovician ostracoderms survived into the Silurian. They were replaced by a diverse fauna consisting of marine and freshwater ostracoderms belonging to several new groups. Although this turnover among the ostracoderms was not part of a global extinction, other marine organisms were certainly affected at that time, most notably the trilobites: of more than 100 trilobite families present in the Cambrian and Ordovician, only three survived into the Silurian.

Devonian fishes suffered three extinction events: at the end of the Early

Devonian, again within the Late Devonian (a major crisis), and again at the close of the Devonian. The first event is not considered part of a global mass extinction, and it mainly affected older (Silurian) ostracoderm and placoderm lineages. In the Middle Devonian, antiarchs and arthrodires diversified and became widespread, replacing localized faunas (the galeaspids of Asia, for example) with more cosmopolitan ones. Pelagic sharks, placoderms and osteichthyans "conquered" the open seas, by moving into unoccupied or underoccupied habitats, much as pterosaurs and birds "conquered" the skies during the Mesozoic.

The Late Devonian extinction was far more catastrophic, for it devastated almost 20% of all marine animal families, including almost three quarters of the fishes. The last bony ostracoderms disappeared, along with 13 of 22 placoderm families, 10 families of lobe-finned fishes, and some sharks and ray-fin families. [Plate 121] Few new groups of fishes appeared immediately after this event, and fish diversity was slow to recover. This extinction event coincided with an abrupt drop in global sea levels (they had been climbing progressively through the Devonian until then) that, coupled with a rise in the level of oxygen-poor bottom waters, probably squeezed many specialized shelf faunas out of existence.

The terminal Devonian extinction involved fewer families than the previous crisis and was accompanied by the appearance of many new families of sharks and ray-finned fishes, so that overall diversity was almost unaffected, even though the placoderms were virtually eliminated. Furthermore, the Devonian extinction of fishes was not mirrored by a corresponding crisis among invertebrate animals or terrestrial vertebrates, and it was therefore not such a global event.

Sharks in particular increased dramatically, from 10 families in the Late Devonian to about two dozen, with two episodes of diversification in the Early and Late Carboniferous.

The Permian mass extinction affected many terrestrial vertebrates and marine invertebrates. Its impact on fishes is harder to assess. Acanthodians finally died out in the Permian, but they had been represented by only a single lineage since the end of the Carboniferous. *Ectosteorhachis*, the last surviving lobe-finned tetrapod, died in the Early Permian, so we cannot link the demise of these fishes to the Late Permian extinction. Many sharks became extinct during the Permian, and freshwater xenacanths, which were cosmopolitan before the crisis, were represented afterward by only a few isolated Triassic survivors (for example, in India). Other Triassic survivors included holocephalans and hybodonts, and the latter were to become the most succesful group of sharks during the Jurassic. The rise of neoselachians in the Triassic may also have been linked to the extinction of other sharks in the Permian. Many Paleozoic ray-finned fishes became extinct, but there were also stragglers that hung on into the Triassic, such as the deep-bodied platysomoids. The first neopterygian fishes appeared long before this mass extinction occurred, but their subsequent success may in part be attributed to increased opportunities for diversification after the mass extinction.

There is little perturbation of the fish fossil record at the end of the Triassic, and many groups made a smooth transition into the early Jurassic. Such varied groups as the hybodont sharks, saurichthyids, semionotids, pycnodontids, primitive pholidophorid teleosts, primitive relatives of bowfins, and lungfishes and coelacanths all swam on serenely. It is consequently difficult to demonstrate any impact of the Triassic extinction on fishes, although its effects elsewhere were strong.

Many terrestrial and aquatic vertebrates and marine invertebrates became

PLATE 121
◐

This unique specimen represents a fossilized slice of life from the Late Devonian of Miguasha, Quebec, about 375 million years ago. It includes examples of *Scaumenacia* (a lungfish), *Eusthenopteron* (an extinct relative of tetrapods), *Bothriolepis* (a placoderm), and *Archaeopteris*, a fernlike fond of a land plant distantly related to modern conifers.

extinct at the end of the Cretaceous. Primitive teleosts such as pachycormids (see page 165) became extinct, and ichthyodectids and aspidorhynchids (see pages 165, 171) suffered such a dramatic decline that for many years it was believed they, too, had fallen victim to the Late Cretaceous extinction (new fossil discoveries suggest they staggered into the Eocene). Coelacanths disappeared from freshwater and shallow marine environments, along with the last hybodonts and semionotids. On the other hand, many fishes weathered the Cretaceous extinction apparently unscathed, including pycnodontids, reedfishes, chondrosteans, gars, bowfins, and all the major living groups of teleosts. But although its impact on fish extinction was uneven, the extinction nevertheless prefaced a dramatic increase in the diversity and abundance of teleosts, and a lesser increase among sharks.

We have discovered, then, that overall periods of high extinction among fishes and among other animals have coincided only three times in the past 500 million years: once within the Late Devonian, again at the end of the Permian, and again at the end of the Cretaceous. In both the Permian and the Cretaceous extinctions, some fishes were strongly affected while others barely faltered, which suggests that no single causal factor is involved. The Late Triassic extinction went virtually unnoticed by many groups of fishes. Conversely, fishes have suffered at least three periods of conspicuously high extinction, all in the Paleozoic, that did not coincide with major global extinctions. If there is a discovery here, it is simply that the factors causing major extinctions among terrestrial vertebrates, marine invertebrates, and most fishes are largely independent.

Fishes and Continental Drift

Of course, the extinction of one group may influence the subsequent success of another, either positively or negatively, but the impact of some global event (for example, altered sea levels) will clearly affect terrestrial and aquatic creatures differently, depending on their particular vulnerabilities. A single, gargantuan supercontinent has about one-third less coastline than three smaller separate continents, so, in a very crude way, continental collisions are bad for shelf-sea inhabitants and continental separations are good. If diversity among freshwater fishes of the African rift valley is an indication, even the *incipient* separation of continents is an impetus for high rates of speciation under certain conditions.

We can detect vestiges of biogeographic distribution patterns even in the earliest ostracoderms from the Ordovician, for those from the southern continents are different from *Astraspis* in the north. By the Silurian and Early Devonian, fairly distinctive patterns among freshwater fishes already existed, for example in the northern Old Red Continent with its cephalaspids, and in an Asiatic province with galeaspids. So we can assume that similar geographic and environmental factors influenced fishes then as now, although we may not know exactly what those factors were. We also see occasions when the barriers broke down, as when *Bothriolepis* rampaged across the world, like an armorplated *Tilapia* let loose in a fragile lake full of cichlids. The analogy may be fanciful, but it is appropriate: the aggressive cosmopolitan generalist plowing through the structured niches of myriad specialist species.

We can also detect biogeographic patterns among later fishes, for example among those of the southern continents during the Cretaceous. In this case there is an interesting parallel between freshwater and marine fishes, because both include many endemic forms known only from the southern continents. Some are more widespread than others: the marine teleost *Vinctifer*, for example, was spread all the way from Venezuela to eastern Australia, but the small ostariophysan *Dastilbe* lived only in lakes associated with the rift between Brazil and Africa. The distribution of Early Cretaceous freshwater fishes in Africa and South America offers compelling support for the former connection of these continents. But the distinctive southern-water marine fauna requires further explanation, because sea fishes are not so constrained as those living in fresh water. The South Atlantic of the Early Cretaceous was blind-ending, without a connection to the North Atlantic, at least until about 120 million years ago. After that time, microscopic fossils such as foraminiferans reveal an invasion of northerly waters from the Caribbean region, into the South Atlantic. Along with these microscopic creatures came fishes, and by the Late Cretaceous the marine fishes of Brazil and Australia resembled those found everywhere else. It seems that establishing an equatorial Atlantic seaway sealed the fate of the endemic southern fishes. If things had gone the other way, maybe the Late Cretaceous seas covering North America would have been filled with *Vinctifer* and *Calamopleurus*.

≡⫟⊳ The Human Fish

Sacabambaspis is not so much a primitive Ordovician fish as an image of our own origins. The later evolution of humans (along with other air-breathing tetrapods) can be traced through a series of increasingly specialized fishes that ultimately turned away from the water about 350 million years ago. Another discovery, then, is that we cannot define fishes in a scientific way without including ourselves, and the origins and evolution of chordates, craniates, and gnathostomes are as much a part of our heritage as is the rise of mammals or primates.

We are fishes, whether we like it or not. It is more than a semantic issue, for our anatomy bears the indelible traces of our fish ancestry: the vestiges of the incompressible notochord, our spinal cord with all its myelin-coated nerves, our internal and external bony skeletons, our highly modified pectoral and pelvic fins—the list is much longer, but the point is made. Our embryos develop using special tissues that first evolved in aquatic creatures, providing them with sophisticated sensory systems and skeletons, giving them an edge in a hostile watery world.

We are tetrapods, and we represent the status quo of a long evolutionary path on land, but our closest living relatives are the lungfishes and Old Fourlegs, the coelacanth. We would do well to protect and nurture those few relatives, for the gap between us extends back some 350 million years. If those half-dozen species become extinct, our next nearest relatives would be the ray-finned fishes, with over 400 million years separating us.

The oceans may be 4 billion years old, but they have held fishes for less than one-eighth of that time. Since then, fishes have evolved in and adapted to an almost unchanged environment, and only the tetrapods broke their link with it. In our anthropocentric way, we humans have focused on a peripheral feature of tetrapods, their toes, instead of on their most powerful adaptation, the switch to obligate air breathing. Once that step was taken, there could be no permanent return to the water, no matter how finlike the limbs became or how long the animal could hold its breath. Fishes are the supreme backboned animals of the water, and they have maintained their preeminence for their entire evolutionary history. More abundant and more diverse than their air-breathing cousins, fishes today dominate the seas and fresh waters of Earth. Through their fossils we can discover a staggering half-billion-year history in which lies our own watery origins.

Acanthodians A group of extinct bony fishes with fin spines in front of all fins except the tail, known only from strata of Paleozoic age.

Acanthomorphs Spiny-rayed teleost fishes, the largest living group with over 11,000 species, and with fossils that first become common in the Late Cretaceous.

Actinopterygians Ray-finned bony fishes, in which the internal skeleton of the fin lies within the body wall and only the fin rays project outward.

Advanced In evolutionary terms, a state derived from a more primitive one; a relative term, involving a comparison of two (sometimes more) states.

Aerobic Respiration process involving the use of molecular oxygen.

Agnathans Primitive craniates lacking movable jaws, including extinct ostracoderms plus modern lampreys and hagfishes.

Amiids Ray-finned fishes belonging to the same family as *Amia*, the modern bowfin.

Amphioxus A popular but semi-technical name, dating from 1836, for the living lancelet, a primitive marine chordate animal; scientific priority is given to the earlier (1834) name *Branchiostoma*.

Anal fin An unpaired fin beneath a fish, located behind the cloaca and in front of the tail; occurs only in gnathostomes, and is absent in several groups.

Anoxic Pertaining to the absence of molecular oxygen.

Arthrodires A major group representing 60% of the extinct armored placoderms; characterized by the presence of two pairs of upper tooth plates instead of a single pair; mostly known from the Devonian.

Benthic Bottom-dwelling, living on or near the bed of aquatic environments.

Bichirs Common name for polypterids, a group thought to be the most primitive living ray-finned fishes, found in lakes and rivers of Africa.

Bony fishes Popular name for the osteichthyans (all ray-finned and lobe-finned fishes), originally intended to distinguish them from "cartilaginous fishes" such as sharks and paddlefishes.

Bowfins Popular name for amiids, derived from the long dorsal fin of *Amia*.

Chimaeroids Rabbitfishes, marine relatives of sharks and rays.

Chondrichthyans Sharks, skates, rays and rabbitfishes (chimaeroids); a group of gnathostomes in which the cartilaginous internal skeleton has a unique pattern of prismatic calcification.

Chondrosteans A group of primitive ray-finned fishes that includes sturgeons and paddlefishes.

Chordates Animals with a notochord, pharyngeal clefts, and a dorsal hollow central nerve tube in the embryo and/or adult.

Cladistic analysis (phylogenetic analysis) Procedure using evolutionary advanced features instead of total similarity to establish relationships among organisms.

Clupeomorphs Herrings and their relatives, a group comprising over 330 living species, first known from the Early Cretaceous.

Coelacanths Popular name of *Latimeria chalumnae* and its fossil relatives; derived from *Coelacanthus*, a Permian fossil named by Louis Agassiz in the mid-19th century.

Conodont Properly, a microscopic toothlike fossil found in marine sediments from the Cambrian to the Triassic; nowadays also used in reference to the animal that bore these structures.

Conserved In evolutionary terms, the equivalent of primitive; a feature that has been retained even though other evolutionary change has occurred.

Convergence The independent evolution of anatomically and functionally similar features in two (or more) species that are not each other's closest relatives.

Craniate Group of chordates characterized by the presence of a distinct head end containing a brain, cranial nerves and sensory capsules, enclosed in a protective braincase of cartilage or bone.

Denticles Microscopic toothlike scales in the skin, covering much of the body in sharks and extinct thelodonts, also occurring inside the mouth; some scientists have suggested that shark teeth evolved from such denticles in the mouth.

Derived In evolutionary terms, the equivalent of advanced and the opposite of primitive; a relative term, involving a comparison of two (sometimes more) states.

Dermal skeleton Bony plates and scales that are formed in the skin, beneath the outer epidermis, usually superficial in position, and not pre-formed in cartilage.

Dorsal fin An unpaired fin located on the back of a fish; there are two such fins in many fishes.

Drag The resistance that a medium (water or air, for example) offers to the motion of an object.

Endoskeleton The internal skeleton of a craniate, made either of cartilage or (secondarily) partly of bone, and usually formed deeper in the body than the dermal skeleton.

Elopocephalans Large group of teleost fishes whose most primitive members are the elopomorphs (tarpons, bonefish, eels) and also includes the herrings, ostariophysans and neoteleosts (including the acanthomorphs).

Elopomorphs A group of teleosts that includes tarpons, bonefish and eels.

Epidermal placodes Special area of cells in the head region of craniate embryos, from which important structures are derived (for example parts of the eyes).

Evolved A relative term, applied either to a structure, organism or even an entire lineage, suggesting transformation from another condition perceived as primitive.

Expression (of genes) In genetics, the physical *site* and *time* during development where a particular gene is active; also the *product* of a gene's activity.

Femur Thigh bone in tetrapods, recognized in the pelvic fin skeleton of their extinct fishlike relatives.

Gars Popular name of lepisosteids, long-snouted and heavily armored predaceous fishes living today in lakes and rivers of North America, first known from the Early Cretaceous.

Gene Segment of genetic material (DNA) coding for a single protein molecule; fundamental units that regulate development of organisms.

Genome The total genetic material of an organism.

Gill arch Segmentally arranged endoskeletal support of gills, located behind the mouth, with separate movable bars of cartilage in gnathostomes.

Gnathostomes Craniates with movable jaws that define the shape of the mouth, and with paired fins on the body, myelinated nerves and many other evolutionarily advanced features not found in jawless craniates.

Gondwana A gigantic southern-hemisphere supercontinent that included South America, Africa, Antarctica, India and Australia; finally fragmented into its present configuration during the later Mesozoic and Cenozoic.

Hagfish Living marine jawless craniates, similar to but anatomically simpler than lampreys; known from fossils since the Carboniferous.

Homeotic genes Those genes responsible for regulating the fundamental form of the embryo, including anterior and posterior, left and right, dorsal and ventral, and segment arrangement.

Homology General and particular resemblance due to inheritance from common ancestry; frequently, homology is inferred between primitive and advanced features displaying some structural, topographic or developmental similarity.

Hox genes A particular family of regulatory (homeotic) genes that has become duplicated in craniates, and regulates the development of many of their fundamental attributes.

Humerus Upper arm bone of tetrapods, recognized in the pectoral fin skeleton of their extinct fishlike relatives (an example of homology).

Hyoid arch Part of the endoskeleton between the jaws and gill arches, resembling a gill arch but braced to the jaws by ligaments and usually helping attach the jaws to the braincase.

Hyomandibular An upper element of the hyoid arch, usually with one end propped against the braincase and the other attached to the jaw near the jaw-joint.

Hypomere specialized region of cells inside the pharynx of craniate embryos, from which pharyngeal muscles are developed.

Ichthyologist Scientist who studies fishes.

Lamprey Living jawless craniate that has a fresh-water larval stage (the ammocoete) and an adult stage that usually is marine, with a circular sucking mouth.

Lancelet Common name for the primitive chordate, amphioxus, used here in a broader sense to include its extinct relatives such as the Cambrian *Pikaea* and *Yunnanozoon*.

Lobe-finned fishes (lobe-fins) Common name for the division of osteichthyans known scientifically as sarcopterygians, the group to which coelacanths, lungfishes and tetrapods belong.

Lungfishes Popular name for dipnoans, air-breathing lobe-finned fishes restricted today to fresh waters of Australia, Africa and South America, with large ridged toothplates and a lunglike air bladder with many chambers and pouches; the first lungfishes date from the Early Devonian, and many early examples were marine.

Mandible (mandibular) The lower jaw of gnathostomes, hinged at the jaw joint to the upper jaw.

Maxillae (maxillaries) A pair of toothed dermal bones overlying the upper jaw in osteichthyans, primitively forming most of the outer biting arcade of the jaw, and becoming progressively more movable in teleost evolution.

Neopterygians A group including modern gars, the bowfin and all the teleosts, that is thought to have evolved from common ancestry some time during the Late Paleozoic.

Neoselachians A group that includes all modern sharks, skates and rays, but which excludes the rabbitfishes.

Notochord Logitudinal flexible rod of cells that forms an incompressible structure running along the body beneath the dorsal nerve cord in chordates; it is primitively a continuous structure, but becomes segmented and restricted to regions between vertebrae in tetrapods and various groups of fishes.

Neural crest A region along the margins of the developing nerve cord in craniate embryos, from which cells migrate to other parts of the body and help form many unique craniate features, including much of the skeleton .

Ontogeny The developmental life-cycle of an individual organism.

Ostariophysans A group of living teleosts for which no common name exists, but which includes the milkfish and its relatives, plus minnows, loaches, characins and catfishes; in many of these fishes the swim bladder is connected to the ear region by a series of special bones; the earliest members of the group date from the Early Cretaceous.

Osteichthyans Jawed fishes with a well developed dermal skeleton that usually includes several bones associated with the jaws, and an internal swim bladder or lung developed from the wall of the esophagus.

Osteoglossomorphs A group of living teleosts that includes the bonytongues, mooneyes and elephantfishes; characterized by a specialized biting mechanism that involves the tongue and roof of the mouth.

Ostracoderm Colloquial name for any extinct, jawless craniate with a bony dermal skeleton.

Otoliths paired ear-stones, usually composed of calcium carbonate or calcium phosphate, within chambers of the labyrinth organ, used to detect motion and orientation.

Paddlefishes Popular name for the polyodontids of North America and China, primitive ray-finned fishes with a sharklike tail, and in which the snout is expanded into a spoonlike shape.

Pectoral fins Paired fins at the front of the body, attached to the shoulder girdle, found only in gnathostomes and some ostracoderms such as cephalaspids; the fish equivalent of tetrapod forelimbs and human arms.

Pelagic Pertaining to the open sea.

Pelvic fins Paired fins that are usually located toward the rear of the body (in many actinopterygians they are located beneath or even in front of the pectorals), found only in gnathostomes; the fish equivalent of tetrapod hind limbs and human legs.

Pharyngeal pertaining to the pharynx (region in the back of the mouth, in fishes containing the gills).

Phylogenetic analysis Alternative name for cladistic analysis (see above).

Pitch Tendency to turn about the transverse axis, head-up or head-down.

Placoderms Extinct class of primitive gnathostomes that lived during the Silurian and Devonian periods, with an armor of overlapping plates covering parts of the head and trunk.

Plate tectonics Geologic process in which continental and oceanic crust is propelled by underlying movement of material of the Earth's interior.

Platysomoids Extinct, deep-bodied actinopterygians of the Late Paleozoic and Early Mesozoic; these were among the earliest fishes to evolve this body shape.

Premaxilla (premaxillary) A pair of toothed dermal bones, covering the front of the upper jaw, that become increasingly movable during teleost evolution; in many teleosts they replace the maxillaries as the principal upper tooth-bearing bones.

Primitive A relative term involving comparison of two (sometimes more) states of a feature, referring to its supposedly ancestral condition.

Pycnodontids An extinct group of mostly deep-bodied neopterygians that lived from the Triassic to the Eocene, frequently in reef environments.

Quadrate A paired endoskeletal bone at the back of the upper jaw of osteichthyans, forming the articulation with the lower jaw.

Radiation (of species) Relatively rapid speciation from a common ancestry; contrasted with apparently slower rates of speciation within the lineage before and after the event.

Ray-finned fishes (ray-fins) Popular name for actinopterygians (see above), based on the appearance of their paired fins which consist largely of fin rays.

Reedfishes An alternative common name for bichirs (polypterids).

Roll Tendency to rotate about a longitudinal axis.

Sarcopterygians Scientific name for the lobe-finned division of osteichthyans, in which only a single endoskeletal bone of the paired fin is attached to the shoulder girdle and pelvis.

Semionotids An extinct group of neopterygians that lived in seas and fresh waters from the Permian until the Late Cretaceous.

Sharks Chondrichthyans having an elongate body and powerful jaws (a primitive body shape), from which more specialized rabbitfishes and rays evolved.

Species flock A high number of closely related species living in close harmony within a single restricted environment such as a lake or inland sea; usually interpreted as the result of rapid speciation from one or two original colonist species.

Stem (form) A primitive member of an evolutionary lineage, sharing advanced features of the group as a whole but lacking the features of its more specialized members.

Stingray A kind of ray with a venomous barb in the tail.

Sturgeons Primitive actinopterygians with largely cartilaginous skeletons (acipenserids) of the northern hemisphere, that live in the sea but come up river to breed.

Swim bladder Outgrowth of the esophagus in osteichthyans that functions either as an organ of buoyancy, or as a lung, or may even be involved in hearing.

Symplectic bone An endoskeletal bone at the base of the hyomandibular in neopterygians, where it is either associated with the quadrate bone (gars, teleosts), or is articulated with the lower jaw (in *Amia* and its extinct relatives).

Teleosts The largest living group of actinopterygians, with over 23,000 living species, characterized by the presence of small uroneural bones in the tail; the earliest teleosts date from the Triassic, but the main modern groups only appeared in the Cretaceous and Eocene.

Tetrapods A group of sarcopterygians characterized by separate digits at the extremities of their paired fins; ultimately unsuccesful in water, these creatures nevertheless came to dominate terrestrial habitats.

Thelodonts A group of ostracoderms that lacked extensive bony plates, and were covered instead by microscopic sharklike denticles.

Toothplate Large biting structure, covering the occlusal arcas of the jaws in various fishes; different kinds of toothplates occur in placoderms, chimaeroids, rays and lungfishes, and probably evolved independently within each of these groups.

Vertebrate Name, popularly used instead of "craniate," which draws attention to a feature (the backbone) that is absent in the most primitive craniates.

Uroneural bone Splintlike bones overlying the vertebrae at the base of the tail in teleosts, that probably evolved from neural arches above the nerve cord; a diagnostic feature of teleosts.

Weberian ossicles Small bones, representing an evolutionary transformation of the first few vertebrae and ribs in ostariophysan fishes, and serving to transmit sounds from the swim bladder to the ear region.

Yaw Tendency to rotate about a vertical axis, to the left or right.

ACKNOWLEDGMENTS

I would like to thank my colleagues at the American Museum of Natural History and the staff of the Fossil Halls Renovation. The production of this book, simultaneously with planning and installing the major new Hall of Vertebrate Origins, involved a fantastic degree of dedicated cooperation, for which I am tremendously grateful. Many people helped, but I would especially like to thank Radford Arrindell, Jacklyn Beckett, Craig Chesek, Niles Eldredge, Walter B. Elvers, Robert Evander, Denis Finnin, Eugene Gaffney, Frank Ippolito, Jeanne Kelly, Dina Langis, Melissa Posen, Melanie Stiassny, Richard Weber and Patricia Wynne. I would like to acknowledge Jenny Clack, Mike Coates and Elliot Goldfinger for their work on the new *Acanthostega* model photographed in this book. Bobb Schaeffer, Curator Emeritus at the American Museum of Natural History, and my colleague, mentor and friend, was an inspiration as always. I am endebted to Max Hecht, Robert Ho and Robert Schoch for useful discussions about Hox genes, and thank them for their patience. Many thanks are owed to Ben Creisler for his time and effort in rooting out many obscure etymologies, and to Henry Galiano for donating specimens and providing generous counsel. Several of the fossils now on exhibition and illustrated in this book were donated to the American Museum of Natural History by Dr. Herbert R. Axelrod, and his generosity is greatly appreciated. David Miller's lively illustrations and Ivy Rutzky's wonderful portraits have brought the fossils to life. Thanks are due to Marjorie Pannell for her excellent copyediting work, and to José Conde for designing a really elegant book. My great thanks also go to Peter N. Nevraumont and Ann J. Perrini of the Nevraumont Publishing Company, for driving this project along and keeping me on track. The original inspiration for this book came from Paula Kakalecik at Henry Holt Publishers; I hope she isn't disappointed. Thanks also go to Alex, my son, for his perceptive comments about the artwork, and to Gloria de Carvalho for her help and companionship. Finally, a special mention for my mum in England, who with my dad really struggled with the educational establishment many years ago, so I could become a paleontologist.

INDEX

generic names italicized
italicized page numbers = illustrations